WHAT REMAINS

WHAT REMAINS

OBJECT LESSONS IN
LOVE AND LOSS

KAREN VON HAHN

ANANSI

Published in Canada in 2017 by House of Anansi Press Inc.
www.houseofanansi.com

House of Anansi Press is committed to protecting our natural environment.
As part of our efforts, the interior of this book is printed on paper that contains 100%
post-consumer recycled fibres, is acid-free, and is processed chlorine-free.

21 20 19 18 17 1 2 3 4 5

Library and Archives Canada Cataloguing in Publication

Von Hahn, Karen, 1961–, author
What remains : object lessons in love and loss / Karen von Hahn.

Issued in print and electronic formats.
ISBN 978-1-4870-0039-4 (hardcover).—ISBN 978-1-4870-0040-0 (EPUB).—
ISBN 978-1-4870-0041-7 (Kindle)

1. Von Hahn, Karen, 1961–. 2. Von Hahn, Karen, 1961– —Family.
3. Journalists—Ontario—Toronto—Biography. 4. Mothers and daughters—
Ontario—Toronto—Biography. 5. Personal belongings—Psychological
aspects. I. Title.

PN4913.V66A3 2017   070.92   C2016-906675-4
C2016-907026-3

Jacket and text design: Alysia Shewchuk

We acknowledge for their financial support of our publishing program
the Canada Council for the Arts, the Ontario Arts Council, and the Government of
Canada through the Canada Book Fund.

Printed and bound in Canada

To Susan

CONTENTS

In matters of grave importance, style,
not sincerity is the vital thing.
— Oscar Wilde, *The Importance of Being Earnest*

PROLOGUE

EVERYONE HAS A MOTHER. The relationship we have with her is the first, and perhaps most profoundly affecting one we will experience in our lives. And then most of us have to live through the experience of losing her. Although it was hardly unique or, given her declining health, entirely unexpected, the loss of my own beautiful, maddening mother several years ago completely rocked my world. Quite literally, I found myself at sea, afflicted with a mysterious vertigo that left me unable to right myself or keep the world around me from pitching and swaying—an illness so easily read as a metaphor that it is even more annoying that it still occasionally plagues me.

The only redeeming feature that came with this new, untethered state of being was a radical sense of freedom. Since the worst had actually happened, suddenly I could say anything. In fact I wanted from that moment on to say everything, hide nothing, give up on any pretense I'd ever hidden behind, and just tell it like it is. It was like that moment after a dinner party when the last of the guests have found their coats, the music's been turned down, and the candles are snuffed out. I was now in those strangely clear hours after the remains of the red wine is drying in small pools at the bottom of the glasses, and it's just you and your dirty kitchen in the late-night glare of the overhead light.

But how to be true and real in remembering my mother when I'd never entirely understood her in the first place? How could I start to explain, even to myself, the things that had hurt and disappointed us—and our love for each other?

From my earliest recollections she was always a puzzle: at once loving and harsh, exquisite and ugly, powerful and ultimately fragile. Our relationship was hardly perfect, but it was a passionate one. Five years after her death I still yearn for her: a surprisingly physical yearning that I expect will continue until the day I die.

Being a mother, as I discovered myself, is a profoundly *physical* experience. First, your own body is colonized by an entirely separate being, whose bodily demands trump your own. And then, once this new person is born and you've become a mother (a personal, and permanent, transformation), the task of mothering involves constant hands-on nurturing, protection, and care. So involved are you on this deeply physical level in those first months that the two of you are almost locked in an embrace. And as your child grows and you gradually become separate beings, the world you inhabit together is still a profoundly real and material one, dominated by everyday acts like feeding and clothing, washing and sleeping, playing and learning—and, too, on the mother's side, the hunting and gathering of the many things that surround and serve a family's life. All of which take on meaning and become part of the culture of childhood and one's immediate family history.

There is the banged-up silver spoon you ate from as a baby, given to your mother by an old aunt when you were born; your first boyfriend's jacket, the one you wore home that night in the rain and which still hangs in the back of your closet; the robin's-egg blue Scandinavian dish you found for next to nothing at a flea market outside New Orleans. Each thing has a story. And the story is ultimately about us.

Hence the "back story" of every brand and label eager to form a bond with its target market with all the intimacy and loyalty of a true friendship; the dedication of the collector to both the expansion of their personal assemblage and the art of its display; and the enduring power and significance of the souvenir.

It should come as no surprise, then, that *things*—the material objects that surround us in our everyday lives—have come to be our reference points, the vessels of our memories, if not, as the emerging field of material culture would have it, a direct reflection and manifestation of who we are. Museums tell about past cultures through glass-paned vitrines of artefacts; biographies of a kind are written on the histories of everything from string to salt. Contemporary galleries show groupings of seemingly random objects gathered with narrative intention; their "objectness" increasingly the subject of the artists' work. That we look to "read" things

3

as signs and signifiers is not new—even early peoples saw totemic power in objects, so much so that their rituals demanded they be buried alongside them.

It is true that a part of me is gone with my mother. It was from her that I learned about the things that are good and the things that are beautiful; also the things that are hard and the things that are sad. In the end, of course, each of us is left with nothing *but* things. If with each acquisition we are in some way curating our lives, then it must be through a closer examination of these things and what they've come to mean to us that we can get closer to a real understanding of ourselves.

Such an examination seems particularly apt in any telling of the story of my extremely privileged if commensurately volatile childhood home, where my mother, who was an interior decorator and a great woman of style, elevated her choice of things to an art form, and thus the things themselves to a nearly mythical level. Things to us were a language that we shared and a bond between us. She passed her love of beautiful things, and her knowledge about them, on to me. Which might explain how, searching for the horizon in my off-balanced state after my mother's death, I found myself on a sort of scavenger hunt to find her, excavating her life and our relationship with the things that surrounded us, looking for clues.

In writing this memoir, my intention has never been to offer anything like a family history; our story is not so unique as to be remarkable, and my siblings have their own stories to tell. What I have attempted to do here instead is to write the way memory works, which is neither logical nor chronological, but intuitive. In this way, I could also try to think like my mother, whose own personal logic was always significantly more associative than rational. Seeing her things as signs and symbols offered a way to draw my lens in closer to try to capture the "real" her. As a portrait, this one is more impressionistic than representational; more like looking at her through the many-coloured shafts of light thrown by a prism on one of her glass-topped coffee tables than any sort of black-and-white account.

There is little doubt that my mother, who always liked to leave a big impression, would have very much enjoyed being the subject of a book. Whether or not she might have been pleased with this one is ultimately as unknowable as she was. But then, she always believed in maintaining a sense of mystery. When it came to my mother, there never was going to be anything resembling a clear understanding. Whatever possible insights would always be shrouded in a fine grey mist.

What I discovered while writing a book about my mother is that I was, without knowing it, also writing a book about myself. Children, even grown ones, can't ever see their parents as fellow adults without the warp of their childish lens, I suppose. And then any form of memoir can't help being about the one who's doing all the remembering.

And it was all, despite the bruised egos and bits of broken glass, really such fun, so glamorous and so fabulous to have the mother that I did. I had the extraordinary good fortune to grow up in a loving and generous family in the most indulgent time in history in the most peaceful and accommodating country in the world, so in no way here am I asking for anyone's sympathy. Indeed, I have no great uplifting moral lesson to impart. No arc of truth other than that, as my mother would definitely have been the first to say, she taught me everything I know about love and life — for better or worse.

One

PEARLS

THE LAST WORD I ever heard from my mother was "pearls."
Though I didn't actually *hear* it; rather, the letters P-E-A-R-L-S
were slowly spelled out, with much effort, by pointing her
index finger at the letters on a white card printed with the
alphabet that was supplied for this purpose by the nursing
staff in the ICU. My mother had a giant clear blue plastic
tube attached to a breathing machine stuck down her throat
and couldn't speak.

Which didn't in any way prevent her from making herself understood. Always one for the grand gesture, the sly
brow, the dark look, the giant sweep of a hand, the pointing finger — hers, now, crooked like a witch's on a hand so
swollen the skin looked tightly stuffed, like a sausage — our
mother made, to the three of us kids standing around her
bed at Mount Sinai Hospital next to the deafening suck-and-
whoosh of the ventilator heaving her chest up and down, two

things perfectly clear. First, that she, Susan May Lambert Young, wanted to die, and that I, her eldest, was the one who should get her pearls.

TO BE PERFECTLY HONEST, I had always admired them. Unlike those graduated sweetheart necklaces that make you look like a college co-ed circa 1956 (kind of uptight, even if in a Mary McCarthy sort of way), or those comically gumball-sized Barbara Bush chokers with the jewelled clasps everyone wore in the '80s courtesy of Kenneth Jay Lane, my mother's pearls are fabulously, perfectly, art deco soigné. Fat and creamy, but elegantly flapper-length and so evenly sized, they always looked like Chanel fakes on my mother's tall, slim, square-shouldered, and small-chested frame.

Of all the precious stones, pearls have got to be the most feminine. Formed from a vexatious piece of grit the uvula-like oyster can't quite manage to cough up, the pearl-to-be is trapped to fulminate in Venus's shell until it becomes a globe as pink-white and glowing as a runaway breast in a Rubens painting. A diver's rare prize, won only after searching the liquid deep, the pearl, once strung, becomes the precious trapping of womanhood. Seemingly lit from within, it is as unknowable and fascinating as the moon, the fallen tear of an enchanted princess in a fairy tale, the drop earring on the mysterious girl in the Vermeer whose gaze from any angle is always turned to you.

As a collar to tradition, pearls are both chain and mantle, gathered and strung around the neck like the kinky accessory of a favoured pet—a reminder of the tether that comes with being desired. Yes, pearls are girls. They are unuttered thoughts and dreams trapped inside shells; planets and globes and orbs and milky breasts. And then, naturally, you drape this creamy strand of luminous globes across your own.

The story of how my mother, who emerged Venus-like to the amazement and admiration of her small-town Ontario family in 1939, managed to land such a prize set was one of the pearls she might pull out at parties. With a glass of red in one hand and a Craven "A" dripping its ash in the other, she would grab at the creamy strand dangling just beneath the deep V of her silk blouse, arch her dark brows dramatically, lower her lids till her eyes were half-closed like a psychic in a trance leading a séance and offer, as if she were sharing a closely guarded secret amongst the world's top gemologists: "You know, pearls as good as these no longer even exist."

Gripping at your wrist to ensure your continued attention, she would go on: "These used to belong to the woman who ran that European jewellery store. You know her, the one with the terrific taste. She wouldn't even consider selling them to us because they were so absolutely perfect. But of course, Perce went back to the store afterwards, and the woman wasn't there, so her own husband, who I always thought was a bit of a suspicious character—I think he had a gambling problem, she was the one who really ran that business—pulled them out from under the counter and sold them to Perce while his poor wife was out at lunch!"

Perce would be my father, the princely youngest child of Russian Jewish émigrés so fancifully named by his two much older European-born sisters that he was forever after misidentified by others as Percy or Pierce. But no, a beautiful alien from another planet entirely, he came with a name invented just for him. In some unconscious way, I always imagined Perce stood for "persistence" because, even before everything went haywire inside his perfectly square-jawed head, that was his most marked quality, and thus the point of many of my mother's best stories.

My mother had a similar yarn about the fabulous old house my parents lived in for many years — a graceful Palladian villa in the highly established Rosedale neighbourhood of Toronto. My husband and I were married there in a grand, black-tie party for two hundred and fifty of our nearest and dearest on a record-breakingly sweltering summer night in a record-breaking July heat wave. Everyone drank so much, the next morning the place looked like a frat house. One of the beautifully panelled interior doors had been broken down with an axe to free a trapped and panicking guest from an upstairs bathroom (we have the pictures, of my father and brother, stripped to the waist in their tuxedos like a pair of axe-toting dancers from Chippendales). And random eggplants from the Tuscan-themed tabletop arrangements (what can I say, it was the '80s) were strewn all over the lawn.

My mother, naturally, took over the planning of this world-historic event, along with her gay pal Van (a lovely man, a florist with a Roman background who grew up in Niagara Falls and used to make us fried artichokes *alla Romana* before he died, too young, of HIV/AIDS). So over the top were the results of this signature Susan Young production that she complained bitterly for years afterward that none of the guests even noticed the frozen vodka caviar station melting under the chandelier in the dining room. "All that beautiful caviar, and it was eaten by the band!"

The house, which was white, had Palladian windows and overlooked a park. It was the kind of house that would prompt interior decorators like my mother to talk admiringly about its "bones." The story was that it had been built in the '20s and six decades later, it was still inhabited by its original owner. When my parents drove by one day and knocked on the door to inquire whether she might ever consider selling it, the elderly woman who answered the door told them that the house had been built for her by her parents as a wedding gift, and she would have to be dragged out the front door in a coffin before it was to be sold.

"And a week later, she died!" my mother would laugh, banging a nearby tabletop or unprotected upper arm with one of her pavé diamond Liberace rings for emphasis.

Yes, my mother was a gay icon.

AS A FAMILY, we moved a lot. And usually on to bigger and, after my mother worked her mojo on them, better places. In Toronto in the '70s, you had to be virtually mentally incompetent not to make money just buying houses, fixing them up, and selling them again. When I came along, my parents were living in a rental apartment on Christie Street. In our next place, a duplex on fashionable Cluny Drive, I remember a bold black-and-white trellis pattern wallpaper my mother installed on the stairs to our upper-level digs. In our first house—an old wreck on Millbank Avenue in the old-money enclave of Forest Hill that my parents virtually stole out from underneath the last, deeply alcoholic heir to a WASP Establishment family who was living like Grey Gardens' Edie Beale amongst the cobweb-covered Georgian silver—she painted the dining-room ceiling tomato red and papered the walls with Mylar.

After Millbank came a grander residence blocks away I will refer to as the Fuck-You Forest Hill House, then it was off to the white Rosedale Palladian, followed by an empty-nest downsizing to a brick Victorian semi nearby, before the double-whammy of their dwindling finances and my mother's declining mobility landed them in what would be their final destination—a two-bedroom condo in an old-school midtown building swankily named the Benvenuto.

As a decorator, much like in life, my mother's specialty was (in her words) "making a statement." But it was in that fine-boned Rosedale Palladian that her signature style reached its zenith. Absolutely everything in the interior, from the walls to the silk satin sofas to the soft broadloom, was in the same exact shade of pearl-grey. Almost every surface glistened with glass, steel, satin and mirror, a cool, endlessly reflective monochromatic palette that was featured on the cover of décor magazines and that she took along with her through successively smaller, identically pearl-grey residences till the grave.

IN THE MONTHS LEADING up to my mother's last stop in the ICU, it was already hard for her to keep anything down. Always a bit of a choker, just like her mother before her, and prone to unattractive fits of coughing up vitamins in the sink just after swallowing them, it had become almost routine to observe her across the table in a fancy restaurant quietly spitting up her lunch into a white linen napkin.

My father, whose dementia had by this point made him challenging to lunch with, let alone live with, must have become an even harder pill for her to swallow. Right before she ended up in hospital, my mother, worn down by his rages and, possibly (one never really knew), truly afraid for her life, had finally called the police to have him arrested. At lunch with a friend, I glanced down at my phone to see a message from my sister that our seventy-eight-year-old father with dementia was in jail.

Once my mother was at Mount Sinai, our dad, now installed in an assisted-living apartment in a senior's residence, would still insist on driving himself there every day (despite the fact that he shouldn't have been driving at all), as well as parking his Jeep, as per his custom, right in the emergency entrance where the ambulances pull in. Like an aging Peter Beard on safari or a model in a Ralph Lauren ad, he would arrive extremely tanned and wearing loafers with no socks.

I hated going to the hospital. There was nowhere to park, the elevators took forever, it smelled like people's old clothes and disinfectant, and the creepy taupe wipe-down Rubbermaid surfaces seemed tired and worn having to contain all that sickness. Some days, I just couldn't bring myself to go and visit. Others I might reward myself with a Valium stolen from my mother's bedside drawer before heading out the door. The whole drive down I would delay the inevitable by stopping to pick up crustless tea sandwiches or ginger ale or shortbread cookies—the nursery comfort foods of my mother's Anglican, postwar childhood that, at least before they shoved a tube down her throat, she might still be able to pick at.

In the weeks before landing in the hospital, my mother was virtually a shut-in, complaining of pain in her shoulder and, after finally kicking my dad out, spending her days in bed and not answering the phone. On my dreaded visits to my parents' apartment, where my mother now lived, lame, argumentative, and alone, I guiltily stocked the fridge with prepared foods like chicken pot pie that she never ate and I had to throw out after their best-before dates had expired. I'd get calls: from the building's concierge, that my mother had fallen and needed help to get back into bed (only to rush over and find her giggling and smirking over my concern); or from the caregiver we had hired to check in on her every afternoon, that my mother was asking her to buy bottles of vodka.

But the thing about my mother was that you could never fully count her out. One morning when I had arranged to take her to the doctor to have him look at her shoulder, fully expecting to have to drag her out of bed or to have her simply refuse to answer the door, I pulled into the drive in front of her building and there she was, waiting for me in lipstick and pearls and looking like a million bucks, despite the ugly walker we had forced on her.

HAD SHE FALLEN OR had my father pulled her arm in anger and twisted it, as she claimed? Either way, there was a microscopic tear in the ligaments of her shoulder that was causing her almost unbearable pain. The first operation to mend it was unsuccessful. After the second attempt, which left my mother in an oxygen mask, struggling for breath, the surgeon came in to tell us how pleased he was with the result. For once, I actually happened to be in the room when the doctor was making his rounds.

"You can see the incision is healing nicely," he says, casually lifting the sleeve of a dying seventy-three-year-old woman's blue hospital gown to display his handiwork. Nodding amiably at my half-naked mother who, despite the impediment of her mask, is clearly glaring back at him with dark intensity above the elastic straps, he adds, "I think the operation went really very well," before leaving to enact another heartless charade with his next patient.

It's around this point that things start to get scary and serious. My brother Josh, who has been summoned to her bedside, starts to feel weird about heading back to New York and changes his flight. He's staying with us in our second-floor guest room and, since he arrived with only a carry-on, he's started wearing our son Philip's clothes. Mornings we meet our sister Jen at the ICU, armed with sustaining flagons of takeout coffee. After long, bleak March afternoons at the hospital, we fortify ourselves with greasy takeout and single malt. In a weak attempt at crisis humour, our living room, where my husband Thomas keeps a constant fire burning and keeps re-filling our glasses, has been re-named the Whiskey Lounge.

Even before they call Code Blue and send my mother up to the intensive care floor, my father's main preoccupation in the hospital is bed linen maintenance. At his post by my mother's side he keeps pulling up her turmeric-coloured pashmina blanket and tucking it in around the business at her neck until it looks like she's suffocating. Once she's actually pinned to the bed through the trachea like a butterfly in a nineteenth-century gentleman's curio cabinet, my mother seems to be struggling even more to free herself from the sheets. Nonetheless, in some weird repetitive tic, he keeps tucking her in around the neck, as if adequate blanket coverage is the problem. Just watching it makes me want to scream.

"She can't seem to relax," the nurses in the ICU complain to us. "Unless we totally knock her out, she's always pulling at her breathing tube trying to take it out."

As per the chief intensive care nurse's recommendation, my brother Josh and I are at Best Buy, trying to find a boom box and headphones that might soothe the savage wildness of her obvious discomfort with music. She's always loved the opera! Surely the EMI Classics recording of Callas singing *La Traviata* is the ticket. Giddy with the brief hall pass from Crisis Watch, my brother holds up a bright red pair of Beats by Dr. Dre and a Rasta pair from House of Marley, asking which one Mom would prefer.

Back at the ICU, it is super clear to us that my mother doesn't give a rat's ass for our opera selection. She wants unplugging and she wants it *now*. This is less clear to the doctors, who, unlike Jen and Josh and me, have not been raised by a goddess who could smite all three of us dead in our tracks with a single raised eyebrow. And then there's the problem of our father, who is clearly well past understanding what is going on.

"But what about the Wonder Drugs?" asks our dad, who must, at that moment, have suddenly been able to recall the headline of an article on the miraculous strides in health care he'd once read in Time magazine back in 1979.

Since it seems weird somehow to talk about removing our mother from life support right there in front of her, we head down the hall to some sort of event space where we find a round table we can sit at even though it's topped with dirty linens. There must have been some kind of hospital fundraiser here earlier, but nobody has been in yet to clear the tables. The party, such as it was, is clearly over.

IN PICTURES AS A GIRL, my mother was almost impossibly beautiful. Dark hair, long nose, high cheekbones, hazel eyes that would brighten when she smiled her wide, white smile. With her sporty, square-shouldered build, long limbs, martini-glass tits, and perfect calves, American sportswear was made for her. Once, in my teens on a girls' weekend in New York, just the two of us, the designer Bill Blass— a complete stranger—actually stopped us at a street corner to tell her how terrific she looked. I remember, even when I was little, admiring her tan, bony feet in thong sandals, her braless nipples through deep-cut jersey and silk, wishing one day I too would have elegant veins on my child's feet and hands, that my laugh would sound as throaty and chic as hers.

Of course, I never could smoke, no matter how much I tried, wheezing over a stale, stolen cigarette of my mother's at thirteen, trying to blow the smoke out the window of my Flower Power–wallpapered third-floor bedroom. After taking it up in her teens, my mother never could really quit. Years after she had supposedly given it up, the inside seam of her handbag would be lined with shreds of tobacco, and you might surprise her in the kitchen of my parents' condo sneaking a quick one, blowing the incriminating smoke into the oven vent hood.

After her death, the word my father used, over and over, pulling the now-yellow laminated picture of my mother as a teenager from the front pocket of his jeans, was "captivating." As in, "Your mother was the most captivating woman I ever met."

The art of being captivating is one that I observed from childhood and yet, perhaps as a result, is one that has always remained beyond my grasp. Should you want to leave everyone awestruck long after you are gone, I highly recommend uttering each and every statement you make during your lifetime — whether right or simply wrong — with total and complete conviction, like a cross between Stalin and Diana Vreeland. It also helps to be eerily psychic and working on a different, more intuitive level than most other people, whether or not such gifts might occasionally lead to being misunderstood.

Once, when I was in high school, I came home to find the family room sofa oddly deconstructed. "Home" at that point in our lives was a grandly overblown faux-Tudor chateau in fancy Forest Hill that even my mother thought was in terrible taste. My father had gone ahead and bought it anyway in a fit of macho pique after its extremely wealthy owner, the builder of the haut-bourgeois monstrosity, told him that we would never be able to afford it (hence its appellation as our "Fuck-You Forest Hill House"). In her appointment of the interior, however, which involved the liberal application of dark woods and louche velvets in the manner of a '70s Milanese palazzo, my mother certainly rose to the occasion.

What passed for our "family room" was a sunken, heavily panelled enclave, each panel of which my mother had mirrored for an infinitely reflective effect like the Hall of Mirrors at Versailles. To enter, you had to step down from the vast empty foyer as if you were entering a nightclub, which in a way it was, most afternoons, for a party of one. The one being my mother, who, dressed in her uniform of that era—a cowl-neck cashmere sweater over grey flannel trousers, accessorized with multiple ropes of gold chains, her hair blown out into the tousled mane of a lioness—would be fully ensconced in the depths of one massively overstuffed velvet sofa, smoking and drinking red wine while on the phone.

I remember coming home from school one dark weekday afternoon in winter.

"Hi, Mum," I yell from the mudroom by the side door, dropping my backpack and slipping off my slushy boots onto the rustic Spanish-tile floor. (Nobody in the house ever uses the actual front entrance, preferring the less daunting trek from the side door to navigating the formidable foyer, which was covered in so much travertine it was about as welcoming as an Egyptian pharaoh's tomb.)

Entering the nightclub/family room where my mother is, as usual, admiring her reflection from the depths of the velvet, I had a vague sense of something being a bit off. This slight, subconscious impression must somehow have registered on my face because my mother, hanging up the phone and leaping off the sofa, suddenly declares, with a bold sweep of one arm as if she were Catherine the Great astride a rearing horse on the palace steps liberating St. Petersburg for the Russian people, "Back pillows are out!"

So alarmingly emphatic is this statement, and so strange the after-school greeting, with its lack of an introductory article and odd emphasis on "out," that I actually think for a moment that what she is saying is that current fashions in interiors now demand the immediate, and potentially permanent, removal of all back sofa cushions.

Momentarily speechless, I stand there in my damp socks on the fur rug, a picture of confusion reflected endlessly in the cruel mirrored panels, trying to come up with the appropriate response. It is true that the pillows on the back of the sofa do seem to be missing. But what does this somewhat unremarkable situation, which my captivating mother has remarked on so very emphatically, actually mean? Maybe this is one of her famous pronouncements, most of which have to do with her stylistic "vision"?

"So...back pillows are, like, *out*?"

"Yes, dear," says Mum, turning back to the phone after eyeing me with what appears to be pity for my hopeless failure to follow even the most basic rules of conversation. "They're out for dry cleaning."

These little miscommunications between slow, ordinary me,

stranded on planet earth with all the other average humans, and the cosmic transmissions that informed my mother's everyday conversation were common. But such was her style of delivery.

Every time I try anything on in a change room, apply moisturizer, or make myself a pot of tea, I can still hear my mother's pearls of wisdom, delivered, always, as if she, Susan May Young (née Lambert, an entirely self-invented diva from a nice Anglican family in St. Catharines, Ontario) was some sort of oracle and such proclamations were being delivered from Style's highest Mount.

"Never underestimate the value of a fashion investment." A "fashion investment" could be anything from a "*really good* haircut" to a pair of sunglasses, black pants, or a trench coat (feel free to substitute any classic, *really good* item here).

"A touch of black can be grounding."

"Finding the right blue can be difficult."

"Never say that you 'hate' a colour like orange, because you never know what you will love next."

While watching someone try on clothes in front of a mirror, my mother might instruct: "Wear it! Don't let an item of clothing wear you." Or, "She's just jealous" — about anyone who failed to include us or seemed ill-disposed. Her trademark riposte, after hearing from anyone on the mend from the flu or an unfortunate bout of food poisoning, was: "No matter how sick you are, there isn't a woman alive who doesn't think, for just a moment, 'Well, at least I might have lost a little weight.'"

And her very favourite, typically delivered with a side-long, withering glance for raised-in-the-'70s, flannel-shirted, free-to-be me: "*Try* to maintain a sense of mystery."

I swear that my mother—who lived for beauty and surrounded all of us in such an exquisitely curated envelope of it, as if its talismanic power could shield us from all the ugliness in the world—once actually said at the mere mention of someone, "I hate her, she's ugly."

Which is not to suggest that her penchant for overemphasis was always entirely negative. She was also immensely generous, almost overly so, loading us down with every imaginable gift and superlative, which always made me suspicious of her praise.

She was almost never dull or uninteresting, and she was fabulously indulgent with everyone, most of all herself. And she loved us big, and boldly. Her kisses were loud and wet. Her laughter came easily and was as uninhibited as her fury. And her signature signoff, whether whispered loudly in one's ear following a kiss, before hanging up the phone, or quickly scribbled on a written note or letter—always near-impossible to read in her looping scrawl—was "Love, love, love you."

MY MOTHER WAS MADE up entirely of estrogen: intuitive and mercurial, witchy and dark, earthy and glamorous, manipulative and beautiful, childlike and wise, loving, and harsh, messy and gorgeous, emphatic, dramatic, operatic, and terrifying. And, yes, captivating. There was no room she entered that did not feel her presence. And no scarf, glove, coat, book, umbrella, sweater, or handbag that failed to exude her perfume long after she had gone.

It is hard for me now to wear her pearls. Not just because I miss her—and I do, still, every day—just as much as I am grateful that for her, the pain, the suffering, and most of all, the terrible indignity of growing old and sick is finally over and done. No, it's literally hard for me to wear the pearls because, unlike my mother, I am no Gatsby girl. I emerged from my own shell a woman with big round Russian Jewish breasts. Breasts I immediately loathed, that made me the object of an unwanted kind of attention, and insistently defied with their protuberance all efforts at a chic silhouette. And so her legacy, the subject of her last words on earth, these precious fetishes of the woman who nursed me, just slide around like marbles across my own generous bosom and refuse to hang just so, the way they always did on her tan, bony chest.

Every time I slip them on, I feel like an impostor. Despite being the same age now as my mother was when she became a grandmother, I still don't feel grown-up enough to wear them. A perplexing state of affairs that only confirms that, despite being her daughter — or, perhaps, because of it — I am, in so many ways, not the woman she was.

Almost five years now after her death, the tragic-comic scene in which we finally managed to convince the authorities that she desperately wanted off the machine is still vivid. It took so long after the unplugging for her to finally stop breathing on her own (although they gave her morphine, they wouldn't remove that bloody tube down her throat till after she died — a failure on my part to have negotiated her full release from being pinned to the bed like a dying butterfly that still haunts me)...so long that the four of us gathered around her bedside began to lose focus. So freaking long that out of sheer exhaustion and boredom my father and brother started idly snacking on the Melba toasts in the official family care package the nurses had left us, dropping crumbs over the terrible baby blue polyester bed sheets as she lay there dying.

Almost five years later and every time I pull out her pearls I'm still left wondering whether this means I don't measure up, or whether I should be eternally grateful.

Two

THE BLUE GLASS BOTTLE

MY FATHER NOW LIVES on a locked floor of a Jewish senior's residence called Baycrest. Everything about the place is depressing, from its bleak, windswept location off the highway to the fact that it's a last stop for people who have become so impossible to deal with that they have to be locked in. Each of the aging and infirm residents, some of whom moan repeatedly or pace the halls like my dad, are considered lucky given the long government wait lists to be billeted to a single room on the floor. The rooms have built-in locked closets and ugly hospital-style beds; the side table and chair look like they come from a used office supply company. At six foot four, my father is too tall for his ugly bed, which has a footboard. Sometimes, when he stops his pacing long enough to submit to a nap, he puts his long, thin legs up alongside the bed on the cheap little chair.

My mother would have been appalled.

Beside the door to my father's room, as with every other door on this floor, is a glass cabinet. Inside, beneath each patient's name, are photos of their loved ones and family mementoes. The photos we provided for my dad's personal cabinet have yellow Post-it notes on the back with all of our names written out so that the caregivers can remind my dad who we all are. Next door, in Raphael Nissenbaum's cabinet, is a pair of bronzed baby shoes; each time I catch a glimpse of them I can't help but wonder whether they belong to a grandchild or whether the tiny brass shoes were once his.

Just before Christmas, my dad's caregivers, a revolving team of saint-like Filipino women, gave my sister and I a schmaltzy Christmas card that they claimed my dad, who never would have chosen such a thing, had picked out for us and signed all by himself. Inside, under the Jesus-y blessing, written in pen in my father's unmistakable and still surprisingly clear, strong hand, was written, "Love, Fraser."

There is absolutely no one in our family named Fraser, nor a single person I can think of that we might know with that name.

THE STORY OF HOW my parents met has all the hallmarks of a Susan Young production. According to my mother, it was at a wedding in Niagara Falls. My mother had been raised in proper, Anglo-Canadian St. Catharines, Ontario, a town known as the "Garden City" with a Victorian band-shell in its main park under the maple trees; my father in neighbouring, dodgier Welland, notable chiefly for its canal.

Niagara Falls in the '50s, apparently, was the height of glam.

"I had come with a date. I couldn't even tell you whose wedding it was, but I was wearing…"

It can safely be said there was no moment in my mother's life, earth-shattering or entirely insignificant, for which she could not immediately recall—and describe in full detail, as if she were emcee-ing a fashion show—the outfit she had on.

"It was cream, not white, but much softer, and more flattering. A bone or ivory colour, in a really lovely cashmere—not the cheap stuff that pills the moment you wear it but the real three-ply Scottish kind—and rib-knit, with a slightly scooped neckline." she would say, tracing the outline of the dress or sweater with a pointed index finger as if drawing the garment on her skin. "I had been working at a ladies' store on St. Paul Street so I would get a discount on all of these really wonderful skirts and sweaters…"

And then the recollection of her first glimpse of my father would interrupt her fashion narration. "Of course Perce walked right up to us, tall and blonde with that big square jaw and in these dark sunglasses and chinos, and he asked me what I wanted to drink before sending my date for the evening off to fetch drinks for all of us—and off the jerk actually went!"

It was hard to say where exactly my parents came by their special brand of arrogance. Neither of them was particularly, as my mother would have said, laying on a posh accent, "to the manor born."

My father, the new-world afterthought of Russian Jewish émigrés who'd come with their two small daughters to Canada in the 1920s, grew up lonely, with immigrant parents and two much older sisters and used to get beat up for being Jewish on his way home from Welland High and Vocational. His tiny mother Dora doted on her princeling, serving him his favourite "steak with eggs on top" (a sort of breaded schnitzel) to fatten him up in his skinny teen years. After surviving both childhood TB and a harrowing exodus from Europe, she died fairly young, around when my sister was born, of breast cancer. His father, Sam, was tall and blonde and suave in the manner of a Russian-Jewish Bing Crosby. Like Bing, he favoured a pipe and even—as documented in a jerky super-8 film of their annual Miami Beach vacation—a white-billed captain's hat, worn jauntily to one side. A sharp hand at cards with an ear for languages, my zayda could play a game of rummy or sell a ladies' coat in Hungarian, Ukrainian, Polish, Russian, or Yiddish. He loved *The Ed Sullivan Show* and an old-fashioned peanut brittle called Poppycock that came in a round tin and he called my father "Sonny boy." According to my father, whenever his only son would ask to do anything vigorously outdoorsy or "Canadian," like play hockey or learn to ski, Sam's customary response, presumably delivered with a shrug and a pull at his pipe stuffed with Sobranie, was: "*Vut* do you need it for?"

The house my father was raised in, on Welland's Parkway Drive, I recall as almost a model of '50s style—down to the clear plastic that covered all the rust-velvet furniture in the sunken living room with its wall-to-wall drapes and my Russian zayda's curiously Anglophile collection of Toby jugs mounted on a plate rail on the curved glass-block wall of the den.

Sam started out as a peddler in Toronto's Kensington

Market, eventually moving to Welland and opening his own ladies' store — Exclusive — where he would showcase the latest every season from the garment wholesalers and furriers that then lined Spadina Avenue. If you walk down Welland's now shuttered and desolate main street, you can still see "Exclusive Ladies Wear" embedded in script on the pavement at what used to be its entrance.

My mysteriously dark mother, with her outsized personality and a full head taller than her parents, must have always seemed too big for Margaret and Raymond Lambert's little bay-windowed house on the cul-de-sac of St. Catharines' Queen Mary Drive. She must have felt like Alice in Wonderland after eating the wrong mushrooms — particularly next to a petite, blonde '50s dream girl like her older sister Ann. Next up after my mother was her brother Bill, whom my mother most closely resembled and always credited with giving her a lifelong fear of citrus fruit by tormenting her with views of his pulpy teeth after eating oranges; then her baby sister Mary, who, in family photos as a child, looked exactly like the freckle-faced girl in pigtails on the faded cover of *Maggie Muggins* on my grandparents' bookshelves that I used to read whenever we would visit.

My grandpa Ray raised his family of four on an auto foreman's salary, and yet the Lamberts were members of the St. Catharines Golf and Country Club and spent their summers at a rented cottage on the Muskoka lakes. The GM plant was mere blocks from their house; each and every work day Ray walked home for lunch, which was unfailingly served on the everyday English china at his own dining room table by his wife Marg — my nana, who, growing up as the youngest daughter of English immigrants in Oshawa, was known as Molly Timmins.

Many years later, not so long after Nana ended up putting her car—always a GM—in drive, rather than reverse, in the driveway beside their house and the car crashed through the back of the garage, sailing through the air until it finally landed at the bottom of their steep garden, Nana was diagnosed with Alzheimer's. Once she was moved into a care home, my grandpa Ray, who was totally fine mentally, packed up his few things—chiefly big band recordings and the extremely thick, black-framed, amber-tinted eyeglasses he wore to correct his extremely poor vision—and moved in with her.

"She's still Molly Timmins, the prettiest girl I ever met," said my grandpa Ray, as, to my mother's horror, my nana lay curled in a fetal position, insensate and drooling, in the bed next to his for a cruel number of years.

To hear my parents speak of their relatively insignificant nests, it seemed as if they both believed their childhood circumstances had been some sort of accident—the stork blown off course in his delivery of their swaddled infant selves. Less a product of their backgrounds than their own inventions, misunderstood by their families if not underappreciated, they were, at least in their own minds, two swan's eggs kindly, if ineptly, raised amongst the dazzled ducks and hens.

The two rare birds, however, found each other. Neither was ever supposed to end up with the other. My mother's family, who had probably never even met a Jew before they met my father, were by all accounts shocked my mother would go ahead and marry one. As for my father's family, it helped that the *shiksa* (my mother) was young, good looking, and knew how to dress.

In pictures of their May, 1960 wedding in comparatively cosmopolitan Toronto, where my parents high-tailed it not long after they met, my twenty-one-year-old mother looks like a young Jackie O in an ivory two-piece silk suit with a portrait neckline and a hat shaped like a small lampshade. My father, who is in his first year of law school and has a buzz cut like a shorn chick, looks about sixteen as he is about to break the glass.

The group portrait taken by a photographer from Eaton's College Street shows the new in-laws looking ill-matched, if not uncomfortable, in the same room, let alone the same family— although both my fair, fine-boned maternal grandmother Marg and my short, dark, bosomy Bubba Dora are wearing nearly identical fur shawls over shiny taffeta dresses, each accessorized with exceedingly proper little white gloves, stiletto-heeled pumps, and the requisite collar-length strand of white pearls.

Like all Jewish weddings, my parents'—even though my mother was a convert—must have ended with the breaking of a glass. "Congratulations!" or "Mazel Tov!" everybody yells, as if a bottle of champagne has been cracked open, which gives the feeling it's meant for luck, like the Jewish equivalent of "Cheers!"

In my parents' case, this ritual was like a bottle of champagne ceremonially launched against the side of a ship that, over its many years at sea, was to catch so much more shattered debris in its wake.

31

WHEN I ARRIVE, rather abruptly, the next spring, it is clear that I am the plaything of these two only slightly more responsible children. It is 1961 and we are living in a rented one-bedroom apartment on Christie Street in Toronto, where the kindly elderly neighbours, many of them Holocaust survivors from Europe, occasionally offer to help my clueless young mother, a mere twenty-one years old at the time, with babysitting. My dad is a law student, staying up late every night smoking cigarettes and reading for his bar admission exams at Osgoode Hall.

With little money or time for outside amusements, my young parents wake me up from my crib late at night to dance for them in my snap-front, quilted, vinyl-footed cotton pyjamas. According to my mother, I was a lively addition if not an early genius. The story goes that as soon as I learn to talk, I call "Susan!" rather than "Mommy" from my crib, in infant imitation of my father. It didn't take me long to learn calling "Mommmmmy" over and over wasn't getting me anywhere.

Or that when he called, she would come.

MY OWN EARLIEST MEMORY is of a big blue glass bottle on the landing of our apartment. I must have been around three years old because my sister wasn't born yet, and we, the original three, were living in the old WASP Establishment neighbourhood of Rosedale, in the upper floors of a rented duplex someone had carved out of drywall from a Tudor-style brick Upper Canadian family home. It was early in the swinging '60s. By the stereo, we had *A Hard*

Day's Night, with its groovy solarized cover featuring the Beatles' hairdos, as well as the fascinating woman on the cover of *Whipped Cream & Other Delights* by Herb Alpert & the Tijuana Brass, wearing what looked like a wedding dress made of icing and saucily licking her fingers. My father was just starting out as a young lawyer at Levinter, Grosberg (one of the few Bay Street firms that would accept Jews at the time). And my mother, with her dreams of carrying the torch lit by such stars in the firmament of great American decorating as Dorothy Draper or Elsie de Wolfe put on hold by my arrival, had updated our digs by filling vintage bottles with sprigs of trailing ivy and peacock feathers and hanging a mod Carnaby Street–inspired wallpaper up and down the stairs. A buyer for the glamorous home décor department at Eaton's College Street, a job she adored, she was abruptly fired when a customer complained after seeing her cross the showroom floor. My mother was pregnant, which, of course, a young working woman was not permitted to be at the time. And so now she was mostly home with me, teaching interior design at a community college while trying to drum up decorating jobs, which, for her, meant smoking and reading Russian novels through the long winter afternoons as I played.

I remember the blue bottle as being giant, although size in recollection is notoriously unreliable. In childhood, scale and perspective are off, coming as they do from a shorter, more mystified place. In any event, the bottle seemed big to me. It was made of clear blue glass and vaguely gourd-shaped, with a long neck and a sturdy, articulated rim like a beer bottle. It was probably an authentic version of the kind of ethnic-chic decorative accent (designed in collaboration with the women of a remote tribe and made to benefit a grassroots development initiative) that's now readily available online or, with 15 percent of its sales going toward the initiative, at Pottery Barn or West Elm—all of which, of course, did not exist at the time.

I also remember our house being huge, which I now know it was not, and, growing up in snowy Toronto, being packed into a debilitating snowsuit before being dragged, zipped up, and overheated into submission, on a sled to the store amongst canyons of snow so deep and white it was like a scene from *The Nutcracker*, which we used to go and see at the O'Keefe Centre every year.

Even though by all reports she had a busy three-year-old, my mother must have placed the big glass bottle on the otherwise empty landing to "Make a Design Statement."

To whom, I don't know, because I certainly can't recall many glamorous parties with important style arbiters as guests in that Early Childhood Era. Dinner was usually something like chicken, served late, on our white Athena plates with their ribbed rims set on navy vinyl placemats in the kitchen, when my dad finally made it home. Which never stopped Mum from insisting that we never, ever do anything so ugly as place a carton of milk or a bottle of ketchup directly on the Danish Modern dining table or, for that matter, that everything she liked or found beautiful made a Design Statement.

Some sort of statement must have been made, as the blue glass bottle did have a weird magic. When I think of it now, it seems like something Picasso might have painted beside a sad, thin boy during his Blue period. At the right times

34

of day it would catch the sun and send azure shafts of light across the black-and-white walls of the hall and the hardwood floor. Vaguely artisanal, it was probably made from hand-blown glass as its surface was bubbly with imperfections; looking through it made the world all wonky. The glass was cool and smooth and had an almost mineral smell, just like its colour, if blue gave off a smell. It was so strange and so pretty, I wanted to be close to it. It was fun to climb up in my stretchy tights and press myself against it and pull its tapered neck down to touch my teeth. And because it was almost my size, like a blue glass twin that I could stand next to and embrace, I also couldn't resist grabbing its neck and spinning it on its fat bottom.

"Stop playing with that," my mother, strangely aware, though on the telephone, would yell up the stairs in between drags of her Craven "A" cigarette. "It's not a toy."

Of course I had other things to play with. My Fisher-Price popcorn mower, for instance, which pleasingly popped away whether you mowed it along the floor or over your hair and down your shirt. An Etch A Sketch, shaped like the front of a TV set, with some sort of graphite dust you could hear shifting inside when you shook it blank, and nipple-like knobs you could twist and turn to make zig-zagging pictures on its screen. An early incarnation of Mr. Potato Head, a kit which gave you freaky plastic ears, eyes, and hair accessories to plug into a real tuber that oozed milky white blood when you stuck them in. Also a yellow plastic View-Master that looked like a pair of sci-fi goggles. When you held it up to your face, you could click through slides of Disney movies and the Grand Canyon via a plastic lever on the side, the pull of which made a satisfying ping. Or my portable record player, which I would scare myself silly with by starting the dark overture of *Peter and the Wolf,* until, heart in my throat, I would gouge the needle across the black surface of the vinyl to make it stop.

On TV, which was black and white with three channels you had to get up and physically turn a knob to switch, there was *The Friendly Giant,* with his tall giraffe friend Jerome, peeking into a medieval-looking tower and rearranging the tiny chairs through the castle window with his fat hands. And *Chez Hélène,* who had a little talking mouse named Suzie and spoke to us in CBC-mandated French while seeming somehow annoyed that we couldn't understand. I read through stacks of Dr. Seuss we got from the library and cut out paper dolls from books with outfits from different eras designed to fit over their awkwardly posed arms with foldable tabs. When these things got boring my mother, who never said no to a messy craft project, would make a paste of flour and water and salt I'd use to collage bits of old magazines together. Or she'd let me sort the tools of her trade like boxes of paint chips and odd buttons, or, best of all, use the Mixmaster to whip white mountainous peaks out of dish soap. But there was something about that blue bottle on the landing that drew me.

One afternoon, inevitably, it wobbled dangerously close to the wall. As soon as she heard the crash, my mother was on her hands and knees on the landing surrounded by bits of blue glass in tears.

"Don't you understand it was the only good thing I own!" she howled, with an intensity that scared me more than the crash. "The only good thing!"

It was a sad sight, the splinters and shards of glass where the Statement used to be. But my mother, who never cared if I made a mess and always said "We never cry over spilt milk" whenever I knocked over my glass at the kitchen table, seemed very mad.

I think I was fed dinner early that night, something warmed from a can, and sent to bed. She was right: it was not a toy. It was special and important and now it was broken.

At the time it seemed entirely possible that I had ruined everything.

AN EARLY MEASURE OF how important things were in our house is that when she was a baby, my little sister Jen was already a hoarder. Or perhaps "magpie" is a better word. But before she could even walk or talk, my tiny sister would spend her days whizzing around our apartment in a treacherous wheeled device with a seat and tray called a "walker" (now outlawed as a serious hazard around stairs, but wildly popular amongst the toddler set back in the lackadaisical '60s), which operated as her ladder and getaway car.

So efficient was this rig for snagging whatever might be bright and shiny that whenever anything in the house went astray (car keys, wallet, lipstick), my mother would immediately check Jen's toy box, where the missing item would regularly turn up concealed amongst her things. Small but focused, she never left any traces and, if confronted, would deny any knowledge of the missing item's whereabouts with her giant, denim-blue eyes.

Once our baby brother Joshua arrived, four years later,

he too exhibited an early attraction to the squirrelling away of shiny things. Wandering, presumably unsupervised, for hours through the dangerous minefield of our first house, which was constantly under renovation, clad only in diapers and a small tool belt for protection that our mother had purchased so that he could look just like one of the many construction workers on the premises, Josh had discovered a small opening in the floor that operated beautifully as a chute for anything slim-lined, like, say, our Dansk flatware. For the longest time, my mother couldn't figure out where all of our knives and forks were disappearing to until she found his secret cache in the unfinished basement.

But then, Josh never would have given her any clues, because he was famously silent until he was three. My mother was actually concerned that there might be something wrong with him until he finally just came out with a fully formed sentence. Later, it was revealed that when he was a baby he had been operating under the odd personal illusion that there were only so many words each of us were permitted to use in our lifetimes and that he hadn't wanted to use up his allotment prematurely.

My mother, when telling this story to anyone who would listen, would always finish by saying, "The poor thing must have been shocked at my extravagance considering how much talking I was doing, keeping up both ends of the conversation the entire time!"

And then there was my father, whom I fully adored, and who would take six-year-old me along with him everywhere. To drugstores, his all-time favourite places, to buy intriguing new shampoos and moisturizers to add to his collection. To outdoor football games in the fall, where he would gently, precisely, zip up my jacket and adjust my wool hat for maximum warmth and coverage, and where we would share bags of peanuts in the shell and make a mess in the stalls. To Switzer's Deli on Spadina Avenue, where he went when he was a student and where you could still get a good pastrami sandwich, old dills, and an extra-strength ginger ale he favoured called Vernors. On these outings, my father was both breathtakingly thoughtless—I could be left waiting, hot and dressed, for hours in a stuffy office or car—and extraordinarily kind. He patiently and carefully taught me basically everything, from how to ride a bike to how to form an argument. Like the rest of us in our house, the one thing I wanted most was his approval, perhaps because it was always going to be out of reach.

But this is not a story about him. For once, it is my mother's.

THE THING ABOUT GLASS is that it, too, leaves you hanging. Is it a liquid or a solid? The Victorians, who were transfixed by it and were witness to its early mass production, saw it as the very breath of life solidified, a manifestation of unearthly spirit that fascinates and distracts with surface reflection and revelations of depth.

At first glance, glass may appear transparent, but its true nature is deceptive, invisibly bouncing light back, reflecting and refracting, all the while obscuring its essential alchemy: a chemical reaction of hot blobs of liquid made sharply solid, a barely-there illusion of something real and material made only from simple sand melted under extreme heat until cooled into cutting shards. Alongside the bold lie of its transparency is its inherent unreliability—you cannot tell from the icy perfection of its smooth, hard surface how fragile glass truly is.

This underlying tension was one that my mother liked to play to extremes, in both her famous decorating strategy and most everything else in her life. For my mother, being more careful or keeping us from harm was never a priority. We could be cut and bleeding and showered in shards of glass, but there would be no steering her away from Making a Design Statement. Or from living or loving the way she wanted to.

"CHILDREN WHO GROW UP surrounded by beautiful things learn to respect them," she would say about her deadly, glass-topped coffee tables with their glittering display of precious, fragile things.

I'm not sure when or where, exactly, my mother acquired her fascination with glass coffee tables, but they became such a signature of her style, their laser-sharp edges such a constant and lurking danger in every house my parents ever lived in—regardless of their threat to unprotected shins, the heads of wrestling children, and the confusion of emerging pets from underneath all the light-reflecting and unforgiving surfaces—that it was a wonder that any of us survived intact.

On top of these tables, alongside a stack of coffee-table art books, would be a rotating collection of other (reflective, razor-sharp, and extremely fragile) precious glass things: a pair of glass obelisks; a grouping of glass candlesticks in varying heights (always equipped with off-white Concord candles, their wicks decoratively pre-burnt — white candles and raw wicks from the box being major faux pas as far as my mother was concerned); a luminous white stone Buddha on a glass pedestal; a Lalique or other cut-glass vase (always filled with pink-and-white rubrum lilies); a heavy, faceted Baccarat ashtray; and a Victorian glass doorstop so solid and weighty you could easily fell an intruder with it in one hand.

"It's all about bouncing light and reflection around a room," my mother would say, with an accompanying karate chop of one manicured and diamond-clad hand to underline her point.

When it came to a question of design or placement, the very air was no match for my mother's certainty. It would simply have to be cleaved into shards with a single gesture.

BEFORE DINNER THERE WOULD always be cheese and crackers (typically a runny French Brie or a three-year-old crumbling white cheddar and Carr's Table Water crackers, with a bunch of green seedless grapes for colour) placed artfully on a silver tray between the bibelots on one of my mother's glass coffee tables. And wine — back in the '80s, in those enormous balloon glasses the size of a child's head, but almost always in tippy, thin-stemmed glasses. Or on special occasions, champagne, in chilled, and equally precarious, glass flutes.

So frequently was there some sort of catastrophe with this set-up (a dog's wagging tail waving a glass of red off the table top, a carelessly knocked-over *objet* cracking a chunk off the bevelled edge of the table, a wineglass breaking at its stem after being imprecisely replaced in the light effect of the tabletop's dizzying surface) that we developed a five-minute emergency stain-removal family protocol involving the quick assembly of warm water, white vinegar, dishwashing liquid, and a roll of paper towels.

"Don't rub! Press!!" my mother would exhort, demonstrating with a forceful, two-handed gesture that looked like something from the St. John's Ambulance posters for emergency CPR, as we were all jolted into carpet-rescue mode.

Years later, when we were finally taking apart my parent's condo and packing everything up, it was amazing, on closer inspection, to see how chipped, stained, and ruined everything really was, despite our rescue efforts. The Modigliani-style bust that I had always thought looked like my mother had the bashed nose of a prizefighter (but then, by the end of her life, unfortunately, so did my mother). The Georgian clock I had always admired? Its lovely golden sundial pendulum was unattached and its dark wood base was missing half its fine trim.

What did they do? Throw the stuff at each other? Literally, there was almost nothing from the wreckage to emerge unscathed.

And then my mother herself. Always so wildly accident-prone over the years — forever bashing her shins on an open dishwasher or slicing her foot on a chunk of broken glass — that I almost always remember her cut and bleeding from somewhere, while at the same time completely oblivious to both her injury and the trail of blood in her wake.

GIVEN THE SCALE OF the damage, I often wondered if perhaps there was some kind of force field of destruction around my parents. Starting with a family I will call the Steinbergs, our nearest and dearest friends whom I was encouraged to think of as family—up until the day we never spoke to them again. We rented summer cottages with them up at Lake Simcoe, my parents vacationed with Jerry and Iona in Acapulco, and then we moved in right next door to them: only to end up worrying about how awkward it would be if we were ever to bump into them on the street. And then came a succession of others who would be quickly taken up as our dear and special friends before those friendships, too, shattered completely.

Ian and Cynthia, Ann and Charlie—gregarious, sporty Charlie taught my brother to skate, while fragile Ann ended up alone, drinking copious amounts of vodka with my mother in the afternoons. The Geists—my parents hosted their wedding at our house—are they even still married? Groovy Alex, who was originally a hairdresser, and his Brit-born fashion-designer wife, Susie. A stunning couple, they had a fabulous boutique in the brutalist Manulife Centre on Toronto's mink mile where they sold the black jersey pieces by Jean Muir and the Krizia and Sonia Rykiel animal-print sweaters my mother collected (and wore—never much of a believer in dry cleaning—reeking of perfume and flecked with fallen bits of food).

There are beautiful black and white pictures of the four of them in black tie drinking champagne on my dad's fortieth birthday out at Cherry Beach (unknown to all, Alex had arranged not only the champagne picnic on the sand,

43

but a hidden photographer). They used to come up north for weekends at my parents' cottage on Georgian Bay and Alex, an early adopter of Florentine *sprezzatura* thanks to his fashion travels in Italy, would cook us big Italian dinners. When I flipped my parents' black Mercedes convertible on my way to visit my boyfriend at summer camp, and my head and scalp emerged from the wreckage all scratched and bloody (I still have the clearest image of climbing out of the ruined car after the accident and stepping out onto the cleanly ejected windshield, a perfect sheet of glass that then shattered under my feet), Alex kindly came over and carefully washed and cut my ruined hair. After my parents moved in with them for a few months when my dad's development company tanked and they were in between houses, Alex and Susie split up, and not only our parents, but we three children—with the increasingly familiar sense of embarrassment of somehow being in the wrong by association combined with confusion as to what had actually taken place—just moved on.

But the worst of these cold wars was the one that developed with my father's sister Edith and her husband Bunny, whose real name was Bernard. Twelve years older than my father, with grown-up children and the same heavy-lidded Russian blue eyes, Edith was statuesque and so blonde she had to draw in eyebrows so she didn't look, in her words, "like a boiled egg." Early on, Edith claimed me as her own, sitting me in her lap and telling me that I looked like her. After my father's mother died, Edith and Bunny became our de facto grandparents, their large home in Welland the place we all gathered with our cousins for the Jewish

44

holidays. My whippet-thin, droll, and glamorous Aunt Eve and my bearded, professorial Uncle Len would come up from Philadelphia with their three kids: silent genius Daniel, beautiful hippie Kit, and baby Suzanne. Close in age, Suzanne and I would share our grown-up cousin Liz's bedroom (which turned scary in the dark thanks to the '60s hair extension — back then referred to as a "fall" — that Liz had left atop a Styrofoam mannequin head on her French provincial desk when she moved to Vancouver Island to join a radical hippie commune). After services at the tiny Welland synagogue, we would all walk home together, a big extended family in our new fall outfits parting the autumn leaves behind us like the Red Sea.

When we got bored with the adult conversation, we would watch our teenage cousin Matthew play ping-pong in the basement or football on the lawn with Johnny Ennis, who lived across the street. Or Matthew would "interview" Suzanne and me in the voice of a radio broadcaster, using his balled-up fist as a microphone — which Suzanne and I, probably six or seven years old at the time, found extremely witty. Light and defenceless, we would also frequently be snatched up by Uncle Bunny — a cigar-chomping Jewish Yosemite Sam with abundant black hair springing from his chest and his ears and an ever-present soggy butt between his tobacco-stained teeth — who would joylessly throw us in the air with intensifying height and ferocity until finally heeding my aunt's shrieks to stop and put us down. Edith was famous for her constant state of near-hysteria and her recipe for sweet-and-sour meatballs. My mother decorated their home when they did their '70s reno and my older cousin

Matthew would take me out record shopping downtown at Sam the Record Man when he was in Toronto. Then Bunny fell out with my father over their home building business, and we never celebrated holidays together or even spoke to any of them ever again.

IN THE EARLY STAGES of my mother's lifelong commitment to renovation and redevelopment, one of her first large-scale efforts involved completing the back of our Millbank house with an "addition." Back in the determinedly casual '70s, everybody was furiously "adding on"—mostly, family rooms off the kitchen, where everybody ended up actually living, turning their living rooms back into the rarely entered formal parlours they'd been when most of the houses in our turn-of-the-century neighbourhood were originally built.

Our very first edition of these additions was a glassed-in rectangle we called the "sunroom." The sunroom had a built-in TV and stereo along what used to be the exterior wall of the house outside the living room (my mother absolutely lived for "built-ins"—everything in the houses we lived in forever after was built in, including the custom-made shutters over all of the upper-floor windows that effectively blocked off all views of the outside world), and sliding-glass doors (another dangerous, reflective trick of my mother's). This new room, which met all my personal needs, served as my childhood office. At lunch I would come home from school and eat my grilled cheese and Campbell's tomato soup in front of *The Flintstones*. After dinner, the sun having set behind the trees, I danced for hours in red headphones and the latest jeans from Denim Connection, practicing my moves in my darkened reflection in the sliding glass doors, which now looked out onto a swimming pool.

Pleasingly azure and rectangular, with a view out into the trees of the park below, the pool was a sign that we had arrived. "This is the life!" my father would shout, on breaking the surface, smoothing the wet strands of his long blonde hair off his square-jawed, suntanned face before laying himself out to broil in the sun.

IN THE SUMMER OF 1974, to celebrate the occasion of my Bat Mitzvah, my parents invited what must have been two or three hundred of their friends to our newly renovated Millbank Avenue home. The party, which my mother had determined would have a Gatsby theme, followed a ceremony at our synagogue, for which I had memorized the ancient words and the tune of my Torah reading as if it were a pop song—because despite several years of attending Hebrew school, I could neither speak nor read Hebrew. The festivities were held in the back yard, where the caterers installed round tables for eight around the pool and topped them with Beverley Hills Hotel–inspired pink tablecloths.

In keeping with my mother's theme, we were all dressed in white linens with a '20s silhouette for the occasion, custom-made for us all by a local designer of repute at the time, Maggy Reeves. My dress was white linen, sailor style, with a middy collar and a pink ribbon at the dropped waist; tiny Jen's was a matching 6X tunic, and my baby brother Josh was in a white linen Christopher Robin–style suit jacket with short pants. My mother wafted through the pretty crowd in chiffon and her pearls. True to theme, my coming-of-age celebration was a champagne-soaked event, with much dancing to a live band. Clearly the guests were inspired to behave with Fitzgerald-like abandon: for months afterward, until we fell out with the Steinbergs and moved on to our grander, fuck-you house, we were fishing bits of broken champagne glasses out of the pool.

MANY YEARS LATER, in another house, a Victorian semi on a hillside lot, with the pool deep below in the garden, my parents, who by that time were both grandparents and empty-nesters, introduced a dramatic new way to spread more bits of glass around. On their return from a mid-life "sabbatical" in London, where my mother had gone, possibly to get away from my father and ostensibly to take the Christie's fine-art course, they came back with a swashbuckling new party trick for opening champagne they had picked up from some posh Knightsbridge types. (True to type, and never one to miss out on an adventure, my father ended up following her.)

"It's how the Napoleonic soldiers did it, with their sabres, probably on horseback!" my mother reported, as enthusiastically as Auntie Mame returned from her world travels (and ever enraptured, just like Patrick Dennis's notoriously flamboyant character, by anything that could be referred to as "Napoleonic").

The trick, according to my father, was to find the seam in the bottle and move one's wrist to follow exactly along its neck to the point where it thins, and then to sabre off the cork in a single dramatic swoop. If performed correctly, the entire cap arrangement — cork, wire, foil, and all — would shoot off in one piece, like a bullet. We were all to be schooled in the practice. And while we didn't own any sabres, we did have kitchen knives. Soon the garden was littered with these cork-and-foil arrangements.

"Isn't this just smashing?" my mother would yell out into the garden, her teeth glowing white in the dark as we gathered on another anniversary or birthday around the sheared remains of another beheaded bottle of Veuve, trying to catch the foaming spew in our flutes.

True, glamour — and what the loathsome TV host Robin Leach would have dubbed "the champagne lifestyle" — were never in short supply. Bottled up in it, however, was always a commensurate volatility.

ONE OF THE MOST unsettling things about my mother, particularly when I was young, was that as a fantasist who held no particular stock or interest in reality, sometimes she would just outright lie. As a liar, she was brilliant, because she never felt she was lying. No matter how outrageous the lie, she could never be caught out or embarrassed by being exposed, because she was always so convinced of her own version. And what the hell was the point, exactly, in "the truth"?

One memorable example of her complicated relationship with transparency involved a set of crystal glasses by a Bohemian manufacturer called Peill. The pattern name, now discontinued, was Felicia. I know this because I was asked to choose them as a wedding gift by mother's friend Jeanne. Admittedly, up to that point, I hadn't ever thought of owning crystal goblets, but as it was Jeanne's very generous offer, my husband-to-be and I went with it, booking our registry appointment at the very proper William Ashley China, and, of course, having our very first real fight right there on the dangerously well-stocked shop floor.

Weeks later, when the Ashley shipment arrived, I could tell my mother was impressed. True, they were beauties. Simple and almost Georgian-looking, with a square, faceted bowl on a chandelier drop stem (a fetching lightness on their feet, which unfortunately left them rather precarious), they looked like relics from an eighteenth-century pirate ship or manor house. It didn't take long for my mother to order a set of her own—and then ask to "borrow" some of ours for a party she was hosting. Unbelievably, I never saw them again.

"I don't know what you're talking about," she would insist, whenever I asked after them. "The crystal I have here is all mine."

She literally held out until her death on this point. It wasn't until we were cleaning out my parents' condo that I was finally able to get my wedding crystal back, which didn't feel like any kind of victory.

Other hurtful bits of glass surfaced from hidden places, as it always had: a bottle of vodka in a shopping bag under the sink with lipstick around its rim, like my mother's Listerine bottles in her purse. Not that the constant swishes of Listerine or liberal applications of perfume ever really disguised the fug of liquor that, particularly in her later years, seemed to emanate from her pores. Emptying their condo, we found half-drunk bottles in the laundry and behind the sofa in the spare room. Always glass bottles, turning up like uninvited guests around the house or in the car. One never really knew with her; that was a part of her allure. Her morning cup of black coffee might turn out to be mostly Scotch. Or not.

And then there were the accusatory and self-pitying notes written out on foolscap in my mother's loopy scrawl, presumably very late into her dark nights. Addressed opaquely to our father, but transparent in my mother's intention that they be read by us, her children, the accusations were wild and various, of abuse and treachery both mental and physical, and as impossible for us not to read with our Corn Flakes and orange juice as they were to believe, given the questionable reliability of our narrator. What was clear was that even though it didn't look like it, our mother was a very sad person and she wanted us all to know just how disappointed and unhappy she was, without giving a damn how it might make her children feel.

Of course it was clear to all of us without her even saying it that the contents of these letters were never really to be discussed, even amongst ourselves. And that when we were out together as a family, at a restaurant or a play or museum, and we were to bump into anybody we knew and they were to ask us how we were doing, we were all to smile and say, "Everything's great, everyone's doing marvellously, thank you."

Even years later, when we were all too old to have to play along in this game, we still found ourselves trapped in the psychic bell jar of having to appear as if everything in our lives was just perfect. And then toward the end of her life, despite the fact that it had likely taken her hours to get herself sufficiently together to leave the house, and had visibly limped in the door earlier on the arm of our father, our mother would be the first to insist on the lie that she was just fine.

Because as much as we were all supposed to share in the pain of her shattered dreams and bruised ego, her larger story, as far as she was concerned, was going to be one of shining magnificence. The psychic weight of growing up under a parent fully prepared to burden us with her issues, yet insistent on maintaining a fantasy of perfection, was one we would just have to learn to bear.

IT TOOK ME YEARS to appreciate that perhaps my mother was so enamoured with glass because she saw herself in it. Not only literally, in terms of admiring her reflection (more on that later), but seeing something of her sparkling, mutable self in its glittering surfaces, so secretly volatile and dangerously brittle.

I swear to you that one night, we were at home in our Fuck-You Forest Hill chateau—at least my mother and the three of us kids were at home; during this high-flying era at the height of the '70s real estate boom, my father was usually working late or travelling, and my mother would annoy us by getting weepy and stupid, drinking vodka (and probably popping a couple Valium), feeling sorry for herself, and applying endless amounts of expensive moisturizer in front of the television—and this really happened:

"Who *is* that woman?" asks my mother, pointing at the television. "She looks exactly like that other one, you know, the one with the hair."

I am possibly fourteen, so already exasperated. We have just finished dinner; it's a school night in the winter and the three of us kids are watching TV on the ivory twill sofa arrangement in my parents' master bedroom, the only comfortable place in the giant tomb of our house to watch TV. My mother, who has plopped herself down on one of the sofas to join us, is in a satin robe with socks and a huge glob of white cream that isn't successfully rubbed in on one side of her face. "Come on, you know her. You do. She has that hair!"

My mother's own hair tonight, a night when we just want to zone out in front of the latest episode of *Hart to Hart*, is greasily standing up off her head after being plastered with Hellmann's mayonnaise as a "hair treatment."

"Come on, kids, you know exactly who I mean," says my mother, now digging one hand deep into an oval jar of moisturizer and messily slathering its unctuous, perfumed contents onto both her décolletage and the arm of the sofa. "You know — the one with the hair."

Trying our best to ignore her and her weirdness, we redouble our focus on this week's mystery, but the air around us is thickening. At any moment, one of us is going to have to tell her to shut up.

"Who is responsible for the design of the outfits on this show?" asks my mother loudly, so loudly that it is getting hard to hear what's going on. Bored silly stuck here with only us as the audience, she would clearly prefer the evening end in some kind of drama. "What kind of person would you have to be to put that redhead in a rust-coloured ensemble? Of all of the people in the world, why would they choose her to put on TV? They could never convince me that *anybody* should ever wear anything so impossibly hideous let alone someone as unfortunate looking as this poor thing. This is almost painful to watch!"

Just as I am about to shout that yes, it is getting painful to watch, we are interrupted by what sounds like a very loud "ping," followed by an enormous, echoing crash coming from the master ensuite.

"What the hell?" yells my mother, momentarily sidetracked from her one-woman performance piece.

Running over to the master bathroom to investigate, my brother and I look at each other in amazement. Every surface of the room, from the marble countertop of the vanity to the floor, is now covered in bits of glass. In the corner, where the walk-in shower once stood, the floor-to-ceiling enclosure is now just an empty frame, like a pair of eyeglasses with the lenses knocked out. Unbelievably, and without any prior visible signs of weakening, the double-width tempered-glass walk-in shower has spontaneously exploded. What is even weirder, though, is the transformation in the glass itself. Somehow, in the process of the tempered glass losing its temper, or whatever sudden and unfathomable chemical reaction has occurred, each of the thousands of glass particles comprising the shower stall has thickened into something chunkier, uneven, and more like rocks or hail.

Apparently the glass itself couldn't stand it any longer either.

Three

CRAVEN "A" KING SIZE LARGE

CLEANING OUT MY MOTHER's closets after she died, I was sad to find nearly a dozen pairs of "comfortable" shoes of questionable curb appeal lying on the closet floor. Never one to consider comfort before style, my poor mother must have been in such agony after three failed knee replacements and a disastrous back surgery that left her listing like a pirate whenever she tried to get around that she was forced to bend her own rules. Struggling with pain and mobility, she must have spent the last months of her life fruitlessly searching for a pair of shoes she might miraculously have been able to walk in. Given that all of this charmless footwear looked barely worn, it didn't appear that any of them had been particularly successful.

Over her last couple of years, there had been some attempts at trying out an ivory-topped cane, which my mother found suitably eccentric, but a walker or wheelchair was simply out the question. As my mother had always (frivolously, it turns out) joked to my father in her earlier, carefree days whenever they passed any poor soul in a wheelchair, "If it ever comes to that, just push me up to the top of a hill and let go."

Unfortunately, as life tends to work, it gets harder to find the humour in the punch line. At a certain point in her life, my mother mostly opted to just stay in bed, telling all her appointments and lunch dates that she was feeling "a little off," or simply not answering the phone or the front door, even to me, for days.

The worst was the back operation—a terrifically misjudged decision on the part of my parents, who were so committed to being proactive on all health matters (and who were so in awe of "top specialists" that they would follow even the most ridiculous of their recommendations) that they believed a seventy-year-old woman crippled after decades of inhaling burning toxins would be good as new after a surgical procedure that involved cutting away the spinal cord from its intricate bed of nerve roots and stitching it back together again. My mother was always a tough customer when it came to pain, and of course her predilection for self-medication on a constant basis didn't hurt. But I have never in my life seen anyone scream and writhe in sheer anguish the way she did after coming to from that procedure. She wasn't even human anymore, more like a wild animal yowling and writhing, caught in the jagged teeth of a cruel metal trap. Or a medieval martyr, burning alive at the stake.

And then she went from bad to worse.

MY MOTHER SMOKED LIKE a film noir heroine. Watching her strike a match and then inhale deeply, eyes closing with pleasure as her entire being took in the suck and burn of her cigarette, should have been X-rated. And I was the under-age audience—a captive audience of one who would bask in the smoke and glow of her torch as if it were incense.

Winter mornings, after we dropped my dad at his downtown office, she would take me, still in my pyjamas underneath my ski jacket, to an old-school classic lunch counter in the lower level of a now-defunct department store called Kresge's. With nowhere in particular to rush off to, the two of us would sit at the metal counter on rotating stools with red vinyl seats and I would get a grilled cheese and spin around and she would get a black coffee and then light up a cigarette. The spark and smell of the struck match and the whoosh of the cigarette's first draw were enchant-ing, the orchestral prelude to stories and observations drawn out between thoughtful inhalations, a hypnotic red-tipped white wand dancing in space like a conductor's baton. Out flew magic ribbons of smoke that curled in mid-air before falling into grey ashes onto my plate of half-finished grilled cheese as if they were a condiment.

"The reason we still remember Katharine Hepburn is that she was a woman who really knew how to wear pants," my mother would offer instructively, her ash lengthening with another deep draw of her cigarette.

"There were others who were great beauties—of course Greta Garbo, or when I was a girl, Deanna Durbin—but ever since I saw her play Jo in *Little Women*, I always thought Katharine Hepburn truly had style."

Rapt with attention despite the fact that, as a preschooler in pyjamas, I hadn't the slightest idea who she was talking about, I would take another sip of my orange juice—in those days, bitter and foamy with formerly frozen reconstituted pulp—awaiting further clarification.

"Some might say it was Audrey Hepburn whose style is truly iconic, and it is true that she does make a boat neck and perhaps a capri-length pant look great, but you cannot say she truly understands drape..."

This last observation is left hanging as she gazes out into the middle distance of the diner, her thoughts forming in the ribbon of smoke from the burning torch between her long fingers, curling upwards in the fluorescent lighting like a question mark.

My mother's ashes were epic. She was never one of those fussy, tense smokers, regularly tending the butt end with a stylized flick. But then, for her, tobacco was like opium (funnily enough, she did go through a phase where she nearly asphyxiated us with the liberal application of Yves Saint Laurent's fragrance of the same name). When she smoked, she was as relaxed as a junkie nodding off with a needle still in one arm. So oblivious was she to the state of her lengthening ash that it became riveting to watch its gravity-defiant cling as she continued to wave it about for emphasis. Like watching a high-wire act, it was impossible to exhale. I suspect she rather liked it that way. All the better to ensure the rapt attention of her audience.

Her brand of choice, Craven "A," was—interestingly—also the favourite of the actress Tallulah Bankhead, who, if you believe the Hollywood legend, smoked one hundred of them daily, liberally washed down with Old Grand-Dad bourbon. Though neither Ms. Bankhead nor my mother could ever be accused of being the least bit craven.

Even though I never successfully became a smoker of anything other than weed no matter how much I tried, I always found myself drawn to the smokers at the party. If I'd ever got beyond being a mere enabler, standing out in the cold with my much cooler smoking friends in front of a bar or a restaurant, Craven "A" would have been my choice too. I always enjoyed its bull's-eye red label along with the glamorous loucheness of addiction and dependency implied by the use of the word "craven" and its associations of "craving" — though legend has it that this most popular brand with GIs during World War Two was actually named back in 1860 after the Third Earl of Craven. You would be hard-pressed to find a pack of Craven "A"s kicking around now, unless you were visiting Vietnam or Jamaica, but according to aficionados, "The cigarettes exhibit the English-style flavour of a Virginia-tobacco dominant blend, with that plant's attendant nutty sweetness."

And what better definition, really, of my mother's own blend of charm?

"Remember, you would like one pack of Craven 'A' King Size — *Large* — not just King Size," my mother would say, drawing out the "Laaa-arge" for emphasis, as soon as I was old enough to go to the Vill on my banana seat bike.

All the kids in the neighbourhood, for whom "the Vill" meant the Village Cigar Store, were allowed to ride their bikes to the store on their own as soon as they learned to ride. There were no such things as safety helmets or bike locks; we would just leave our bikes lying right there on the curb outside. Before going in to buy smokes for our mothers. And now there is no such thing as the Village Cigar Store.

The Village Cigar store had a bell on the screen door that rang when you opened it. Inside it was a mottled billiard green with wood floors and it sold cigarettes and comic books next to adult magazines displayed on scarred wooden racks. On the glass counter were jars of penny candy, like the big, soft strawberries made from sugar and Red dye No. 2, and artificial "bananas" that tasted more like banana than the fruit ever did. For a quarter — the big one with a moose on it, I would remind myself — I could get a bag of chips and a blue Popsicle or some Rain-Blo bubble gum. The grey-haired lady behind the till would take the cash from my mum that I had been gripping tightly in one hand against my bike handlebars, and when I asked her, as instructed, for a pack of Craven "A" King Size *Large*, she would simply hand a pack of smokes — barely looking up from her racing form — over to a six-year-old who could barely reach the counter. No questions like "Would this be for your mother?" ever entering the equation.

Sometimes after we went to the Vill on our bikes we kids would take our sugary haul into the ravine, where we looked at the boobs in the adult magazines and tried to smoke the cigarettes. It was scary and thrilling and maybe five hundred yards away from my house.

This was our Millbank house, our first real one, a big brick wreck of a thing that backed onto a ravine on a family-friendly street in the grand old neighbourhood of Forest Hill, which my parents could only afford because it was in such extreme disrepair that it looked haunted. The only real rules of this house were that there weren't any. Except, of course, that my parents knew absolutely everything and that anybody who might be of a different opinion was simply nuts.

GROWING UP IN THE '70s was a blast. Everything was exploding—rules about how to dress and how to live and how to behave were being torched and cast aside. There were no seatbelts for the ride—definitely not in my dad's vintage Jag, the back door of which would dependably open whenever we turned a corner—and definitely no sunscreen protection. When it came to the sun (particularly in my near-albino state) it was Burn, Baby, Burn. On our family trips down south over the Christmas holidays, or by the pool or a northern lake in summer, whenever my dad would catch me—already red and blistering—in the shade, he would yell, "What are you doing inside? It's beautiful out there!"

According to *LIFE* magazine which, like *National Geographic* and *The New Yorker*, we subscribed to and I read, cover to cover, spread out on the wall-to-wall broadloom on my tummy, bras were burning—entire cities were burning!—and giant rockets aimed into space were being set on fire. And not only were we kids happily doused in second-hand smoke, snacking on artificially flavoured toxins and fully exposed to every known politically incorrect adult notion, we were bred for a revolution that never really happened.

At school they promised a world of greater understanding, where we would all live together as One. On Hallowe'en we dutifully collected pennies for UNICEF in little slotted boxes which hung from strings around our small necks over our costumes. But as hard as we were encouraged to sing about it, the grown-ups never really did give peace a chance. Instead, everybody just made loads of money, tuned into the voices of their inner child, filed for divorce and went shopping. The upside of being raised on this bonfire was that everything was fun and wrong and there were really no rules. Or none that applied to us, anyway. Rule-following led to being ordinary, a state of being which, according to my mother, we were to avoid at all costs.

The only bibles or domestic manuals we had in the house were written by the liberal Drs. Seuss and Spock, both of whom my mother could quote entire passages from by heart even years later. In keeping with her chosen gurus, my mother believed she held insights into the childish imagination, and that her ability to get what "made us tick" would foster creativity in us — a value which, along with taste and discernment, she made clear trumped all others, including, but definitely not limited to, respect for authority, moderation, and timeliness.

The upshot was that I never had any particular bedtime, and by the time I was in grade three or five (having skipped a grade, I missed the fourth entirely), I was typically the last one in the house to turn out the lights and head up to bed. Nobody ever taught us table manners, but it was understood that we all were to learn by example. Nor did any of us ever have a weekly allowance, both of my parents finding the idea of fiscal responsibility in the young (and pretty much fiscal responsibility altogether) petty and pointless. Whenever any of us wanted money for candy, we would just ask for it. A specially-designated drawer in the kitchen for our yield on these excursions was dubbed the "candy drawer" and we had access to it at any time.

We may have been able to eat as many sweets as we wanted, but there were no apologies or explanations for any of the bitterness. Voices could be raised, doors slammed, phone receivers crashed down in fury in the middle of a conversation — an unsettling penchant for drama that we all were to learn by example too. And lessons, even amidst all the tasteful grandeur and largesse, that proved hard for us to ever forget.

MOST DAYS WE WOULD come home from school to find our mother safely on the phone, a smoke in one hand, gesticulating wildly, a glass of red atop a Lucite side table by the other. Other afternoons we might open the door to find a coven of her women friends gathered around her in the sunroom to console her as she sobbed theatrically. Whatever was the matter, we had learned at that point to go straight to our rooms before the real fireworks started. Even though I would get evil stares from some of her girlfriends for my apparent hard-heartedness in the face of whatever melodrama my mother was embroiled in, by the time I was in grade school I already knew to steer clear of the sparks.

And then there was the stage where, through child development sessions via the Home and School Association at our neighbourhood public school, my mother had come under the sway of a fashionable child psychologist by the name of Rudolf Dreikurs. To this day, I know little about the child development theories of Dr. Dreikurs, but he did not prove to be the most winning dinner guest.

"Don't think I don't know what you are up to," my mother would say, following me around the kitchen with a dangerously fiery expression when I had absolutely no idea what she was talking about. "This manipulation game you are playing. Well, I have news for you: this is NOT all about you children! I am a human being here too!" Consciousness-raising cocktails sparked the same sort of night. It was never clear what we had done wrong, except to thwart her with our very existence.

The night our soft-spoken neighbour Linda died (a dead ringer for Linda McCartney, with three look-alike blonde daughters around my age, she had swallowed a bucketful of pills, it was rumoured, after having learned something awful — I never knew exactly what — about her husband), I remember being frightened to hear my mother's animal-like sobbing from downstairs. "The bastard!" she screamed, over and over, from my father's lap. "He killed her!" This was also compellingly mysterious, as I didn't recall my mother being all that close to the vague Linda. I do, however, remember their dog, fat, a sweet-tempered yellow Lab who was the unofficial street mascot. Her name was Lucky.

AMIDST ALL THE DRAMA and the largely benign neglect, there was indulgence. On our birthdays, from the time we were little until we left home for college, each of us three kids would wake up to a silver tray of presents at the foot of the bed, a flamboyant invention of my mother's designed to enhance our feeling of specialness on our special day.

By the time I got to junior high, I could borrow my mother's credit card to go shopping for a new pair of jeans or a cool peasant top to wear to a party. All you needed back then to use your mother's credit card was a signed note of permission. And then by grade eight, I had my very own MasterCard, meant for "emergencies," with which I would sometimes take a friend to lunch at the kind of ritzy places in Yorkville that my parents frequented: the Courtyard Café, Bemelmans, or Noodles, where they would serve us wine without asking for any ID because we were cute and we could pay for it.

To say that we were merely entitled would be to miss the point. My mother didn't believe you could spoil a child by giving any of them too much, but rather that people who denied their children were acting from a meanness of spirit. It is true that we lived in a bubble of privilege, but this too came with its own expectations and obligations. While this was never fully articulated as a rule, it was always clear that our end of the deal was that we kids were to do well in school, be above what my parents considered "cheap" or low-class tastes and entertainments (one early example being comic books, which I was not allowed to buy and had to read on the sly at my friends' houses), and always present as attractive, appealing accessories to our stylish and socially ambitious parents.

Which is not to say there was any real sort of agenda. It was an era of blissfully free-range parenting, and so after school we kids ran around in unsupervised packs to rifle through each other's refrigerators, read our parents' dirty books, and play jump rope and four-square on the street, which luckily for us rarely had any cars driving by. Mothers — who had become mothers almost as soon as they were able to leave their parents' homes, and hadn't had a chance yet to become anything else — were either busy making a stab at a career (like mine, with her part-time decorating, or Carole across the street, whom my mother admired because she had started her own successful business), or else they were just vague and inattentive, like poor Linda, whose three blonde little girls ran around with tangled hair and dirty T-shirts and were never called in after dinner.

But most of all, mothers were too busy being grownups with their own glamorous lives to run around begging us to just try a little bite of the organic kale or spend all night working on our school projects, the way our generation ended up parenting — as if it were such an active verb that our very lives depended upon it. For my mother and her friends, being a parent wasn't a calling; it just came along with being a grown-up, like cocktails and mortgages.

My mother spent her days zipping around town picking up wallpaper and dropping off fabric samples in an olive-green Mustang convertible, which in nice weather would sit with the top down in the driveway next to our house so we kids could easily climb in and play in it. One time, lost in some fantasy, I must have pulled the gearshift out of park, because the Mustang started rolling down the driveway, which had a slight incline, and into the street with me in it. I jumped out of the moving car and ran to the front door calling frantically for my mother, who merely looked up, exasperated that I had interrupted her phone conversation. Until she saw her car, now rolled to a stop—thankfully without having killed anyone or hit anything—right in the middle of our street. Upon which she yelled out, "For God's sake! What do I have to do to have a moment to myself here without one of you trying to kill yourself?"

My mother loved to recount the story of the cranky neighbour next door, an elderly man who once actually called the police after my apparently entirely unsupervised little sister picked some of the flowers from his beautiful garden. The tiny, blue-eyed culprit clutching a small bouquet in her fat hands was returned home by two police officers who gave her a stern and serious reprimand at the front door—which my mother found absolutely hilarious.

"Can you believe anybody would call the police on a three-year-old!" my mother would hoot. "And for picking flowers!"

Caught up in the mood of their time, neither of my parents ever had much faith in the police or policing in general. While I can recall them regularly incensed by incidents of police brutality in the newspaper, I cannot think of a single occasion on which they told me to ask for the help of a policeman should I ever find myself in any trouble.

Another family down the street named Stern with three ill-behaved boys who ran in a pack like wolves that my mother called "the Stern gang" were, however, to be avoided at all costs.

I AM SMALL FOR my age, always in the middle of the front row—beside the sign for the class—in school photographs, not particularly sporty, and kind of a browner. I have long blonde hair parted in the middle, and my mother dresses me in hippie turtlenecks and fringed suede miniskirts. I love my first-grade teacher, Mrs. Graham, who is blonde and pretty and seems to think I am very clever for having written a poem about how the world is very large and there are a lot of different people on it. My poem and the accompanying picture I have painted in poster paints, of a happy blue planet with people sticking out of it like cloves in an orange, are put up on the board for parent-teacher night.

I read everything I can get my hands on, including things I can't understand like *The New Yorker*'s "Talk of the Town" section and books like *Tropic of Cancer* and *Catch-22* from the wall-to-wall bookshelves in our second-floor guest room. So absorbed am I in whatever I might happen to be reading that my mother jokes she can't get my attention at the breakfast table because I am so deeply absorbed in reading the side of the cereal box.

One day I am walking home from school, in my own world, as usual, swinging my book bag at a line of shrubs or singing the words from a TV jingle in my head, and I don't immediately notice that the entire Stern gang has run up right behind me. One of them, maybe the Stern from my class, suddenly shoves me without warning from behind so that I fly face-first across the pavement, which really hurts. Getting up, I see that my knee is bleeding and there is dirt and gravel in the scrape. All three boys laugh as I gather up my bag and run for home.

"What the hell happened to your face?" my dad yells that night as he joins us at the head of the dinner table. Dinner is a flank steak marinated in soy sauce, served on these glossy black vinyl placemats I love to make imprints in with my fork and watch fade away again.

"Um, nothing," I say, swinging one knee-socked leg under the table and concentrating on my placemat. The long scrape that had started to show up on the side of my face feels hot and itchy, and my knee is burning. But I am starting to be concerned about where this is headed.

"Who did that to you? Who!" My father looks very mad, like it's my fault and I'm going to be in trouble.

"She says it was one of those Stern boys from down the street," says Mum, gesturing in the vague direction of the Stern house with her fork. "You know those boys, Perce — the father is a psychiatrist? God knows what the mother does. And of course they are totally wild."

"Jesus Christ!" yells Dad, banging the flat of his hand sharply against the tabletop of the grand, Georgian-style mahogany dining table we inherited when we bought the house, along with all the former family's old silver.

"It's not that bad," I offer. "Really."

"Tomorrow morning before you leave the house for school I want you to point them out to me," he says, getting up from the table.

"I don't even know them," I plead. But my father is having none of it.

"You know, when boys do that it means one of them must like you," says my Mum, gathering the plates while opening her eyes wide and tilting her head toward me in a gesture I know I am meant to understand as indicating her superior insight and knowledge, although this particular insight of hers seems so obviously dumb.

"But they don't even talk to me! Why would they like me?"

Nobody answers. My dad gets up from the table and says darkly, "You point those boys out to me tomorrow."

The next morning, to my great embarrassment, I am positioned in the front window of our house waiting for the Stern gang to pass by on the way to school. My dad is right behind me, waiting and breathing. There doesn't seem to be anything I can do to avoid this.

"There they are," I say weakly, pointing out the three dark-haired boys who looked way meaner and bigger laughing at me the day before. This morning they just look like any other kids.

My father, who is fully dressed for work in his double-breasted navy suit, French cuffs, and striped tie, steps out the door and stops the three boys right in front of our house. The tallest one doesn't even come to his belt buckle.

"You!" yells my Dad. "You three come right here."

Stopped in their tracks by an enormous angry stranger, the three little boys meekly comply. "Did you push my daughter? Did you??"

Taking their bowed, quiet heads for assent, my father, who now seems even bigger and angrier than he did moments ago, leans down and looks each one of them in the eye.

"If any one of you so much as lays a finger on her ever again, I swear to God, I will kill you," says my Dad, scarily and slow, the veins in his neck bulging.

The Stern gang, such as it is, runs off. And not one of them ever so much as looks my way or even speaks to me ever again.

My father is all-powerful. He can transform in an instant from just being my dad into a fire-breathing dragon.

MILLBANK WAS LINED WITH families like ours: the Goldens, the Drakes, the Oguses, and, yes, the Sterns. Everybody's grandparents were recent arrivals from Europe. Everybody's dad had grown up in Canada and was an architect or a doctor or a lawyer. Whether or not the mothers also worked, everyone had a cleaning lady. We kids all attended the same public school, went to each other's houses for lunch, and played on the street after dinner.

On the weekends, our parents had each other over for dinner parties for which the mothers would get their hair teased into topiaries and try to outdo each other with complicated recipes from *Mastering the Art of French Cooking*. My mother's go-to first course was Coquilles St.-Jacques, which she would serve on real buttered scallop shells, just like the French — not that my mother actually knew first-hand what anyone from Europe ate or how, because she hadn't been there yet.

During the long afternoons of preparation, when my mother would be dutifully, if messily, following Julia Child's rigorous steps for *suprêmes de volaille* or rice pilaf, the house would be warm and the air rich with the pungency of scallions browning in butter. And my mother, bright-eyed and full of energy, would call upstairs to ask for my help in choosing a tablecloth or setting out her flower arrangements, usually cut tulips in pinks and whites, which she would pull free of their leaves and set in glass bowls in a spare and gestural fashion.

The lead-up was all so exciting that I would have difficulty sitting still to eat my own early kids' dinner with my little sister and brother in the kitchen. And then we three would be sent upstairs to play and read in our rooms once the first of the guests — basically our neighbours — arrived at our door. We had just seen these same people pull into their own driveways as they did every other night of the week, but now here they were in loud voices and party clothes, the men in turtlenecks or wide ties, the women in false eyelashes and scoop-neck dresses in wild prints.

Being left out of this action I remember as unbearable. A child insomniac with early FOMO, I would take in as much of the adult fun as I could, listening intently from the landing in my PJs and sucking my thumb, clutching a pillow for safety in the dark of our centre hall.

"Sue! Karen's up," a passing guest/neighbour with shocking pink lipstick and a vertiginous updo would inform my mother after having caught me awake, despite my best efforts to be as quiet as Harriet the Spy. From the other room I would hear my mother deliver the punchline to whatever tale she'd just been recounting, the living room would fill with loud peals of grown-up, fake-sounding laughter, and then, looking back at her appreciative audience and smiling, she would spin into view. So sparkling and beautiful in her plum jersey halter dress and gold hoop earrings under the light of the front hall chandelier, just like my favourite Troll

Fairy Princess doll in its lilac-scented, see-through collect-
ible case, she would hold out her arms and call up to me:

"Are you still awake, darling? Okay, you can come down
and join us just for a minute and then you are going to have
to go right back up to bed."

Suddenly shy and feeling small in my pyjamas in front of
the room full of scary adults, I would nod in solemn agree-
ment, still clutching my pillow as the talk picked up again.
Anything, so long as I can be downstairs for even a little
while to listen to the grown-ups.

"Are you hungry? Do you want a little taste of the pilaf?"
My mother's sticky sweet rice pilaf, nut-brown and boiled
down with cans of consommé, was my absolute favourite.
In the kitchen, which would be a tangle of dirty pots and
glasses with cigarettes floating in them, I would get a spoon-
ful on a salad plate.

After the pilaf and my brief sojourn in the sparkle of the
candlelit room brightened with grown-up conversation, I
would be sent back upstairs only to fall asleep on the hall
carpet outside my bedroom to the hum coming from downstairs. My eyelids getting heavier, their voices getting louder
over James Taylor and Carole King and the crackling of
another log being thrown on the fire. And there would be
another familiar party smell besides that of the wood burning in the fireplace, another smell of burning that wasn't
quite the smell of cigarettes, but also something that adults
smoked at parties.

On the glass coffee table in the morning, amidst the
half-full lipstick-marked glasses and smelly ashtrays filled
with the bent, burnt ends of cigarettes, there might be a few

black paper slips still left in the box of After Eights, wafer-thin after-dinner mints coated in chocolate which I adored and gorged myself on whenever I had the chance. And a mostly empty bottle of Chivas Regal, with which I was still unfamiliar, even though we used one of the blue velvet bags it came in to store our Scrabble tiles.

ALTHOUGH I KNOW MY mother would have wanted me to say that she was my guru in everything, the truth is that everything I know I learned from watching *Jeopardy!*

South Prep, as our neighbourhood public school from senior kindergarten to junior high was then called, with its antebellum architecture and water-stained marigold draperies, was stuck in some British colonial postwar film. There was "God Save the Queen" in the mornings before "Oh, Canada." And teachers named Macpherson in kilts, with pursed lips and sour expressions who would make the kids they didn't like come up to the front of the class and open their palms so they could strike their hands with a ruler. Not to mention the other, unfathomable children, who seemed to know things like who had the cooties but who couldn't read aloud without spelling out every syllable. Since it was mostly freezing out anyway and I was already on to reading inappropriate novels, my mother often let me stay home.

It is hard to overstate the importance of TV for someone of my generation, the first, really, to be raised fully in front of it. TV was our cell phone, our laptop, our Facebook, our Instagram. It was what we rushed home to after school, what we ran our evenings around when there was a miniseries on or a Peanuts special. If we kids had such a thing as a water cooler, what was on TV last night would be what we would have talked about around it. When important things were happening out in the world, like the Apollo landing or the Canada-Russia hockey series final, our teachers, or the guy from the school's AV department, would wheel a laughably small and boxy TV set into the classroom for us all to watch it on. That was what we did and how we learned: we *watched*.

These exquisite days of staying home "sick" always started with my mentor Alex Trebek, a font of general knowledge who could pronounce the names of Italian operas, African generals, and Polish rivers as if he were a native of Milan, Djibouti, and Warsaw. They then lowered their IQ with goofy game shows like *The Newlywed Game*, on which just-married army captains and their newly recruited wives, sitting together in what looked like marital bumper cars, had to guess the answer their new spouse might have given to questions peppered with bedroom humour. Or *Let's Make A Deal*, where adults dressed like cowboys and M&Ms practically peed themselves with excitement at being able to choose between Doors Number 1, 2, or 3.

At noon, sick or even just home for lunch from school, it was always time for my first bewitching taste of satire with *The Flintstones*, which portrayed *The Honeymooners* in the Stone Age with cars made of rocks and stars re-named Gina Lolabrickida and Gary Granite (its Saturday-morning counterpart being the futuristic *Jetsons*).

Hollywood Squares was a bright light with its wisecracking, world-weary old New York comedians like Rose Marie and Morey Amsterdam, piled atop each other in neon squares like residents of a celebrity condo. The best was when the super-high-camp guests would make a special appearance, like the manic shimmying Charo or Paul Lynde, with his little yellow neck scarf and bitchy put-downs.

Of course it was never explicitly explained to us that this was gayness, but we always knew that Lynde—like Charles Nelson Reilly on the deliciously off-colour *Match Game*, with its suggestive "blankety-blanks"—was somehow *different*. And in a way that looked way more fun.

I have zero recollection of my mother ever interrupting this reverie of completely bad-for-you television, other than to enter occasionally with sick-room trays of ginger ale and Campbell's tomato soup. So my education in the ways of the world would continue uninterrupted in the afternoons with the madcap shenanigans of the seemingly witless-yet-adorable Marlo Thomas on *That Girl* (the lesson being that girls cannot possibly cope on their own in a big city like New York without an endlessly patient, kind-of-boring male chaperone, in this case a not particularly attractive boyfriend named Donald). Next up would be *I Dream of Jeannie* wherein the similarly naïf Barbara Eden, a fabulously slutty-looking Playmate in harem pyjamas and a magically bouncy blonde ponytail, would be summoned from a bottle by her "Master" Larry Hagman, who could stuff her back inside whenever she asked any questions.

As Eva Gabor swanned around the farm in jewels on *Green Acres* (boring—even in grade school I recognized it as a one-note show), I might quickly grab an optically glaring snack of toast with Cheez Whiz and a glass of Tang (the beverage of choice of the Apollo astronauts) because I never wanted to miss even a second of the swinging, sexy set piece *Love, American Style*. Or the almost meta-ironic *Hogan's Heroes*, with Bob Crane as the smart, studly American in a German POW camp that actually looked kind of fun.

The movies they showed us at Hebrew school, which I reluctantly attended three days a week—it cut into my TV-viewing schedule, plus the deeply crabby Mrs. Nili used to scream and fire pieces of chalk at us for not listening (among the very few phrases I ever learned in Hebrew: "*Sheket bevakashah!*" or "Please shut up!")—told a rather different story of the war.

I don't know if it's just post-traumatic stress talking here, but in my recollection we Jew-*ish* kids did very little in all those hours of Hebrew school at our conservative synagogue—Mondays and Wednesdays after school and Sunday afternoon every single week—except watch Holocaust films. And I don't mean Hollywood versions by Steven Spielberg (which of course hadn't even been written yet), but the pure, unadulterated documentary-style straight goods, featuring the neat piles of dead people's shoes, eyeglasses, and gold teeth, carefully sorted for re-gifting to the Germans (their skin, we were told, would be re-used as lampshades). Literally nothing was considered TMI for children's consumption: in grade school we were shown people's naked bodies being stacked like firewood outside the kilns at Auschwitz and bulldozers tossing the limp forms of firing-squad victims into ditches at Mauthausen. And then the mad, starved stick figures in filthy striped pyjamas clinging to the gates when the liberators finally arrived at Bergen-Belsen and Birkenau.

"Never forget!" was obviously their educational goal. And in this, they were extremely successful.

IN HER MANY OPINIONS, my mother, of course, was always completely unedited, if not unfiltered.

"Don't I sound exactly like Cher?" I once asked her, playing back a version of "Gypsies, Tramps and Thieves" that I had just recorded on my (portable, canary-yellow plastic) cassette player up in my pink-and-orange Pop-art flowered bedroom that I thought this time had really hit the mark. I had even worked out Cher's accompanying dance moves, and was considering my fringed Indian princess outfit.

"No," she said, without the slightest hesitation, or even a little regretful smile or encouraging parental pat on the back. "No, you don't sound like Cher even one little bit."

Or not all that many years later, my mother rubbing the side of her face, asking, "Don't you find giving blow jobs makes your jaw hurt?" (Full and frank discussions of sex—not just in general, but the unedited particulars of my parents' own sex life—were not just permitted in our house, but near-mandated.) I kid you not that one summer when I was home from college my father spent an entire lunch date outlining in full, illustrated detail, on a paper napkin with his Montblanc Meisterstück, a medical procedure he planned to undergo involving his penis. So much did my mother badger me from the day I got my first period to just tell her whenever I might want to start the birth control pill that I think I was already on it for months before I shared the news. But then my mother, who saw herself and my father as involved in a grand and legendary love affair on, say, the world-historic level of Antony and Cleopatra or, at the very least, Elizabeth Taylor and Richard Burton, was always way more interested in sharing the details of her own romantic life than she was in anyone else's.

My mother actually once said (to the astonishment of my sister-in-law) that of my sister-in-law's two young children — a son and a daughter — it was lucky that her daughter had turned out to be the attractive one. A friend of mine swears that the very first time she ever met my mother, my mother offered, "You know, you should really have that mole looked at." Another jewel she once offered to that very same girl-friend (who, by the way, she always adored) was, "Your problem, sweetheart, is that you are stuck in an era."

Being "stuck in an era" was a common failing as far as my mother was concerned. I remember she used the charge against her old friend Toby, who, decades later, always dressed, styled her hair, and wore her makeup — down to the exact shade of pink lipstick — as she had when my mother first met her in the early '6os.

If my mother ended up "stuck in an era" herself, it wasn't so much a problem of style as a problem of attitude. By the end of her life she had abandoned first her Krizia, then her tailored Armani and Chanel, for black leggings — senior's comfort by way of Marcel Marceau (with the red lips and scary black eyeliner, shakily applied, to match). But spiritu-ally and essentially, she was always a child of the '7os. Until the day she died, fuck the bores and damn the sparks that flew, she just had to shoot from the hip and get the truth party started.

The unfortunate fallout from this take-no-prisoners attitude was that as much as it made her great fun at a party, it also cost her some friendships. Her great pal Ann, for instance, who had emigrated from South Africa in the early '60s because she and her architect husband Ken were opposed to the regime, and wore, on her ring finger on the plane over (in my mother's words) "a diamond the size of an ashtray" to fund their new life in Canada.

Many afternoons when I came home from school, Ann would be there in the living room with my mother, the two of them smoking and laughing uproariously. The ashtray on the glass coffee table would be full, and there would be lipstick marks on the rims of their wineglasses, which had clearly seen some heavy lifting throughout the afternoon. Ann had a peculiar, overdramatic style of speaking — somewhat like my mother's — wherein she would close her eyes and, with her prominent mouth and big white teeth, draw certain words out for emphasis in her strong South "Efrican" accent.

"Sue! You are *tew much*!" I would hear her scream with husky laughter after my mother had said something particularly outrageous. Soul sisters, the two women drank and smoked and laughed (and cried) over the phone if they weren't actually together in the afternoons.

After their family became more established, Ann and Ken and their two boys moved further uptown to proper Lawrence Park, which my mother disapproved of for being uptight and conventional. (Basically, my mother's personal boundaries were rigidly dismissive of anywhere north of Eglinton Avenue.) Over the years they saw less and less of each other and I remember my mother complaining that Ann had quit smoking and wasn't as much fun. When my sister, who was by that time in high school, told my mother that she had heard Ann's eldest son, who went to the neighbouring boys' school, was a "druggie" (or what today might be called a "heavy partier"), my mother unwisely decided to share this with her friend.

Needless to say, this particular newsflash was not well received. And whether or not my mother had somehow wanted to set the torch, another friendship went down in flames.

IT COULD BE EMBARRASSING, on occasion, to have my mother pull up at school to pick me up in her green Mustang convertible with the top down. She never looked like the other mothers, with her oversized sunglasses and, perhaps, a paisley-print peasant blouse from Yves Saint Laurent's Russian collection, topped with vintage gold chains from which might be dangling an enormous South African coin or a pair of folding nineteenth-century opera glasses which I have known, courtesy of my mother, since grade school, as a *lorgnette*. (For travelling by plane, she would wear one of these blouses, a man-tailored double-breasted jacket, and a pair of YSL pleated wool trousers — "Yves really does cut the best woman's pant," she would say, as if they were the greatest of friends, or at least amiable colleagues; "They are so comfortable, I could wear them to bed.")

And yet it was kind of cool that, once my parents got beyond the hand-to-mouth student stage financially, my mother never cared about stupid things like whether we tracked dirt into the house or broke anything or were properly attired for bad weather or used the "good" china for cereal (an admirably laissez-faire attitude I was unable to entirely pull off with my two children). She didn't care if I brought ten friends home for a messy baking project or whether we made a fort with the satin pillows in the living room. She didn't give a damn what the teachers said or what anybody thought about us: we were geniuses and they were just jealous.

Part of my mother's allure was that she fully believed in her own pyrotechnics and illusion. Our houses were beautiful and she was always beautifully dressed, but the inside of her purse was always a disaster. And God forbid you ever looked in the trunk of her car—and not only because it might be a mess. There might be secret contraband she'd tucked away to avoid detection and potential criticism—expensive clothes with the price tags still dangling from them (much like a lot of clothes in my mother's closet, even sometimes, like an upscale Minnie Pearl, the clothes she was wearing); a hidden half-empty liquor bottle; maybe even a lit cigarette.

For years after my father gave up smoking, which was, really, his entire adult life from his late-twenties onwards, the one thing absolutely guaranteed to set him off was the smell of cigarettes. Which meant that my mother, who really had zero interest in quitting even once it became clear to all concerned that smoking was a terrible health hazard, was required to become extremely inventive.

One weekend many years later when my kids were small and we were all up at the cottage, my mother went into town, ostensibly to get some groceries. It was an opportunity to slip out of range and, also, of course, provided her a brief interlude in which she might enjoy a couple of undetected puffs on a cigarette. This time, however, she must have cut it too close and actually lit up in the driveway right outside our cottage. Because when my father came out to help her bring in the groceries, he was surprised to find a lit cigarette smoking up the trunk of her car.

"I haven't the slightest idea how that got in there," my mother said, defiantly, when confronted with the still-burning cigarette. "Maybe it blew in from somewhere and just landed in the open trunk?"

My mother wasn't ever subdued, or the slightest bit apologetic, even when she'd behaved like a crazy person. After an inferno she herself had set, she would just hide away until the fire had died down and she could emerge from the ashes, triumphant — if only because she had gotten away with it.

Truthfully she managed to keep a lot of dark secrets, even what a mess she really was, hidden from view. Years later, at her graveside after her funeral, I found myself totally dumbfounded when her good friends actually came up to me to ask what on earth had happened.

"But I don't understand," says one of my mother's closest girlfriends. "We talked over the phone just a couple of weeks ago."

"She had an appointment to come see me but she kept cancelling it," adds the friend's husband, a semi-retired surgeon, shaking his head at my mother's nuttiness as if to cast off any responsibility that might land on his shoulders. "Something about having to get her hair done."

I want to scream, "Where have you been? You didn't notice she hasn't been in the greatest shape, for, oh, the past decade?" But, of course, having been raised to play pretend around others, to smile through all anguish and humiliation, I don't do anything of the sort.

Instead I reassure these guilty, frightened souls beside my crazy, beautiful mother's freshly dug grave.

It isn't until I turn around and see the faces of my mother's sister Mary, her brother Bill, and his wife Nancy that I completely lose it. Sobbing into their arms with the sheer relief that they have actually shown up.

THE RELATIONSHIP BETWEEN MY parents could best be described as volatile. Though they would often spend weekend afternoons in their master bedroom "sleeping," with the doors locked, there was always a possibility that things could heat up in a bad way. My mother, quite frankly, was obsessed with my father, and with whatever he might think about any given situation. Constantly bringing him up in conversation—"Well, of course, Perce says…"— as if he were her personal guru, if not one of the great observers of our age. But whenever he was referred to, with distaste and in the third person, as "your father," it was a clue that her grudges against him were mounting, that the fire that turned her hazel eyes a cat-like yellow had for some reason been lit within, and that, at any given moment, they might start screaming at each other.

No matter. I had my stereo in my room, where I played my recording of the theatrical production of *Hair* over and over until I knew every single word. Even though, when it came to the part that went "sod-o-my, fell-a-ti-o, cun-ni-Lin-gus, ped-er-asty," I would have to sing along phonetically, without the slightest comprehension, somewhat like learning my Bat Mitzvah portion.

Of course I had my little brother and sister to hide away with. In Jen's room, because it was the largest and had the bay window looking out onto the street, we would drag her sheep-skin rug and all her tiny wicker kid furniture up onto her huge, built-in desk, which worked as a sort of elevated stage and play boarding school where I was the heartless headmistress and Jen the poor orphan child who had to do everything I said.

And I also had the spare room, lined in floor-to-ceiling bookcases full of paperbacks, where I could curl up on the black and white checked tweed pull-out, comforted by the smell of books and the shafts of bright, warm sunlight that would pour in through the south-facing window. Still too young to do much more than flip through the paperbacks for the steamy parts, I would memorize the names on the spines (Baldwin, Bellow, McCarthy, Miller, Michener, Updike, Uris) and their titles.

Some years later, when I was already a mother myself, on a girl's getaway at a spa in the Arizona desert, I signed up for a craniosacral treatment from a visiting expert. Ten minutes into the treatment, which basically consisted of him gently holding the back of my head, hot tears were pouring down my face and there was a burning wedge of what felt like a piece of un-chewed meat at the back of my throat. The therapist asked gently, "Your home, growing up was it, um...unpredictable?"

ONE AFTERNOON WHEN I was still in grade school, I remember my father gathering a bunch of the neighbourhood kids in from the street to our new family room. He gave us all crayons and pieces of white paper and asked us to draw a house. The winner—a bright and happy child's version of the ideal house, crudely rendered in primary colours, with a classically peaked roof and surrounded by trees and a green lawn—ended up being the logo for his new company. The company was to be called Whitehall Homes, and together with our next-door neighbour Jerry, who was an architect, along with a fellow lawyer my dad had grown up with in Welland named Saul and my Uncle Bunny, they would build subdivisions of brick homes in the new suburbs cropping up on what used to be farmland around Toronto.

On weekends we would drive out to the muddy building sites and I would play with the *objets* in the glamorously appointed model homes, which were, of course, the handiwork of my decorator mother. Prospective buyers got to choose which style of home they wanted from a selection of different faux-colonial styles, each with grand, old-world names like The Hardwick, The Canterbury, or The Chartwell.

Things went great guns for a time; it was the high-flying '70s and my parents, whose own parents had never been anywhere more exotic than Florida, started to travel to glittering places like London and New York and Rome, where my mom would return armed with gold chains from Bulgari, David Hicks carpets, Jean Muir capes, and (for me) suede fringed miniskirts from Biba. They would come back with tales of cocktails with James Baldwin in Saint-Tropez and lunch with Andy Warhol at his Factory (where they were actually served Campbell's tomato soup from a can). And once, after I had entered my teens and got my period (an embarrassing episode involving my father offering his hearty congratulations), they presented me with a white Braun Lady Shaver from Europe, with which I was presumably to start immediately removing the unsightly body hair I hadn't even noticed yet.

At Christmas, we would fly down south to spend two weeks at Settlers Beach in Barbados, where the other guests might include the heartthrob crooner Tom Jones (who would appear at the beach in the tiniest of black bikinis) and his incredibly plain Welsh wife (who, much to the amusement of my mother, wore her fur stole to the beachside restaurant at dinner), or the dazzlingly beautiful Engelbert Humperdinck family—even Philip Roth and Claire Bloom (when my parents had them over to our villa for cocktails, I secretly kept, and wore for years, the otherwise unremarkable grey athletic Hanes T-shirt the writer left behind). After a few days at the beach, everyone would be perfectly sun-kissed, and my mother would toss on a pair of white jeans and a ribbed French T-shirt, her white teeth and gold hoop earrings shining in the dark as we climbed into our Mini Moke to drive to dinner somewhere louche and groovy in the hills, like the famously swinging spot where the ex-pat Brit owner swanned around in caftans and the only thing on the menu was fondue. Wednesday nights we would dress up and walk down the beach barefoot, carrying our sandals, to the old-school glam Coral Reef Club, where I once saw our former Prime Minister John Diefenbaker and his lily-pale wife at the fancy Calypso BBQ buffet, famous for its live steel-drum band and flaming limbo.

Back at home we joined the tennis club—not the Lawn, which back then didn't let in Jews, but York Racquets, where everyone else was also Jewish and a real estate developer. Under the ski hills at Collingwood on Georgian Bay, we built a '70s Modern cottage with multiple views of the lake through its many sliding glass doors. My mother appointed it with slate-blue leather modular sofas, stoneware lamps, and antique quilts on the walls. Like all the other Forest Hill families, we joined the club at Alpine, where the hills were more like mounds than mountains. Still, we all behaved like it was Aspen, clumping around on the wood floors of the chalet-style lodge in our heavy boots and neon one-piece ski suits, picnicking from straw Provençal baskets carried in for lunch, and gathering around the outdoor fire for après-ski at the bottom of the hill. On weekends in the summer, my dad would make what he called a "shore breakfast" of eggs, bacon, and fried potatoes with onions burnt to a crisp over a wood fire in the fieldstone fireplace by the lake, and then we would spend the afternoons searing ourselves in the sun on our white mesh Knoll chaises. After dinner at our long pine harvest table by the glass doors facing onto the dark-ened lake, we roasted marshmallows on enormous bonfires in the trucked-in sand, oblivious to the dangerous sparks that were flying around us.

THINGS CERTAINLY SEEMED TO be going our way—until matters started to heat up amongst the partners at Whitehall and the whole arrangement went down in flames of litigation, accusation, and late-night phone calls, my parents screaming at each other across the house at all hours. At one point in the long struggle, my always dangerously explosive father, blood boiling at the sight of one of his former partners, pulled over his car and started beating him up on the street outside our school. Or at least that's what we heard later. From everyone.

Whatever. We moved away from the house next door to the Steinbergs to a fancier, timbered chateau-style house with an indoor swimming pool and sauna in the basement that offered the perfect fuck-you, even if my mother always found it gauche.

True to the emerging lingo of the Gordon Gekko era, my dad started calling himself an "entrepreneur" and built hotels in Florida with partners from Houston and LA. There was talk of leaving Toronto entirely for California. I remember a trial visit where we stayed at a house in Laguna Beach, right on the Pacific, owned by some new business connection of my father's. In the top drawer of the bedside table in the room I was sleeping in (I think I had opened it looking for some Kleenex), I was amazed to see a real live handgun.

We kids never really knew what happened, other than that we were never to speak to either the Steinbergs or my Aunt Edith and Uncle Bunny ever again. We never did leave Toronto; true to form, my parents just brazened it out. Nonetheless my dad, who had made us notorious, never ceased to ask me, even decades later, whenever he learned that I had met someone socially important, "Did you tell them you were my daughter?"

YEARS LATER, at an engagement party for friends of ours that was being held at the home of their parents, I saw my Aunt Edith across the room. Hot with embarrassment, I considered leaving. I wondered if she would acknowledge me (it's funny, the shame of the entirely innocent). By the smoked salmon and bagels at the buffet, I found myself standing next to her. She looked years older, of course, but still with that lovely, familiar eyebrow-less face, so much like my father's (and, as I had been told, my own).

"I never would have recognized you," was what my father's sister, the aunt who had cooed over me in her lap, said to me after twenty-five years—me, a woman who has looked almost comically the same, if older and more faded, in every single picture since I was born. My mother was always the one who was quick on her feet and unafraid of telling it like it is, but I, for once, had the perfect comeback: "I would have known you anywhere," I said, in truth.

As my kids would say: "Burn!"

Four

THE WISEMANS

AFTER OUR MOTHER DIED, there was no question in our minds that her final resting place was not going to be the grim and treeless Jewish cemetery up in the nouveau ghetto of North York.

Our mother, who lived for beauty, had always loathed the colourlessness of the suburbs and loved Toronto, which, for her, comprised the area between the Annex and Rosedale, with occasional excursions south of Bloor Street to a hot new restaurant, a film festival gala, or the opera. Even though it had been the fashion, when they were just starting out, for young couples like my parents to move to the new planned community in North York called Don Mills, my mother used to recount how, when she and my father had merely driven up to take a look at it, she'd burst into tears.

Besides, as far as "the community" was concerned, our mother, although officially a convert to the faith, wasn't ever considered fully Jewish. Why should she have to lie there for eternity in between some small-minded Yids who would have looked down on her for being born a *goy*?

Our father, however, was of a different opinion. By this point in his dementia and general disappointment with life, his views had taken on a more radically Zionist, if not highly paranoid, hue than he had ever exhibited in his younger, saner moments. And then, of course, with his lifelong need to call all the shots, my mother couldn't even be free to go and die without his controlling the outcome. In his view, the final resting place for Susan May, née Lambert, would have to be beside him in some schleppy, tree-less yard neither of them would ever have felt the least bit drawn to while she was alive.

Which was why, less than twenty-four hours after our mother's death, we were racing over to Mount Pleasant Cemetery to see if there was any way we could head our father off at the pass.

In post-colonial Canada, class snobbery is still so engrained, it outlasts even death. Mount Pleasant Cemetery in Toronto is where the grand old Canadian families are buried, under old heritage elms and willows in beautiful stone crypts notable for their historical architectural vogues. The Eatons are buried there, in a neo-Georgian stone temple, and the Masseys, in an earlier Richardsonian rustic cottage covered in ivy. So pleasant are the cemetery's meandering paths that on a sunny day, it's full of joggers, kids learning to ride their bikes, and people pushing prams as if they were out for a walk in a pretty park instead of a cemetery.

Officially Mount Pleasant doesn't discriminate — in

reflection of the diverse, multicultural city it has served, there are also rows of tombstones with "ethnic" names, many engraved in Chinese characters. But these tombstones of the city's later arrivals tend to be housed in the newer, less established grounds of the cemetery which, in the landscaping expression of the social hierarchy, just happen to sit in the treeless field beneath the grand family crypts on the hilltop, where the names are all easily pronounceable ones from the British Isles.

I'm not sure how it happened but, to the shock of some of our more Establishment friends and acquaintances (who could not stop remarking about it throughout the gathering after the burial), we somehow scored possibly the last remaining spot in the posh, older, and greener part of the cemetery that our mother would have loved. The only hitch was getting a rabbi there to perform the rites as Mount Pleasant doesn't have one on its Rolodex.

On a cloudless day, eerily warm for March and just days shy of what would have been her seventy-fourth birthday, we buried our mother in a lovely spot right under the long branches of a beautiful old silver maple. A rabbi-for-hire recited the prayers of mourning for us heathens beside the shockingly deep grave. Unknown to our father, we had also secured the plot right next to hers for him one day. A posthumous win for her side that might have come too late for her to enjoy, but still felt like some kind of redress.

IT'S CHRISTMAS, and we are all packed into the Mercedes in our best outfits to drive to my grandparents' in

St. Catharines. Except it's not really Christmas. At Christmas, we will be on the beach in Barbados, where we go every year for the holidays because we Jews don't celebrate the birthday party of Jesus. So we are on our way to a Christmas party at my mother's parents' house in advance of the actual occasion — a faux-Christmas that my grandparents host every year just for us before we leave.

My sister and I are dressed up under our coats in navy smocked dresses with Peter Pan collars and white tights with our little leather Mary Janes that my mother finds for us at the Italian shoe stores along St. Clair. My brother and my father are both in grey flannel pants and Oxford button-downs (my brother, at this point, has taken to accessorizing all excursions outside of the home with his Hot Wheels collection in a briefcase). I think my mother might be in her steel-grey Jean Muir crepe dress with the cut-suede appliqué at the neckline and cuffs (were she here beside me as I write, she could have verified this in an instant).

Our gifts in the trunk for our grandparents, aunts, uncle, and cousins, however, are almost guaranteed to be flamboyantly, if sloppily, wrapped, in expensive silver metallic paper inexpertly secured with bandages of Scotch tape and a limp bow of marine blue ribbon. My mother always buys nice paper and ribbon, but her gifts still manage to look as though they've been dragged behind the car.

I am bouncing in the back seat with excitement over the afternoon ahead — I love Christmas, even though my dad, who won't let us have a tree and shouts at the endless seasonal Canadian Tire commercials that Christmas is nothing but a sad ruse that makes poor people feel they have to spend money. Also because it's rare that I get to go to my grandparents', and because none of us are—ever, really—wearing seatbelts.

I love my grandparents' house—the cheese buns and the glass relish tray that will be there when we arrive and the beautiful, serious big doll with the porcelain head named Binnie that I am allowed to play with if I am very careful and which is kept, together with her many outfits (all made by my nana), neatly stored in zippered cases in the upstairs bedroom closet.

I love everything about this drive across the dizzying Burlington bridge and into the Niagara farms with their gnarled fruit trees by the highway along the lake which is dedicated to the Queen and lit with elegantly arching metal light standards decorated with the curving letters "E" and "R" for *Elizabeth Regina*. My mother, in the front seat, is dead asleep. It's barely ten in the morning, we've only just hit the road, and her head is lolling from side to side with the car's movement as if she had just been felled by the dart of a tranquilizer gun.

Looking back as a mother and wife myself, I now realize she was probably exhausted from pulling all the gifts together and getting us ready, but this sudden narcolepsy was a weird quality amongst many other puzzling aspects of my mother: while entirely adult in her glamour and scarily wise to whatever others might be up to, she could also fall asleep with the complete and total surrender of a toddler.

And there were other ways too, in which my mother was surprisingly childish. She would never have admitted it—always picking at her plate, finding it more elegant never to appear too interested in eating—but she really preferred nursery food over anything complicated: crustless tea sandwiches and hamburgers (medium rare with ketchup, no tomato, best accompanied with a glass of red wine), things she could pick up and eat with her fingers, like asparagus and Bridge Mix. She loved card and board games (at Scrabble she was a virtuoso) and played heartlessly to win—even against her grandchildren (and though she would vigorously deny it, she was also known to occasionally cheat). She was petulant if she was not the centre of attention, self-pitying, and a sore loser. Just like a child, she would insistently refuse to admit even the most glaring mistake. Yet she was also playful and joyous, and brilliant with small children because she never really grew up herself. She was always up for a game and never forgot the words to a nursery rhyme. And even when she was old and ill and cranky, her eyes would still light up like someone seeing something for the very first time whenever she came across something beautiful and simple, like a tree in bloom or a passing bird. The same quality I see in my daughter's hazel eyes when they brighten with a clear, untroubled joy that, just like her eye colour, must have skipped a generation.

As my nana would always say of my mother, quoting the Mother Goose nursery rhyme on the colourful Royal Worcester figurine representing the bonny second daughter she gave birth to on a Sunday, "But the child who is born on the Sabbath day is fair and wise and good and gay."

Nana was full of such Briticisms and sayings ("Only the boring are bored, dear," being one directed at us), and her shelves and tabletops were full of small-time, un-glamorous tchotchkes like Royal Worcester figurines, which my mother would never even for a minute consider putting out on display.

It sounds funny to say this about such an unrestrained personality as my mother, but style, for her, was the one area of life in which restraint was a rule. Her interiors, while sumptuously appointed, adhered closely to her own strict rules of proportion and what she mysteriously referred to as "flow." Model-thin until sideswiped by menopause, she never really consumed much beyond red wine and black coffee (though the smoking—and the speed, which was fashionable at the time and which she kept in her mess of a purse—probably helped) and she absolutely lived to throw things away. She couldn't stand her mother's Depression-era need to stow every bit and bob, and to waste not, want not.

"My mother kept every single little piece of string and dirty rubber elastic that ever came into her house," she would complain. "It was disgusting, all that *stuff* everywhere and those little bits of leftover food drying out in the fridge. I would come home from school and there my mother would be on one of her 'cleaning days' on her hands and knees with the ugly contents of the bureau spilled out all over the front hall."

So adamant was my mother not to follow suit that she would simply clear an unsightly desktop by dumping everything on its surface directly into the garbage; my Ontario Scholarship together with another un-cashed cheque for my academic achievement in high school were never to be seen again after one of her purges. Years later after we three kids were long gone and she'd finally kicked my father out of their apartment, she directed "the Filipina" we had hired as a companion to simply clear his old office of all the unsightly files and magazines he had piled up everywhere and toss it all, unexamined, straight into the trash. Like all great dictators confronted with their war crimes, she would vigorously deny any involvement whatsoever.

"Your mother was such a beautiful baby," my nana would say, playing with her charm bracelet (another thing my mother would never consider wearing but which I secretly admired) and nodding her little grey, permed head with a sigh. "Honestly, people would just come up to me and stop me on the street when I took her out in the pram, she was so lovely! And such a quiet little thing—she could spend hours lying in her crib, just moving her fingers and looking at her hands."

No kidding, I would think unkindly as a teenager. Probably conjuring some spell or imagining how fabulous her ring finger might look adorned with a little something in the seven-carat range. Because that was another childish thing about my mother: disarmingly warm and generous, she could also be surprisingly, and deliberately, mean. She gave us everything, but she could be a real bitch.

NANA AND GRANDPA'S HOUSE is not large but it is pretty to me, in the centre of the cul-de-sac on Queen Mary Drive, with its bay-coloured walls and its bay window overlooking the ravine. My nana favours framed botanical prints and reproductions of Leonardo da Vinci sketches on the walls, stoneware jugs on the sideboard and mismatched pressed-glass goblets on the dining table—a different universe entirely from the Chagall lithographs and complex, abstract Vasarelys and hanging above the L-shaped chocolate-brown velvet modular sofa in the sunken living room at Uncle Bunny and Aunt Edith's, where we go for the Jewish holidays, or for that matter our own Mylar and blood-red dining room at home, and its Design Statement.

The minute we arrive at my grandparents' and take off our coats in the tiny slate foyer (mine, and my sister Jen's, English, navy, with velvet collars and hemmed to a mod, mini-skirt length), my Nana's famous cheese buns come out piping hot from the oven: open-face white dinner rolls topped with a gooey, orange melted elixir reputed to have its origins in Velveeta (although they could never be properly duplicated by anyone else) and finished with a small square of crisp, sizzling bacon. My father, who would never have eaten this incredibly non-Jewish food growing up, can easily demolish twenty in a sitting, popping them into his wide-open mouth like nuts. A delicate relish tray of divided glass squares for carrots and celery and olives and pickles, all chilled on bits of crushed ice, sits on the coffee table. My grandpa's drink is rum and "Peps"—never Coca Cola—which he enjoys in a frosted grey-green tumbler etched with scenes of Confederation. He and my dad and Uncle Bill talk about the drive from Toronto. Their GM cars are parked in the driveway in front of our expensive German one. During the First World War, my nana's English-born father, George, left his three small children behind in Oshawa to fight in the trenches. There is no way they would ever have a German car of their own in their driveway.

We ladies — my aunts Mary and Nancy, my mother and my grandmother and I — sit at the neat grouping of grey-green armchairs and matching sofa around the marble-topped coffee table facing the fire. My feet in their patent-leather shoes do not reach the ground, so I dangle them on the piped skirt of the sofa. Jen and Josh and our cousins Ginny and Mary-Ann play on the broadloom. Even though it's not really Christmas, the little tree is up, sparkling with shiny glass globes and little birds in the front window, and my absolute favourite holiday decoration — a set of three Wise Men made by my nana out of blown egg shells (for the heads) and bits of old jewellery and scraps of fabric all gilded with a sheen of gold paint — sits on the mantel above the fireplace. Like the familiar, lined faces of my grandparents, it feels good to see them again. I admire the gilded statuesque folds of their outfits and the way my Nana has made each one of their little bejewelled offerings different for the baby Jesus, whom we sing carols about for the holidays at my public school (though sometimes I feel bad singing along because I am not Christian and we don't believe in Him, so I just mouth the words). We have beautiful things at home, but none of them are specially out for Christmas or, for sure, anything my mother has ever made herself.

Unlike at Edith and Bunny's, at Queen Mary Drive there are no stacks of modern art books or *New Yorker* magazines piled on the coffee table — here, an oval of white marble void of reading material and looking like something that was brought in from the garden with its coppery-green iron base. Nobody is lounging with their feet up, smoking a cigar or yelling into another room from the stairs. The adults aren't talking heatedly of real estate or Israel, but instead about what Mary Margesson's two daughters are up to now, who has joined the golf club, and the latest plans for the garden.

(In the words of my mother, my grandparents, who have a lovely steep garden leading onto a ravine, actually garden "themselves!" — a refrain she will hoot, with disdain, on one of her four p.m. calls to a girlfriend, a glass of red and ashtray at the ready, once we are back at home.)

At my grandparents', Glenn Gould is never playing the *Goldberg Variations* with Asperger's intensity in the background, but one can hear the twitter of birds at the feeders my grandpa fills with seeds outside the white-mullioned windows. Also there are no *MAD* magazines upstairs, like there are at Edith and Bunny's, for me to read. There are, however, old children's books with black and white illustrations on the basement shelves and wildflowers drying in bunches from the furnace-room ceiling, flowers my grandmother snips on her walks and makes into the dried clumps of baby's-breath that are all over the house.

My nana has a good friend named Iris Saul whom she once took me to visit. Because her name was Iris, every single item in her house, from the wall-to-wall drapes to the Kleenex-box cover in the bathroom, was either mauve, lilac, or grape-juice coloured. I couldn't get over how glamorous it was.

When I told my mother about it afterwards, she sighed. "Children really have no taste."

I love my nana's bathroom, which smells flowery and has white wicker shelves for her towels and a very deep bathtub that my nana claims she never, ever fills with hot water any higher than her hips because that would just be wasteful, which makes my mother snort with derision.

"You would think, after all that work raising the four of us and all those years of keeping a house and garden, she might at least allow herself a soak every once in a while in a full bathtub!"

Behind my nana and grandpa's bed is a collection of old black-and-white pictures my nana has carefully hung in different little frames that make a pattern on the wall. I don't know all of the people or the dogs in the pictures but sometimes, during the long afternoons of our Christmas visits, I like to go upstairs to my grandparents' room, lie on the bed (which has a cozy white cover with little raised towelly dots on it), and stare up at the frames. Some of the pictures are of my mother when she was little, which must have been a long time ago because they look really old-fashioned.

"Mother, you *really* should consider putting in at least a powder room," I can hear my mother telling her mother downstairs, as she does every time we visit, which isn't often, because "your father just can't stand being in that tiny little house for very long."

"Susan, dear, we have managed perfectly well all these years with four children and just the one bathroom," replies my nana, who has a special intonation for *Su-san,* with a drawn-out emphasis on the "*Su*" that alternates between shocked amusement and pleading exasperation depending on my alien mother's antics. Earlier during our visit, it was the former, when my mother, regaling her sisters with stories of her gay hairdresser, was intent on being risqué.

"According to Frank, it really is true about the size of men's hands," says my mother, raising a sly, dark brow as her sister and sister-in-law break into snorts of laughter. "Of course he should know! You know all the gay men go to these bathhouses where they have sex all night with complete strangers."

"Oh, come on, Susan," giggles my aunt Nancy.

Draining her glass, my mother goes for broke. "I always thought you could tell just from looking at their noses."

Downstairs in the TV room, where Grandpa watches *The Price Is Right* on the cabinet TV under the window and refreshes his rum and Peps at the built-in bar, there is another, larger tree with the presents all set up underneath it, some for us from a mysterious Aunt Winnie, whom I can't remember meeting, but I think is somehow related to us. She does give us some strange presents, like recipe boxes and wooden crochet pegs, even though the wrapping paper is very pretty, with lots of Santas on it. Later, after opening them, we will have an early dinner, always the extremely Gentile combo of a ham with cheesy scalloped, cubed potatoes, buns, and a green salad served from the sideboard, followed by homemade squares in cut-glass dishes and a slice of one of my nana's famous raspberry pies with vanilla ice cream.

So amazingly flaky and delectable were my grandmother's pies that years later, when my mother had joined the Hadassah-WIZO committee and they were compiling a recipe book to raise funds for Israel, my mother asked her mother for her pie recipe. Today, I can find my dear, departed Anglican grandmother's baking tips in my worn, spiral-bound copy of the 1979 *Kinnereth Cook Book*, it's there on the first page of the "Pies & Pastry" section, next to recipes for poppyseed pastries and Israeli strudel, under the heading "Some Random Suggestions by Mrs. Raymond Lambert, St. Catharines."

WHEN MY MOTHER MARRIED my father she became known as Susan May (Lambert) Yanofsky, a mouthful if there ever was one. I was born Karen Naomi Yanofsky, until my dad decided to change our family name to Young. The explanation always offered for this re-naming was that "Young" was easier for people to spell. But of course it was a lot easier, too, to get around the small-mindedness of WASPy old Toronto in the early '60s with a culturally blank name like "Young." And truth be told, "Yanofsky" wasn't my dad's family's real name either. When my father's father emigrated from Russia somehow, amidst his desperate flight and passage, which involved the death of a child from typhus (a brother, Michael, who was never spoken of and whom none of us learned about until many years later, when my brother Joshua was born), the family name morphed from "Zahansky" on all the official documents into the name my father grew up with—the same one my mother assumed when they married and the one I was given when I was born.

Jen, I think, was named after the popular Donovan hit "Jennifer Juniper," and managed to embody the winsome delicacy of the song into adulthood by staying extremely small and fine-boned. When introduced to us, people still don't believe we are sisters. Once, on a trip to Paris with Jen after I finished high school (a graduation present from our parents), a stranger came up to us and complimented me on my pretty daughter. (At exactly three and a half years older, I would have to have been pregnant with her in nursery school).

The name Joshua David for our baby brother, if particularly heroic in a *Jesus Christ Superstar*-meets-Old Testament fashion, was an obvious '70s choice. I, on the other hand, was named Karen (which my mother, to the end of her days, oddly insisted on pronouncing "*Kah-ren*" as if she, and by extension, just the two of us, were actually somehow Scandinavian) after the doomed Zionist heroine in Leon Uris's postwar epic *Exodus*.

Names aside, Judaism wasn't just something my mother converted to when she married my father. She embraced its world-weary irony and sadness as if it were the elixir her parched, Southern-Ontario Anglican soul had always been searching for, growing up in her neat little house on Queen Mary Drive, walking her Beagle, Tipper, and singing on Sundays in the choir.

Perhaps it was the high romanticism of Jewish mysticism, isolation, and persecution that so appealed to her? For Susan May, born on the Sabbath to be "fair and wise and good and gay," came to master the deadpan delivery of the Jewish joke, the making of legendary chicken soup golden with floating orbs of yellow fat and unctuous, garlicky brisket—along with the perfectly delivered guilt trip.

In a way, even though we never were fully accepted as pure-blooded, card-carrying members of our Jewish community—my mother being a convert and all of us being impossibly blonde and somewhat Aryan-looking (although that actually came from my father's side, likely the result of centuries of Cossack rape and pillage)—it was my mother who was the most stereotypically "Jewish"—particularly in her rejection of DIY and handicraft.

Like a natural-born Jewess, what my mother really knew was how to direct others. Gilded though my nana's Wise Men might be, it was nevertheless she who had fashioned their elaborate costumes herself, and from leftover odds and ends. Like all good Canadian WASPs, "make do and mend" was central to my grandmother's style directive; invest in plain things of good quality that will last and even their scraps will always be useful. The unspoken motto was: don't acquire more than you need, nor draw attention to yourself with exhibitions of grandeur lest you be thought vain and selfish. Released from these norms of respectability, it was as if my mother had been set free to let her freak flag of fabulousness fly.

Jews, who are to this day never judged entirely socially acceptable by Establishment rules anyway, simply don't bother with these conventional wisdoms. Why hide your light under a barrel? Or bushel, whatever. If you've got it, flaunt it. And while you're at it, why bother making something yourself when you can get perfectly good people who specialize in that kind of thing to do it for you?

Every surface of our series of glass-covered houses was kept constantly smudge-free and gleaming—never by our mother, but by a succession of recently arrived women from less fortunate circumstances known variously, and together, as "the help." Early on, they were young, adventuring au pairs from England, Finland, and Denmark who would party with under-age me when my parents were away. Later, a rotating chorus of tiny but amazingly strong and steadfast Filipino women, whom my father regularly accused of stealing his white Lacoste shirts to send home to their children in the Philippines. Our laundry—a key category for such professional clothes horses as ourselves—was the exclusive purview of a lovely Italian woman named Mrs. Bicci. A maestro with an iron who hailed from near Turin, Mrs. Bicci had a son named Luciano whom she fretted over, and would regale me with stories of how the first leather shoes she ever wore came courtesy of Mussolini.

Never mind fussing over the sprigs of Sweet William and phlox as per Queen Mary Drive: gardening, for my mother, meant calling the gardening guy to come in and plant, as if she were landscaping Versailles, something in the neighbourhood of four hundred million all-white tulips. "Panache, my dear, is all about making a clear statement and going all the way with it," my mother would instruct, opening her arms wide like Lady Bountiful accepting a congratulatory bouquet at the end of a performance.

LATER IN LIFE, my mother liked to claim that when we were small, she used to make our dresses, a conceit of hers that was about as believable, given her total disinterest in athleticism, as her story that, "before jogging was 'in,'" she used to go running at the private-school track near our house. True, my mother could draw (her specialty being caricatures, mostly of us), and she could certainly pull together an outfit—or a room—on an egg timer, so assured was her stylistic vision. Woe betide anyone, however, who might ask her to help with anything from a child's school project to a potluck potato salad unless they were prepared to deal with a sad-looking and sorry mess. Which was why I also never entirely believed her claims that she baked my birthday cakes herself until the day that I—a tasteless and undiscerning five-year-old—had the gall to ask for one of the ticky-tacky ones from the grocery store bakery department (the one with a real plastic doll standing in the centre of a cake dress every bit as white and fluffy as the one on the album cover of Herb Alpert's *Whipped Cream*). "Why go to all that trouble," my mother would ask rhetorically, "when obviously you kids couldn't even tell the difference?"

When she cooked, which was not every night, since we went out to eat often and there was always "the help" around to throw another chicken in the oven for dinner, the result of her efforts was often startlingly delicious—usually dark and pungent (late in her life, frighteningly so; the other day I pulled out one of her well-cured Le Creuset pots and there was something black and charred still stuck to the bottom)—and the kitchen after these exertions guaranteed to be a total disaster. Things that required a light touch were never her forte; her culinary art lay in signature showstoppers like a brisket so drenched in garlic, paprika, and Lea & Perrins the result was almost prune-coloured; a buttery capon she made for holidays with an extraordinarily rich stuffing of challah bread tossed with sautéed chicken livers; a cabbage borscht with huge marrow bones that I remember congealing in pools of bright-orange fat when she would leave her cooking pots outside because the fridge was too full. The act of grocery shopping yet another area for my mother to exercise her penchant for largesse.

I cannot recall, however, even once seeing my mother wield any type of vacuum, toilet brush, or iron. Her most frequently used household device was her black vinyl spiral-bound address book. Knowing who to call, where to find it, and how to make it happen was her métier.

Indeed, my mother's leading role was as an arbiter of taste. When it came to the applied arts of housekeeping, she saw herself as more of a Producer or Creative Director than any of the little people fiddling with the lights backstage. Knowing where to go for anything from kosher chicken feet to the finest damask was her specialty, and she made full use of the extensive listings of trades and resources in her little black book: a torch of connoisseurship she passed on to me, her eldest, when I was able to land my first writing gig, a *Toronto Life* column actually called "Super Shopper" that I sometimes joked should have come with a cape. But really, as she would have been the first to say, I learned it all from her.

Scarce was the afternoon when I didn't return to find our driveway crammed with trucks and I didn't walk in the door to come upon someone fixing or changing or delivering something. Or unwittingly enter a bathroom to sit down on the toilet only to notice someone outside the window on a ladder silently working on whatever the task at hand was way up there (the eaves?). And this was at every house they ever lived in.

By the sixth or seventh grade, my brother Josh started

prefacing each and every phrase he uttered with the word "fuckin,'" as in "I have no fuckin' idea" or "That fuckin' guy, I know, he's just a jerk." Although swearing was hardly verboten *chez nous*, the ubiquity of this particular phrasing brought it to a whole new level. When asked about the origins of this new off-colour linguistic tic, my brother offered that he had most probably picked it up from the constant litany of swearing tradesmen that were always working on something just outside his windows.

"I know! Isn't it awesome?" said Josh, with enthusiasm. "That's exactly how the guys on the ladders talk to each other whenever they need something. "Hey dickhead, would you pass me the fuckin' hammer?"

Unlike at Queen Mary Drive, at our house nothing ever stayed the same and everything was in a constant state of renovation and revision. And my mother, centre stage, loving all the action, directing her support staff with all the certainty and self-possession of a Tang Dynasty emperor.

IT COULD BE COMPLICATED, at times, being a half-breed. Amidst the mixed messages we were given of how to live, and what exactly the point was in doing so, we three children never really ended up feeling part of any tribe other than our own. It didn't help that we were only Jew-*ish*. We never went to synagogue other than at the High Holidays (and even then we were usually late and typically among the first to leave the moment the *shofar* was blown). With many of our family friends being either non-believers or from a mixed bag of backgrounds, we didn't keep to "our own" the way that many Jewish families did. Given, too, that we kids attended mainstream, Establishment private schools rather than all-Jewish ones, we often felt like interlopers at both ends of the table.

Because we didn't "look" or "act" sufficiently Jewish, whatever that is, one of the oddest things that would happen to us as invisible minorities is that we were regularly mistaken for Gentiles. So much so that people would feel comfortable making anti-Semitic remarks in front of us as if we might actually be inclined to agree.

"Well, the problem with (insert name of formerly desirable neighbourhood or tennis club or school here) is that it's got so *Jewish*," the unsuspecting might complain over cocktails or across the table at a dinner party, with a drawn-out emphasis on the descriptive that made it perfectly clear that this development was not a good thing. It made one feel the need to respond, "But *I'm* Jewish"—as if that would make any difference at all to the limited worldview of the person making the unpleasant observation, other than make them refrain from saying it in front of us.

And then again, I was way too Jewish—and way too progressively raised by my liberal-minded '70s parents—to fit in at my completely inappropriate choice of high school (typical of my laissez-faire upbringing, it had been my idea to apply there after finding out the century-old former all-boys school, which was renowned for its academic rigour, was accepting female students). So traditional and old-school was this academy that before it started admitting girls in my entrance year, the boys used to swim naked, Etonian-style, for gym, in the pool.

Unsurprisingly, the English teachers were roundly suspicious of my attempts to fashion myself as a young bohemian, or to write like Anaïs Nin, whose sexually adventurous, stream-of-consciousness journals I was enraptured with at the time. The math teachers, who used to hand out our test results in order of performance (with mine typically last), advised me to simply quit math entirely—in grade nine. One teacher, a war vet with one glass eye which made him unable to observe the misbehaviour of students in precisely one-half of the schoolroom, actually went by the name of S. H. Bull, and nobody else seemed to find it the least bit funny.

After signing myself in one morning at the principal's office for missing a day of school on Yom Kippur, the principal's secretary, a spiteful, yellowish-grey-haired woman with a disapproving *moue* of a mouth named Mrs. Curle, accused me of lying about the reason for my absence.

"I saw you outside Holt Renfrew with an umbrella," she sneered, clearly deranged. So roundly despised was I by the administration by my graduating year that when a vote was held amongst the student body for class valedictorian and I turned up the winner, they actually held a second vote. My parents, increasingly wrapped up in their own dramas, were of little help in these perplexing situations.

"These people are so *average*," my mother would say, exhaling the word with a smoke ring of disdain, as if that judgement could offer any consolation. "They cannot possibly appreciate anyone as interesting as you."

Thank God for my first boyfriend, a long-haired and lanky Methodist who reminded me of James Taylor on the cover of *Sweet Baby James* and whose musically-inclined family sang grace in three-part harmony before dinner ("Do you eat pork, dear?"). Their cottage, on the sandy shores of Lake Huron in a reassuringly homogenous development restricted since the war to white families of Anglo-Saxon background, had a small sailboat acronymically named "Bageacageada" after their five children: Barbara, George, Cathy, David, and my lovely Alec. A hippie actor and canoe-ist uninclined to the use of deodorant, Alec permeated a musk I found intoxicating. So infused with his natural eau de funk were his button-down shirts, I would wear one of them to bed at night. My parents, however, were some-what less charmed. When he came up for a weekend to our family's cottage, the one with a fake imported beach and an unnamed sailboat, my parents pulled me aside to insist he take a shower. Immediately.

"The smell of him is giving me a headache," complained my mother, pouring herself a glass of wine and lighting another cigarette before attending to the marination of that night's burnt chicken offering.

And then I had to go and marry the boy I sat down beside on the very first day of law school, who turned out to be not only not Jewish, but German. And not just a little bit German, but actually German-speaking, which I only discovered once I overheard him talking to his mother on the phone. On the five-point scale of Germanness he would rank a solid five: an actual baron, from a very old Baltic German family descended from the Teutonic knights, who grew up speaking German at home amongst his five extremely tall and hearty siblings. Bringing him home was like a remake of *Guess Who's Coming to Dinner?*, WWII edition (and, presumably, on his end, something starring Joan Rivers or Woody Allen). Given my parents' liberal politics, I literally could have come home with almost anyone—a woman, someone with a disability, a person of colour—and it would have been less shocking than anyone whose mother tongue was the language of Luther, Nietzsche, Wagner, and *Mein Kampf.*

The first time I met my extraordinary mother-in-law—an almost Brechtian Mother Courage figure who survived the war, raised five children with little help after emigrating from Europe, and still chops her own wood for the fire and mows her own giant lawn well into her nineties—she looked down her long nose at me from her full six feet of height and handed me a colander, to go out and pick raspberries for dessert from the brambles of her own Brothers Grimm garden. This was on my first visit to my husband-to-be's heavily forested family home in Vancouver, and over dinner, Thomas and I, who had been seeing each other for only a year or two and were still in law school, shared our plans to set off on a car camping trip the next morning.

"Have you ever been camping before?" asked my future mother-in-law, sizing me up immediately.

As awkward as I (and she, too, I imagine) found that first encounter, let alone the very idea that anybody would grow and eat raspberries from their very own garden, we did somehow manage over the years to bridge the cultural gap, despite the depth of its chasm. My mother-in-law and I swap good reads, and we both love to argue about politics, which has made for some lively dinners over the years.

And now Thomas and I even have a raspberry patch of our own in our backyard, the thorny branches of which have to be hacked back like fairy-tale vines from encroaching upon our swimming pool. To paraphrase my father, although he would never have idealized this particular, prickly situation, it turns out it really doesn't get any better than this.

When Thomas and I did finally decide to share our own little rowboat and get married, the only certainty as we navigated the unknown waters ahead was that there would be absolutely no conversion of anybody to anyone else's religion. Given how much of herself my mother had to give up in marrying my father — the inevitable result of converting to his faith and turning away from her own family and traditions — there was no way I would insist on the same from my husband, whose family traditions were certainly more longstanding and probably more meaningful to him than whatever we mutts had cobbled together. And besides, wasn't it high time everyone start living in peace and move forward from the accidents of history? Damn convention and the ghetto mentalities of both of our tribes, we would just celebrate and honour everybody's everything as long we did it all together!

After a memorable ceremony on a sweltering midsummer night in my parents' garden — where, after we were joined in matrimony by an incredibly miniature female Unitarian minister (between my giant husband and his even taller brother, and mid-size me and my even smaller sister, it made for a visually comic altar arrangement), followed by the breaking of a glass to get the party started (*L'chaim!*) — came years of pre-Christmas *latkahs* and Easter egg hunts on the tails of Passover Seder dinners. How to navigate this demanding course we learned the hard way.

At the High Holidays, our heathen children would attend synagogue merely to please my parents, who themselves didn't know the Hebrew prayers, and then we would stuff ourselves with my mother's chicken soup and brisket. And at Christmas, we would fly our kids out to Vancouver for the giant family dinner after church on Christmas Eve, where, fuelled by vodka shots and bacon-stuffed *speckkuchen,* my in-laws would not only serve a ham made even less kosher with scalloped potatoes, but risk torching their house entirely by lighting their tree with real, burning candles just like they had every Christmas Eve in Riga for generations.

Which came to the problem of how on earth to celebrate our children's coming of age. Whether you are a nomadic hunter from the last remote corner of the globe or a half-Jewish/half-Lutheran, mostly non-practicing family from Toronto, it seems sad not to mark the occasion of a child's entering adulthood with some kind of ritual appropriate to your own tribe. Jews get bar- or bat-mitzvahed at thirteen; Latin Catholics mark their *quinceañera*; Protestants get confirmed around the same age. Most of these rituals involve some sort of test in front of the larger community. And so, with the wisdom we'd gradually come to over the years, that if we couldn't ever fully satisfy the cultural and spiritual requirements of either of our family backgrounds, we might as well have fun — the occasion of our eldest daughter Sophie's thirteenth birthday clearly called for a party. But one at home, where we could call the shots and set the test.

Since Sophie's birthday happened to fall on a Sunday in November, we decided to make it an afternoon open house with friends and family. A caterer was hired to make dim sum in the kitchen, a bar was set up in the living room, and the test we assigned our first-born was to write a purely secular speech (in English, not Hebrew) and deliver it in front of all of our assembled friends. Not an easy or particularly comfortable assignment for a thirteen-year-old, but hence its soundness as a rite of passage.

Such a success did our customized ritual prove, and so brilliantly delivered and well received was Sophie's speech, that when our son Philip was turning thirteen we followed the same strategy—except that, since his birthday fell on a long weekend in August, we threw the bash in the evening in the garden. In an effort at double-entendre, we called it "Phil's Grill": dinner was an outdoor BBQ, complete with gelato served from a cart. Just like the night he was born, it was so hot and humid that immediately after Philip's speech, which he delivered in style from the diving board, most of our guests followed the young man of the hour, fully dressed, into the swimming pool.

OF COURSE IT WASN'T all a picnic in the grass.

Ever a force governed by her own natural laws, the inevitabilities of aging weren't something that my mother, whose interior design business seemed to be slowing down along with her physical ability to cope with it, was managing particularly gracefully.

Only just entering her fifties once she became a

grandmother to our two children, she wasn't particularly keen to be referred to as "Grandma." "Bubbie," of course, was out of the question.

"I think it might be nice if they called me 'Susan,'" offered my mother one afternoon over a glass of red wine (for her) and a cup of Earl Grey (for me) in her grey velvet lair when I was a few months pregnant with Sophie. "Susan is a nice name."

"Yes, Mom, it is a nice name but it's not exactly how children generally refer to their grandmothers," I did my best to point out. "It sort of suggests that my children will be people you just happen to know, like a neighbour or a client, rather than someone you're actually related to."

"Well, I don't see why we have to do something just because everyone else does," said my mother, with a hoot of disdain. "I think it's a little late for that."

This, even on the heels of her quick dismissal of absolutely each and every baby name I had thus far on my list ("Alberta!—isn't that a province? Why would anyone ever want their child to be named after a province? And then such an uninteresting one!"), was only par-for-the-course annoying.

Somehow we settled on "Nan," which my mother seemed to accept partly because it was close to "Nana," which I had called her mother, and because it came naturally from Sophie. My dad ended up being called "Zade"—short for the Jewish "Zayda" we'd called his own father—and together, known by the cross-cultural moniker of "Nan and Zade," they, just like all the other great tag teams in the bloodsport of family dynamics and struggle, were both wonderful and horrible to my children, who both adored them and were infuriated by them, just as we were.

Weekends would be a game of chicken with my parents, who would have liked nothing better than for us to spend each and every one up at their cottage on the lake with them, no matter how they chose to behave in our presence. Thomas and I, both busy and stressed with work and the demands of raising two young children whenever we weren't working, would hope against hope each weekend during the ski season or in the height of summer that maybe — just maybe — this would be the one where we might get the cottage blissfully to ourselves. Or maybe even be able to spend the weekend with some friends. But each week, my mother would keep us guessing right up to the bitter end. By around Thursday, I might break down and give her a call.

"Hi Mom, so what's happening with you and Dad this week?"

"Well, we were just out last night with Harvey and Sylvia at the pasta bar at Scaramouche. You know how I just love the fish there, it's always so good. And that coconut cream pie! Of course we all had to share a piece."

I can see the coconut cream pie with its Alpine mountain of meringue sitting on a plate in the middle of their candle-lit, white-linen-covered table. Three silver forks are raised around it, my mother prodding the coconut cream with her index finger before licking it off like a child.

"But this morning I am really exhausted. I didn't sleep that well. I may just crawl back into bed right now," says my mother, yawning into the phone. It is ten-thirty in the morning.

"That's great, Mom. So, do you think you and Dad will be going up north this weekend?"

"I'm not sure," says my mother. "Are you guys coming?"

"Well, I don't know, Mom. I was just checking in with you. To see what your plans were."

"I don't know, we haven't really decided yet. The weather isn't really looking all that great," yawns my mother. "And who knows, maybe I'm coming down with something." I can hear the pages of a newspaper rustling in the background. She must still be in bed in her white robe, reading the paper.

Encouraged, I come right out with it. "Well, if you guys thought maybe you weren't going to go up, we wondered if maybe we could invite someone?"

"So you guys are definitely going? Well, then maybe we'll join you," says my mother. "I've got to go back to bed, I can't keep my eyes open." Click and dial tone. Game, set, and match––as usual—to Susan May.

That I was too easy a target never seemed to discourage my mother. Restless and with time on her hands, she would often call wanting to talk, which was hard on my end because I was suffering from the exact opposite problem. But catching up on whatever might be going on with me was never really the reason for her call. No, she wanted to talk, which for her meant making pronouncements.

"I've decided I'm not going to buy anything for any of you for Christmas. I'm going to give each of you something I already own," she would say in her declarative way into the cell phone—too loudly, as she never quite figured out that you don't actually have to speak with your lips pressed into the mouthpiece for others to hear. With some effort, I would make out through the muffled roar that she was asking, "Do you think it's time Sophie had a look at my Yves Saint Laurent tuxedo jacket? I don't think I can even get it on anymore." Or, "Last time I was over, I had a look at that deco table, and it really needs refinishing." Or, recently: "I'm making a list. If you had to choose between any one of our paintings, which one would you want when I'm dead?"

Gifts and their ever-present BFFs — the accompanying guilt trip — aside, the Jewish holidays became more strained, and harder to enjoy, the smaller our family circle got, as my parents wore out more welcomes and my siblings made their escapes — first, to study, and then to live, abroad. And then, the more the elaborate rituals required to celebrate them properly became a burden to my increasingly lame (and increasingly wigged-out on pain meds) mother, who remained insistent on hosting everything, the more the "holidays" became a trial. She would cook all day and be in a terrible mood when we arrived, and then she'd be cross for having forgotten something like the shank bone for the Seder plate, and her food would be weird and over-salted. Dogged, nonetheless, she would continue on, her suffering and disappointment now operatic in its dimensions. Dragging herself and the rest of us through these occasions less out of a sense of duty (never an operating principle) than, I think, a demonstration of her sheer will to remain the centre of attention and action. Her ongoing determination a refusal to entertain or even acknowledge the possibility that she might, one day, have to pass on the torch to me. And yet, it is particularly during our holiday celebrations now, when there is no longer any power struggle over who will be doing what and where, that I miss her so.

AFTER MY GRANDPARENTS' HOUSE on Queen Mary Drive was finally sold, I drove out to St. Catharines one afternoon with my mother to help pack up my grandparents' things. My mother and my Aunt Mary and I spent the day reminiscing over the different dishes and glasses from the cupboards and the little vintage objects my grandmother had found charming that used to be on the bookshelves in the family room. My mother ended up taking a few things: a beautiful blue glass-footed bowl with what looks like earrings on its sides; my grandmother's pressed-glass water goblets; and, of course, the little Royal Worcester figurine of the child born on the Sabbath Day. (All of which, after the death of my own mother, now reside in my own kitchen cabinets.)

As for me, I took the three Wise Men my grandmother had made, and we wrapped up our treasures and packed them in the back of the car for our drive home.

Every year since then, in early December, around what Thomas's family would mark as the First Advent (which usually falls right around the start of Chanukkah), I bring out the faded cardboard box with my grandmother's gilded Wise Men and put them out on our mantel. My children, who have over the years become as charmed by their annual re-appearance as I was, have re-named them: in our home, amongst our tribe, they are referred to as The Wisemans.

Five

BAIN DE SOLEIL

IT IS STRANGE TO me the way one misses someone who has died. Perhaps it has to be someone you were very close to for you to miss them in this way; but nearly five years in, my sense of loss still feels very physical. Like a bump or a bruise or a limp or a sprain, I can actually feel my missing her. It is not just missing what she might have said if she were still here, or what she might have been able to contribute in the way of company or consolation or opinion — although these things, too, you miss when someone so much a part of your own self is gone.

Perhaps because it is my mother that I miss, a body I knew almost as intimately as I know my own — even as her body changed over the years — that, in moments when I feel despondent, and left behind to continue alone, what I miss is her actual, physical presence. The heaviness of her body, the huskiness in her voice, the hot whisper of a secret, the smack of her wet kiss too close, and too loud always, to my ear. The way her hair would be flattened in the back after a nap or her skin would be cool and goose-bumped after a morning swim.

Sometimes I want to be small again, just to be able to curl up beside her, feel her sigh, and breathe in the smell of her. Simply in being, she was my mother, which is something you learn once you become a mother yourself, and something that leaves you so bereft after your own mother is gone.

When she died and we had to clear out everything in my parents' condo, emptying the master bathroom of its contents proved the most difficult task. Not only because it was the sacred temple of my mother's daily self-observance, but also because, of all of the rooms in a house, the bathroom is perhaps the most intimate. As with all their rooms, I tried to be ruthless. The last thing I wanted was for my own house to turn into a museum, particularly one dedicated to the crazy, mixed-up mess they made of their lives. But somehow I couldn't bring myself to throw away a half-empty bottle of my mother's Lancôme makeup remover, slipping it in my handbag to take home. It wasn't that I particularly needed makeup remover. I just wanted it because it was something she had used on herself, dabbing it on a cotton pad or, more likely given her toilette etiquette, a wad of toilet paper, to ineffectively smear away the globs of black mascara around her eyelids every night before she went to bed in one of my dad's extra-large T-shirts and athletic socks, because her feet were always so cold.

Some people might be unable to erase a telephone message or throw away an old birthday card signed by their dear departed. For me, it was the makeup remover. Almost five years later, it's still sitting there in my medicine cabinet, untouched. A half-used remnant in a blue plastic bottle of someone who is still so very corporeal — the sense of her physical presence still so strong — to me.

I AM NINE YEARS OLD, wearing the blue-and-white cotton polka-dot string bikini that my mother bought in matching versions for both my sister and I in the little shop at the white stucco, ivy-covered entrance to Sandy Lane, in Barbados, an island we go to every winter that is burning hot and smells like things on fire from the moment we step onto the rippling tarmac from the plane.

Around my neck is a necklace made of white shells that we bought from a guy in ripped pants balancing a cooler on his head as he walked along the beach. While the adults lie reading and chatting in the hot sun on sun cots with white-and-yellow plastic webbing that makes marks on their backs, I run across the burning white sand straight into the water to cool down. Floating on my back, spread out like a pale white starfish with red stripes of burnt skin, I squint at the sun. The only sound in my ears is the roll and crash of the waves as they hit the sand. With each little wave, my body ripples. Floating is easy but I am trying not to think of sharks. Or the big fish that I can see under the water when we go out for a ride in the glass-bottom boat. If I get scared and start swallowing any seawater, it's so salty in my mouth that I will have to get out of the water and run across the burning sand to the beach bar to wash it down with a Coke immediately.

Careful to steer clear of any big pieces of coral or spiny black sea urchins—which I know will really hurt if I were to step on them and then my dad would make me pee on the spines they will have left in my foot—I make my way back onto the shore without being knocked down by a wave and run across the hot white sand as fast as I can to my mother's lounge chair, which she has positioned to face directly into the rays without any shadows. My mother is wearing a leopard-print one-piece bathing suit with cut-out parts on the sides and her big gold men's watch and earrings. In one hand, dangling beneath the straps of the lounge chair, she has a cigarette, and in the other, a hardcover book in front of her face. Underneath the cigarette hand there is a plastic cup half-wedged in the sand. We have been down south for only a few days, but every single day has been 90 degrees and breezy with a Windex sky meeting the turquoise horizon, and my mother, thanks to her chosen tanning product, which hails from the south of France and dyes your skin orange while offering almost no sun protection, is already mahogany. Against my wet, white legs, her skin is toasty warm and smells like Bain de Soleil.

"Don't get me wet," she says, sliding away from me on the chaise and handing me a towel, her face still in her book.

EVEN NOW WHEN I close my eyes and conjure my mother, I see her at her best, smiling wide with her hazel eyes. Maybe she has her hair, which is still slightly wet after a shower, centre-parted, and she is wearing a navy ribbed T-shirt over a pair of white pants and her big gold hoop earrings. Her bare feet are in thong sandals, the toenails painted a rusty red. Behind one ear she has tucked a pink hibiscus bloom, like her muse of the moment, the loopy LA chanteuse Maria Muldaur. And her skin shines like something roasted from a day spent in the sun.

So obviously glowing was my mother after having internalised the rays after a day down south or a long, hot summer afternoon out on the beach at the cottage that I imagine if I had placed her in a darkroom, her solarised likeness would have magically appeared on photographic paper without any additional light source. And how fitting a portrait would be the boldly graphic result: the high-contrast silhouette of a Warhol silkscreen or the album cover art from the volatile '60s and '70s. A time when every truth had to be uncovered to the point of overexposure, and every position taken had to be taken to extremes.

IF I HAD TO pinpoint the core belief of the house I grew up in, it would be that there is absolutely no point in half-measures. Going all in, headfirst, while throwing caution to the wind, was my family's practice. Immoderation in all things their true shared religion. Particularly when it came to the category of health and beauty, where mere acceptance of one's God-given physical state constituted, at least in my parents' opinion, a particularly reprehensible form of laziness. Nowhere was this more apparent than on the shelves of their master bathroom, which were always kept stocked with as many products as one might find in a small-town drug store—all of them maximum-strength.

No gentle Ivory or lavender Yardley for them; the soap we always had in our shower was Dial, a vigorously antiseptic bar designed to convey a surgical-prep's level of cleanliness that was guaranteed to scour through any and all levels of natural bacteria to reveal new and fresh layers of skin. In my father's case, this high-potency cleanser would be something typically, and topically, employed several times daily, as he not only showered in the mornings, but before going out to dinner, and most definitely before getting ready to go skiing or play a game of tennis, while we all waited, exasperated and ready, in the car.

God forbid you fell and ended up with a splinter or a scraped knee or elbow: first aid was typically administered by my father who, secretly believing himself to have the innate skills, not to mention the full encyclopaedic knowledge, of a trained physician, would take on the sombre, methodical aspect of a laparoscopic surgeon while administering lashings of blisteringly painful iodine or blasts of peroxide straight onto the open wound from the bottle.

Moisturizing was left to Vaseline Intensive Care, for the high-level reassurance of its name alone. Lips were kept from unsightly cracking first with medicinal-tasting, if waxy, applications of Chapstick, and then, after it was discovered on the ski slopes of Colorado in the '80s along with sunshine-tinted Vuarnet sunglasses, little yellow-and-white tubs of even more medicinal-tasting Carmex.

When it came to oral hygiene, there was no product too stringent or rigorously corrective for daily use. Forget regular old toothpaste; long before the mass whitening trend of today, my parents were early adopters of Pearl Drops tooth polish, an alarmingly abrasive paste in a small white bottle that promised to rid the oral field of stains and plaque whilst giving the mouth and tongue a distinct burning sensation.

Even eyes could not escape regular ministrations lest they fail to adequately twinkle. My mother was inordinately fond of a pharmacy-strength and hard-to-score blue liquid vaso-constrictor known as Murine, a couple of brightening drops of which not only eliminated redness, but seemed to operate as a kind of bleaching agent for the whites of one's eyeballs.

One area of technological development with which my parents were always entirely au courant was the latest in elec-tric toothbrushes, and my father was truly addicted to GUM picks, dental floss, and Stim-U-Dents, a lifelong addiction which took on a rather poignant character when, during that apartment-clearing after my mother's death, I discov-ered hordes of electric toothbrush attachments and oral care products, all in their original blister packaging. My father, in the early stages of dementia, must have gone out to pro-cure them, forgetting that he had already done so — and on many different occasions. (It was a similar story with germ-killing antibiotic hand washes, a fairly recent product innovation that proved no less enthusiastically received — in his case, over and over.)

This oral hygiene "procedure" (a clinical word my parents well and truly loved, as in "I'm booked for a medical pro-cedure tomorrow," or, "Doctor so-and-so, a specialist in the field, is recommending the procedure") was followed up with generous swishes of Listerine from the ever-present sink-side jeroboam of the stuff — not the new, brightly coloured, more palatable ones my parents would have inevitably viewed as cop-outs, but the original gold variety, with its punishingly harsh burn and truly awful flavour, because that's when you know it's working. And then my mother would ensure extra freshness, and whiteness, by swishing around a little swig of pure, unadulterated hydrogen peroxide straight from the bottle, an extremely potent and not professionally recommended practice which, somewhat ironically, eventually stripped the lovely white enamel off her teeth entirely, leaving her smile a bit yellowish in her later years. Luckily, by that time, she couldn't really see her reflection in the mirror all that well either.

In every house my family ever lived in, from our cottage to their condo, my mother's bathrooms were always austere, white-tiled clinical laboratories piled with stacks of white towels and a matching pair of his-and-hers giant white cotton-terrycloth bathrobes, the "hers" of which my mother eventually adopted as an at-home, 24/7 uniform.

Mirrors were installed wall-to-wall above the sinks (always two for a two-person bathroom, my mother would counsel, as "the real secret to a successful marriage"). A collection of multiple personal grooming tools, from nail clippers to tweezers of various weights and angles, stood at the ready on the extra-wide vanity counter in a popsicle-stick box with my father's initials spelled out on top in red beads glued together by my sister at summer camp. Neat rows of bottles of shampoo and conditioner, collected by my father on his regular shopping jaunts to the drugstore, lined the white marble shelf of the glass walk-in shower, the chrome handles of which sparkled with "the help's" daily ministrations. The bathroom walls were always tiled a glossy white, while the lighting would have been adequate for the needs of an operating theatre.

Even though all of our houses after the '70s featured Jacuzzis in the master ensuite with jets so powerful they could blast a small child helpless against the side of the tub, nobody ever used them because, as my mother would say, "Showering makes you feel so much *cleaner*." Particularly when, as was the custom in the gay, industrial-strength romp of their time, a shower was followed up with a protective layer of Mitchum 24-hour cream anti-perspirant—a voguish formulation of late '70s deodorant that I recall as so super-effectively drying on contact, it seemed to suck all vital fluids from the body on application.

BESIDES BEING EXTREMELY CLEAN, another thing my parents loved was being crisp. In no particular order, they were highly in favour of: crisp white dress shirts; crisp white cotton bedding with the highest possible thread count; crisp white pants in season (my mother would buy a fresh new pair every spring and before each trip south); crisp dill pickles and crisp autumn apples; crisp salads of iceberg lettuce (for my mother, who would often proclaim the need for "something crisp"); crisply ironed jeans (for my father, who liked his denim ironed to a knife-point centre seam over the knee down to the ankle); and crisp-fried bacon (to be left to rest in the hot pan a couple of minutes after frying, to "crisp up," according to my mother).

But what they really, truly lived for was frying themselves to a crisp in the sun. "As soon as you get out there and get a little sun, you will forget all about it," my mother would say whenever I might express the slightest concern about being too busy with work to go on vacation. Or dread about putting on a bathing suit feeling all white and pasty after a long winter, or somewhat large and puffy after having just had a baby only months before. And she meant it. Pallor, with its intimations of meek and blinking indoor mousiness, was an aesthetic project that called out for attention; something to be worked on and eventually overcome with prolonged and repeated tanning sessions in the sun. In her mind, the sun's blast was a purifying agent that incinerated one's worries while providing the ideal tan.

"Mmmmmm," sighs my mother, in deep, sensual delight like an actress in a porno. Her eyes are closed. Her book is abandoned. Her face, which is void of all expression, is tilted directly into the sun's rays so its fine planes are obliterated by the white light. Like an iguana on a hot rock, her long brown limbs are splayed out on her white mesh sun cot in a caricature of surrender. I have come over to her perfectly positioned deck lounge to ask her something.

"Mum, do you think I could go to Ellen Webber's house for dinner?"

"Hmm, wha'?" says my mother through closed lips, her nut-brown face somewhat glowing with beads of sweat but still in perfect sun-receiving position, like an acolyte reverent to the demands of her planetary deity.

"Could I go to Ellen's house? Tonight, for dinner?" I repeat, with some added emphasis on "tonight" and "dinner."

"Sure," says my mother, still in exaggerated repose, eyes still closed, head still tilted sunward, reaching down now with one hand beside the cot to feel around for her glass like a blind person. "What time is it now, anyway? It's not dinner already, is it?"

In the quest for the ideal tan, no mere sun-kissed peachiness or, worse, tell-tale redness, which marked one as but a nouveau aspirant to the glamorous life, would do. No, what we were aiming for was the moneyed aspect of the bronzed finish common only amongst those who have grown up with family villas by the Mediterranean. The right tan meant leisure and looked like money. Not only was tanned skin more youthful, glowing, and radiant; having a tan meant being more vigorous, conveying a zest for life and a sensualist's appetite for adventure. In my mother's professional opinion, tans were also more chic, more sophisticated, more *sportif*—and, as demonstrated by Jackie O and her sister Lee Radziwill (along with countless other fabulous, jet-setting socialites and actresses in ritzy getaways from Marrakesh to Saint-Tropez), a tan looked even better with bare legs, thong sandals, and lots of gold jewellery.

What's more, getting there was half the fun. Indeed, nothing provided the blissful burn and fetching result my parents so craved better than basking in the rays of their sun god. And, like everything else they did, they did it to extremes, worshipping what they saw as a rejuvenation of their vitality with a devotion and commitment that saw them, in their later years, develop not only deep lines and sun damage, but a shared custom skin tone that, soon after almost any exposure to sunlight, quickly became almost purplish—a deep-mahogany all-over tattoo—with a texture of mottled leather, like the hide of an old African elephant. A look that, thanks to their early and insistent interventions ("It's beautiful out there! What are you doing inside in the shade?"), I too am probably headed toward now, despite having been a blinking, near-albino as a child with skin the natural hue of white asparagus. After my first twenty-four hours forced out under the scorching equatorial sun as a girl, I was not a glowing mahogany or even the sun-kissed peach of a tan Scandinavian, but a blotchy mess of hives and red, peeling skin.

No matter, an icy blast of a skin-numbing spray stored under the powder room sink for such emergencies called Solarcaine would save the day.

IT IS TRUE THAT Toronto, Canada, was not an ideal habitat for such committed sun-worshippers. Apart from the blissful yet all-too-short roasting season of summer, during which they could indulge in their chosen ritual merely by going outside and lying very still for hours on a perfectly positioned sun cot by a lake or beside a swimming pool, some ingenuity was required to maintain the glow. Hence the tanning lamp, an early model, that sat on my parents' bathroom counter next to a baby-blue Lady Schick steam-facial unit from as early as I can remember. The approximate size and appearance of a two-slice toaster, it looked exactly like one of those vintage British-made war-time models with fully exposed electrical coils that burned bright red once you plugged it in — except that instead of grilling bread on the glowing coils, you were supposed to toast your face. This questionable apparatus came with a set of tiny orange goggles on a fine elastic strap so you wouldn't be left with any unsightly white lines from trying to protect your retinas from incineration. It was probably a terrible fire hazard. But during the long winter months, whenever any of us might appear remotely ill, or "peaky," my parents' first prescription, looking up from a book or newspaper to comment on our sickly hue, was to advise us to go upstairs to the bathroom and "take a little sun."

A more flexible, portable option readily available at any drug or hardware store was a cone-shaped, tri-fold device made from cardboard and lined with silver metallic foil referred to as a sun reflector. My father had one called the "Suntana" with a kitschy illustration of a sun-bathing beauty in an old-fashioned looking two-piece bathing suit on its folded exterior that he would carry around in the back pocket of his ironed designer jeans and pull out for use in the most unlikely of settings if the conditions were just right: in a car park outside a convenience store; in front of our cottage in the middle of winter beside an icy berm of snow for wind protection; once, in summer, atop a mountain in the Italian Dolomites so steep that he nearly fell to his death while adjusting his perch in an effort to find the ideal angle. Given that the lack of what they liked to refer to as "a little colour" was in their view tantamount to living only a pale imitation of life, achieving his desired hue was clearly worth even a near-death experience.

AN AD FROM 1965 for a fancy new suntanning gelée called Bain de Soleil invited you to "Have a Love Affair with the

Sun." Framed like a beach towel, with a straw-coloured edge, it featured an illustration of a sun-kissed, long-limbed, wild-haired young woman in a French bandeau bikini posed in what looked like an ecstatic sun salutation. By her side was the secret to both her perfect Riviera tan and her up-for-anything sex appeal: a white tube with rail-thin letters that darkened from orange to chocolate brown as they spelled out the luxuriously hedonistic words *Bain de Soleil*—an enticement to not only get out there and let it all hang out, but actually *bathe* in the sun's rays to achieve that sun-kissed bliss of being truly golden.

Like the concept of "chic" itself, the notion of a tan as desirable is a fairly recent French invention. For centuries, and in almost every culture, a creamy pallor was considered the height of beauty (hence the walls of museums lined with pasty nudes). And then came the roaring '20s, when hemlines were lifted, an emerging youth culture bared its limbs, and the daring Coco Chanel herself sported deeply sun-bronzed skin as a fashion statement. Intending to capitalize on this reversal of attitudes, one Monsieur Antoine of Paris is said to have developed the formula for the orange tanning gelée in 1925, marketing it in Europe under the name "Antoine de Paris" until it was introduced to North America in the '40s by the House of Lanvin under the name it is known by now. The height of its popularity came in the sun-worshipping '60s and '70s, before our fears of skin cancer, and after the newly-chic former fishing village of Saint-Tropez became a community of artists and an international hotspot for the jet set. Aspiration in a bottle, Bain de Soleil even smelled like a vacation only the wealthy could afford.

Before our discovery of Bain de Soleil and its unique selling premise, my father had developed his own special tanning formulation: a 50/50 blend of baby oil mixed with drops of pure iodine he kept in a baby oil bottle under the sink in the downstairs powder room. This custom blend not only failed to provide any sort of sun protection, it actually encouraged immediate burning, particularly when used in conjunction with one of his other prized tanning aids like the aforementioned sun reflector. Each and every time you applied it, you had to shake the bottle beforehand, as the iodine beads never fully dissolved into the baby oil. More like a dye than a skin formula, it tended to darken even the inside of your palms when you rubbed it on.

Bain de Soleil still exists, although less and less of us in the paranoid and fearful North America of today would ever be brazen enough to pull the stuff out of their beach bags now, given that its sun protection factor is only a mild-to-moderate, if not politically incorrect, 4. These days, all my friends are in hats the size of UFOs when they venture out of doors. Despite the damage already done, I am still the first one out there to soak up the rays, albeit now with the hope that a perfunctory dab of SPF 45 on my already sun-spotted trouble spots will be a sufficient offering to the sun gods to keep me safe. But I still recall with an almost sensual fondness the distinctly toasted Mediterranean smell of the orange gelée inside its white metal tube, and the way one had to squeeze, flatten, and roll it out from the bottom like an old-school tube of toothpaste. Transparent and gel-like in consistency, it would melt, erotically, into a dripping, neon-orange body oil as soon as it met with the heat of your hands — admittedly a problem for a product that tended to be left out on a towel or packed in a beach bag for hours under the hot sun. And yet, like nearly everything else that is now "wrong," Bain de Soleil was pure escape.

As powerful in conjuring the smell of my own toasting skin or the yellowing pages of a book being read on my belly on a damp towel in the sand against the regular sound of gulls and crashing waves, it is Bain de Soleil that is my madeleine. A single sniff from its open tube still brings me right back to the beach in the heat. Sitting at the edge of my mother's sun cot dripping wet, fresh out of the water, close enough to bask in the glow of the warmth radiating from her relaxed body and the comforting tang of her walnut skin, still browning under the purifying rays of the hot sun.

THE MOMENT ANYONE EVER walked into one of our family homes, whether they were a total stranger, a dear friend, or a relative, the first question they were inevitably asked was: "Can I get you a cold drink?" Not just a drink, as a puzzled boyfriend of my sister's once pointed out to us, but a *cold* one. The offer of lukewarm beverages obviously (at least to us) having been judged as insufficient in the pursuit of absolute and total refreshment — another value my parents shared *in extremis*.

Like my parents' penchant for always turning the air conditioning to full blast in hot weather until their master bedroom was like a meat locker ("It gets rid of the humidity," according to my mother), or for building a fire so roaring in the fireplace that it could roast a heretic alive, my family's unique emphasis on setting the valve to maximum, even when it came to ascertaining the ideal temperature for refreshment, was another example of their commitment to immoderation in all things.

Scale and proportion was another area that might be affected by this worldview. Why buy just one of those white shirts you really like, when you might as well have twenty? Then you will always be certain to have a perfectly spotless, freshly ironed one at the ready at all times.

Similarly, why hang a couple of light fixtures when your ceiling could be pockmarked with enough recessed lighting to illuminate an airport landing strip at night? Okay, so it's a little bright. At least you can see! Anyhow, they'll all be set on dimmers.

Looking to get comfortable? My mother designed her extra-long down-filled sofas to be so impossibly deep, with pillows so roundly plumped, that once ensconced, your feet would dangle above the floor like a toddler's and it would require significant, if not heroic, effort to climb out of them. So intensely comfortable were they intended to be that sitting in them without actually lying down was almost impossible.

Need to find out something? Nobody ever simply sat down and talked quietly together in our house. Questions were usually hollered from another room, or shouted down the stairs from another floor — the idea apparently only forming, like a thought bubble, whenever one of us was actually to step out of one room and enter another. Given the typical square footage of any of our family homes, such interlocutory challenges were thus conducted across great distances and, therefore, at the highest possible volume.

In the mood for a little snack? Rather than offer a couple of grapes and a neat wedge of cheese, my mother would put out what looked like a machete-cut swath of a vineyard and place an entire wheel of Brie oozing out on a low table—a temptation so lavish that our poor yellow Lab, Dexter, once taking the opportunity at a cocktail party when nobody was looking to scarf down the entire presentation, was ill for days.

Unsure what to order? How about everything on the menu?

IT'S SUNDAY NIGHT, so all of us are dressed and ready to go out for Chinese. I am wearing my best pink top, the one with puffy sleeves that ties at the waist, and my flared, flower-powered elephant pants. As usual, we are going to the House of Chan, where my dad is a part owner with a bunch of guys from the tennis club. More of a Chinese kitsch version of a steakhouse than a real Chinese restaurant, the point in going to the House of Chan is more to see and be seen amongst the local glitterati while dining on USDA prime with chicken-fried rice. The House of Chan has its name spelled out front in campy Grauman's Chinese–era lettering above red doors that look like they came from the set of a Charlie Chan movie. The waiters, who wear buttoned-up imperial red vests over their black trousers and have slicked-back hair like '40s gangsters, greet us as like a mob boss's family.

"Mistah Young, good to see you, good to see you! For you, this special table heah," says the tiny maître d' leading us to our VIP table, a red, channel-quilted banquette in the corner. My dad, in his ironed denim, literally twice his size, patting the shoulders of various other boss-men along the way.

"Looking good, Skip," Dad says to one tan and blow-dried patriarch. "It's been a while, Stan," to another, who is stroking the jewelled and moisturized wrist of what must be his second, much younger wife.

"Do you think that's the nanny?" whispers my mother, not particularly under her breath.

"Nice to see you, Percy. You're doing well? And this must be the family."

The second our bums make contact with the red vinyl quilting of our banquette, the maître d' is clapping for one of the red-vested waiters to bring us a bowl of fried Chinese noodles with plum sauce to dip them in. "Tommy, take Mistah Young ordah!" One of the nervous-looking young waiters, all of whom appear to go by the name "Tommy," immediately rushes over with a pen and a small yellow lined pad of paper.

"Okay, so we have to have some of those ribs, you know the ones that come with salt —"

"Small dry rib or long one?" inquires Tommy, pad in hand.

"Kar, what are those ones called, the ones I liked last time?" my father asks, turning to me, oblivious to the waiter's obviously rising impatience.

"Dry salted ribs, Dad."

"Okay, let's have some of those dry salted ribs. How many orders? Two, or do we need three?"

"But Perce, I don't think I like that kind," says my mother. "I like the BBQ ones."

"Let's get both kinds then. Kids? How many orders?"

"I don't want any ribs," says my sister.

"Can we have egg rolls?" my mother asks.

"I want a Coke," says my brother.

"Okay, who wants Coke?" asks my Dad.

"Is there ginger ale?" I ask the waiter, who nods nervously.

"Tommy, how many ribs come in an order?" asks my Dad, who has a few stock restaurant phrases, like "What are your top three items on the menu?" that he likes to torture waiters with, particularly when they are really busy.

"Six piece," says Tommy, squinting away the sweat behind his thick nerd glasses, his eyes nervously darting around the busy room. "I come back now with your drink, okay?"

Eventually, over my rising embarrassment, we make it through the ordering process and end up with a traffic jam of dishes vying for space over every square inch of the white linen table, from the egg rolls and ribs to bleeding steaks of USDA prime, plastic wooden bowls heaped with fried onions and potatoes, steamed lobster with drawn butter, pale glutinous chop suey, salty fried rice, and tea with fortune cookies. After we have eaten enough for a small Chinese village, the waiters pack up the leftovers for us to bring home for the dog and "the help."

We have driven here in our chocolate-brown Mercedes convertible with the top down, which my Dad has parked right out front—illegally, as he does most everywhere.

ALONG WITH BEING NATURAL-BORN experts in the fine arts of lifestyle and presentation, my parents considered themselves cultural critics, the ultimate authorities on their own lifelong "hot and not" and "best and worst" lists. The point of this long-running sideline, which admittedly formed the core of their ongoing discourse, was for them to take fanatical positions—both obsessively hot and then deadly cold—on their favourite, most incredible music, most amazing dishes, and most fantastic (before inevitably becoming disappointing) friends, stores, museums, hotels, and restaurants that they could then expound upon to others. Opinions, though always potentially subject to 180-degree reversal, that were, naturally, the final word.

"The world's absolute best hamburger is at P. J. Clarke's in New York," my mother would say, with the certainty of a food critic who had made it her life's work to travel the world in search of the Platonic ideal of said culinary expression. Or, "Lee Garden on Spadina is, hands-down, Toronto's best Chinese," my father would assert, brooking no argument on the subject. And then there were the insistent recommendations for the poor sod who happened to mention an upcoming trip to any destination with which my parents might be only passingly familiar. "If you're going to be in Miami," they would say, "you absolutely must go to Joe's for the stone crab, it's incredible." Or it was the sun cots at the pool bar at the Jockey Club (mesh, not webbing, and probably Knoll); the pastrami at Wolfie's Deli (spicy and dry); the beaches of Florida's west coast (wider, nicer sand, and more sea birds); or the service and the selection at Nordstrom (infinitely superior to any other department store). The font of their opinions — their likes and their dislikes, their mad passions and their utter loathing, along with their need to share it with you — was endless.

So fanatical would my parents be about their various "best" lists, that for months you would literally hear nothing else from them but how great the pizza at Terroni was last night, or how fun the bar at the Four Seasons was; until one day, the pizza at Terroni or the bar at the Four Seasons might come up in casual conversation and the unsuspecting unfortunate who had raised it would find him or herself with some explaining to do.

"I don't know, but the last time we were there, I was really disappointed," would be the first phase of disillusionment, accompanied by a regretful sidelong glance, as if the subject under discussion's sudden failure to please one or both of my parents on that singular occasion was almost a personal slight. This would be followed by, "I think it's really gone downhill," ending, inevitably, with, an emphatic "I hate that place" whenever its now besmirched and ruined name might come up. "The food's terrible!"

These fits of extreme passion were not limited to the people we knew or the restaurants we frequented. Musical recordings, too, would be taken up with such enthusiasm that, every time you entered the house, the exact same recording would be playing for months at a time, until, in the case of a vinyl record, its grooves would become impossibly scratched and crackly, or, once records were replaced by CDs, the disc would have to be thrown away because it came to a dead stuttering halt every time you put it on. Either that or, simply to stop our ears from bleeding, one of us kids would have to come up with a new musical offering to be immediately claimed in my parents' manic affections as the new greatest recording of all time.

At least it could be said about them that when they loved something, they loved it hard.

JUST NOW, searching for the words to explain my parents' extreme conviction in everything that they ever said or did, I realize that somehow, I was never able to have the same completely unclouded faith in myself. Or perhaps I had it early on and then lost it somewhere along the way?

Perhaps my tentativeness wasn't exclusively mine, but a part of a generational shift. Friends my age have somehow never entirely assumed the mantle of adult conviction that our mothers wore with ease. Whatever choices our parents' generation made—in how to live, and who to marry, and how to deal with their children and partners—there was never any doubt that they were doing the right thing, regardless of who got hurt or how the chips might fall. Now all of us, their aging children, losing what little conviction we had and in little ways: becoming sad and bitter with disappointment; facing crumbling careers and marriages; fearful of our grown children's every wobble, or worry. Somewhere amidst the mid-life terrors—of becoming irrelevant, of getting sick and old—that wake us in the middle of the night, the small, firm knot of self-belief we had as girls never fully deepened into certainty. Irked by a sense of having somehow failed to assume our roles as matriarchs, we seem to have been blinded by opportunities that never fully materialized.

Unlike our mothers before us, we might have been lucky enough to have our moments in the sun, but in the end we just got burnt. While our mothers, who may only have dreamed of trying to achieve the things we did, somehow managed to maintain their glow.

Was our ambivalence the fallout of their dead certainty? Could it be that the ground shifting beneath us during all those years of change somehow left us off-balance? Sometimes I think I am still searching for an equanimity that my mother never lost.

Straight from all those years when she could still smite us with a cocked eyebrow, right on through to the end when she demanded to be released from this life, my mother never flinched. The blood in her veins ran burning hot or icy cold — but always more than 100 proof, all the way.

Six

DIAMONDS BY THE YARD

A COUPLE OF MONTHS after my mother died, Thomas and I flew down south to join some friends on a sailing trip through the Grenadines—a splurge we hoped might be fun and restorative, and something Thomas had always wanted to do. Turns out the sleeping quarters on even a fair-sized sailboat are still rather tight—at night we had to slip into our shared drawer-like bed like two neatly rolled burritos. In the middle of one of these nights—a hot and rainy one in a famously rough mooring—I sat up in my sweaty burrito drawer with a start, crashing my head into a porthole window frame and, oddly like my mother in her final days, gasping for breath. Just like in the dream I'd just been dreaming, the very worst thing—the thing that I had always been afraid might happen—had actually happened. There was no sense in the dream of what that was, exactly, but of course it was true: my beautiful, strange mother was dead. And I would never ever see her face or hear her pronounce on anything again.

IT IS A RAINY AFTERNOON, and we are hanging around the long harvest table in our open-concept '70s cottage by the lake, playing cards. "A kiss, on the hand, may be quite *con-ti-nen-tal*," sings my mother, dragging out the syllables in her best high-camp imitation of Marilyn Monroe before triumphantly slapping down her winning hand, all diamonds, on the table. "But diamonds are a girl's best friend."

We give up, exasperated. She always wins. "Square-cut, or pear-shaped, these rocks don't lose THEIR shape—" she crows from the kitchen, refilling her glass of wine before raising her long arms in the air like a showgirl for the big finale. "Diamonds are a girl's—best—friend!"

My mother loved to sing (sometimes, of course, entirely in the wrong words), and she loved to win, but no triumph was complete without a victory lap that was worthy of the closing number of a Broadway production. Another thing she well and truly loved, of course, was diamonds. The glitz of them, their singularity and sparkle, answered her need to "make a statement."

Ever since *National Velvet*, which came out when she and its violet-eyed star were just girls, I suspect she rather identified with Elizabeth Taylor, the dark Hollywood seductress who, of course, collected huge diamonds like they were hockey cards and even named her line of gem-inspired perfumes after them (the bestselling—and most prized—being White Diamonds). Just like Liz, no messing around with any rinky-dink, semi-precious, or coloured stones for my mother—no, like an old-school gangster's moll, it was all about the infinite reflection and razzle-dazzle of a brilliantly cut, high-clarity chunk of "ice."

Fully blinged-out before that was even a concept, my mother could certainly have dazzled like an NBA star: on her ears, alternating with her signature 18k gold hoops, a pair of blindingly white diamond studs (brilliant cut, 1.85 cts, VS2 and SI1 clarity); on her ring finger, a dangerously heavy trapezoid of gold and platinum, glittering with five rows of pavé-set rocks like a knuckle-ring custom-made for Liberace and which she would regularly thump us with for emphasis (and with momentum, it packed a wallop); on one pinkie, a more discreet, if substantial, brilliant-cut solitaire, twinkling against a boldly masculine setting of black onyx and gold in a deco style. And, on occasion, around her neck, ever since it was first released by Tiffany & Co. in 1974, a fine gold opera-length strand dotted with bezel-set diamonds designed by Elsa Peretti and rather wittily titled "Diamonds by the Yard."

Like Coco Chanel, Le Corbusier, or David Hicks—or anyone else my mother admired sufficiently to buy into their style project (and then forever after refer to such purchase as "my Chanel suit," "the Corbusier table," or "the David Hicks carpet")—Peretti herself was an icon. An Italian-born former model who had posed for Salvador Dali and Helmut Newton, partied with Andy Warhol and Liza Minnelli at Studio 54, and collaborated with Halston before designing icons of minimal, organically inspired contemporary design such as the silver bone cuff and the bean pendant for Tiffany, the legendary jewellery designer once summed up her fabulously reductive approach as "Style is to be simple." A style directive Peretti shared with fellow style gurus from Chanel to Vreeland, and which, like Mies van der Rohe's dictum, "Less is more," was typically interpreted by my mother, particularly in her later years, as "Go big or go home."

THE EARLIEST WRITINGS ON diamonds come from India. In the *Ratnapariska* of Buddhabhatta, circa 500 A.D., it is written in Sanskrit that "He who wears a diamond will see dangers recede from him whether he be threatened by serpents, fire, poison, sickness, thieves, flood, or evil spirits." Hence India's rulers' historical practice of claiming the largest diamonds for themselves as protective talismans to ensure victory and ward off defeat. The story of almost every world-famous diamond like the Hope was that it once served as the eye in a statue of a Hindu god. Hindus believed the dazzling talisman could significantly improve their current, earthly incarnation; had it served as a god's third eye, such a diamond could eventually lead them to nirvana.

Little wonder they are a girl's BFF. If diamonds first attract our attention with their sparkle, they become perhaps even more valuable to their owners as talismans—just like the song says—their enduring value a hedge against the dimming of one's own brilliance, a dazzling distraction to diffuse the lines that appear with age.

As icons, diamonds stand for exclusivity, being both precious and rare; for wealth—or good fortune, in the Confucian sense of being rich enough to be able to afford them; and for opulence, magnificence, and luxurious splendour. Doubly so, should those dazzlers happen to be designed by a star like Elsa Peretti and come in the similarly iconic robin's egg blue box of Tiffany & Co. In the case of Diamonds by the Yard, it was a style trifecta that my mother would have immediately wanted in on.

For that was how it was with my mother and the things she claimed as her own: never intrigued by the merely pretty, her life's project was a sort of distillation of her own point of view until it became the hard-liquor version—her name writ large for all eternity in indelible ink, her observations set until they crystallized into sparkling stone. For such an icon-in-waiting, the things that were already in some way iconic or essential were must-haves, step one in her own journey toward immortality. Which is not to suggest that my mother was merely a label snob, or a collector of fancy things that already came with a designer guarantee of good taste.

Like the celebrated collector and nonagenarian style icon Iris Apfel, my mother wasn't in the business of seeking approval from others and believed strongly in her own pure vision. Her true gift was an eye for the unique. And she saw the potential for fabulousness everywhere, from the junk vendors at a flea market to the rattan dealers of Chinatown. Because there was also the secondary possibility of my mother conveying importance to something simply through choosing it, her taste and vision like the explosive sparkle in Disney's *Cinderella* when ordinary things are touched with a magic wand. All it took to transform these diamonds-in-the-rough was her recognition of their previously unseen possibilities. Once added to her collection and tossed into the mix with her characteristic panache, any such finds now dazzled as if they really were diamonds. While the appreciation and acquisition of things like Diamonds by the Yard—which already came with their own built-in imprimatur of cachet—were step one in her journey toward icon status. Our education in the particular strains and qualities that conveyed such transformative provenance started early.

"NOW THIS I GOT in a little boutique we just happened to walk into on the Left Bank, because there is nothing as chic as a box-pleated navy skirt," explains my mother. We are in the walk-in cedar closet she has had installed in the basement of our Fuck-You Forest Hill House. The walls and floor of this fashion bunker are fully lined with cedar to protect my parents' clothes against the disfigurement of moths or any unforeseen natural disaster. The scent of cedar is so strong it's as if we have walked right inside a radically blown-up version of the hamster cage in my sister's bedroom. I am supposed to be taking mental notes.

"You can wear it anywhere, under a jacket or with a fitted little sweater, maybe something in a nice navy-and-white stripe for a bit of a nautical look."

The clothes we are perusing as if we were in a boutique or an art gallery are from my mother's personal collection. They are hanging in dry cleaning bags on rolling racks, as they are items that my mother has put away in storage. We are looking through the racks for "inspiration" for the photo shoots my mother styles for newspaper stories on the vintage clothing show she helps organize every year for the Hadassah-WIZO Bazaar charity sale. The stories are always about what great deals you can find at the bazaar but my mother mostly uses the clothes she has on file in the cedar closet, composing quirky *Annie Hall*–inspired outfits out of her vintage designer jackets and my dad's old vests and ties that will be modelled for the paper by our friends' teenage kids.

"I always loved this red cape. It's just amazing what you can do with just a piece of good wool," says my mother, wrapping said bit around herself in creative ways to demonstrate before stopping dead in front of a Creeds Dry Cleaning bag containing a cream silk mini-dress, the shirtfront placket of which is buttoned up with glittering rhinestones. "Now that's the dress I wore when I danced with Trudeau!" (Actually, her tone could be more accurately conveyed as "The Dress I Wore When I Danced With Trudeau" — as if it were the title of a short story or perhaps a one-woman, one-act play.)

Twirling it off the rack and clutching it to her chest with enthusiasm, the memory of her triumph appears as fresh as if it had occurred just the night before. "Honestly, I was a sensation. Everyone in the room stopped to watch us. And he was quite the dancer, the kind who makes you feel like a great dancer yourself" — this next bit delivered in a more confessional, lower register — "although he really was terribly short, and with these tiny little feet!"

Every single thing in my mother's closet, if not our entire house, always had a story. And for the most part, the story was one about my mother — where she had been when she found it; who happened to have noticed her there; or how she, alone, had the singular, transformative vision to know it was something truly amazing, perhaps even a "fashion investment."

Thanks to my mother, I know that "at a certain point in a woman's life," she must really own a Chanel suit. That Walter Steiger really makes the best boots; Hermès the best scarves and ties; and Jean Muir, Sonia Rykiel, and Donna Karan, the best jerseys. A "really smashing" Armani jacket is "an investment that will carry you almost anywhere," and an Yves Saint Laurent tuxedo is "infinitely more chic than any of those fluffy long gowns women wear to galas as if they were dressing up for their prom."

I have also been made aware that silver can—and indeed should—be worn with gold; oversized men's-style watches have more panache than silly little ladies' ones; a boxy hand-bag over your wrist is as dowdy-looking as the Queen; "a bold ethnic touch," like native turquoise jewellery, is always fabulous; mink coats are "too ordinary"; and wearing white hosiery makes you look like a nurse.

WE ARE IN THE change room on the designer floor at Henri Bendel in New York, which my mother pronounces as Ben-*delle*, in the "French fashion," (which I later learned was, like the way she always called Ralph Lauren, "Ralph Lo-*wren*," actually incorrect. But then my mother never cared for precision. She spoke her own intuitive language, with its own linguistic rules). Like a younger acolyte or handmaiden, I am perched on a sort of rose-satin tuffet in the corner, surrounded by our coats and bags, watching my mother try on clothes in the change room's three-way mirror. Watching her dress is something I like to do, even at home in my parents' en-suite. Sometimes I sit at the edge of the tub and watch her putting on her makeup and getting glammed to go out as if it were some kind of ceremonial ritual, and my mother, making her perfect face into the mirror and whisking bronzer into her décolletage with the flourish of an enormous brush, is happy to oblige.

With each exquisite garment from Chloé and Jean Muir and Sonia Rykiel rushed into the room by the clearly impressed saleswoman, whom my mother is ordering about as if she had access to the Swiss bank accounts of the Shah of Iran, my mother has the same routine. Like a cellist raising her bow to begin a solo, or a professional tennis player bouncing the ball in preparation to serve an ace, once she is zipped and buttoned in the suit or dress, she draws herself up to her full height of five foot nine, squares her shoulders, and approaches the centre panel of the mirror. Her head is slightly tilted, her eyebrows are raised, her chin is lowered, and her lips are gathered like a bouquet. Looking over one shoulder into the mirror's side panel, she places a hand on her hip, puts one foot forward, and raises that shoulder to her lowered chin for a side view. She is magnificent, formidable, her eyes focused and intent on her image. It is an extraordinary performance. In this setting, she sparkles, as if each garment was made with only her in mind. But she is not so easily impressed.

"I hate my arms," she says, ripping off a Chloé silk dress with a fluttering cap sleeve. "Too much going on," is her immediate verdict on a complicated Japanese ensemble whisked in by the intimidated saleswoman for her approval. "Now this, I can see," she says, turning in the light in a beaded, midnight-blue Armani jacket fitted just so over her beautiful, bony shoulders and a floaty chiffon dress in the same colour that shows her long, elegant legs.

Beauty like my mother's is an all-access pass. Nobody in the admiring crowd of sales staff gathered around us as we exit knows that we are really just tourists from Canada on a girls' trip for the weekend; that my mother is only a self-taught stylista with a convincing swagger. "Wrap it up," commands my mother, tossing down her Amex as if money were no object. "Now let's go to P. J. Clarke's and get ourselves a hamburger."

BACK IN THE YEARS I was in grade school, every fall, my mother would take me out for a back-to-school shopping spree at this children's wear boutique on Eglinton West where the old, Eastern European owner brought in fashionable clothes from Europe. It being the '70s, everything came in "outfits," with the tops and slacks designed to match, which my mother was a fan of. ("That way you always have a top that works and you always look pulled together.") We're talking brightly coloured macramé vests, flared burgundy or mustard corduroy pants, "denim"-print miniskirts and sweaters with fake dickie collars (such fashion fakery in that back-to-nature era a strange style convergence). My mother insisted that I try each outfit on in the back, which was piled with old cardboard boxes, and then parade it around the store in front of her and the ancient proprietor. Some ensembles were met enthusiastically, with immediate calls for a matching turtleneck, windbreaker, or pair of knee-high socks to complete the look. Others were abandoned outright. But we always left with the trunk of my mother's Mustang convertible piled high with fabulous new clothes, my mother flushed with creativity and the thrill of spending money.

Later that night, I would be required to run upstairs and try on every outfit again for my dad's approval in the dining room after dinner. My mother would provide the narration for each outfit ("Now isn't this little A-line dress terrific? I just love the apple print! Red is so right on blondes! It will be perfect for going out to dinner.") Each ensemble would be remarked upon by my dad, who would still be seated at the head of the table finishing a bowl of ice cream. The finale of my annual modelling performance would inevitably be received with my father's exaggerated applause and a standing ovation, which makes me laugh but also makes the whole thing (the ritual of getting the new clothes, my excitement over them) feel sort of silly.

IN THE YEARS AFTER my father's development business took off and we started living the high life, my mother would invite her sisters to come over for the afternoon. It was a chance for them to have a visit and also, whether as a gesture of generosity or a demonstration of my mother's largesse, for them to take away her old clothes. My mother's elder sister, Ann, wouldn't come because she lived far away in South Carolina and, besides, she too had married well and didn't need anything. But my mother's little sister, Mary, who was a schoolteacher and a single mom, together with my mother's sister-in-law Nancy, would drive in for the day from St. Catharines to spend the afternoon at our house, drinking white wine and going through my mother's closets.

I remember it as a fun gathering, because there was always lots of gossip (though I didn't know half the people they were telling tales about, most of them being old family friends from St. Catharines) and lots of laughter. And of course my mother would be at her best and most supreme, as the hostess serving up a ladies' lunch of quiche Lorraine and a green salad on the good china in the dining room, the table set with the good silver, pink rubrum lilies, and white linen. And then the party would move to my mother's bedroom, where my parents' California King would be piled high with clothes.

"Mary, that camel coat would look just smashing on you," my mother would direct her smaller, plainer little sister, who would dutifully try it on in the adjoining bathroom and then do a little turn in my parents' spacious bedroom, which had a sofa and sitting room at one end where we, the fashion judges, were seated. My mother would opine generally on the benefits of having a good camel coat in one's closet, as well as on the finer points of this particular model currently being worn by her sister. And then it would be my Aunt Nancy's turn. Even though she was dark and petite and my mother's sister-in-law, married to my Uncle Bill, I always thought she looked and seemed like my mother's real sister. "And Nancy, I thought of that navy dress for you."

The afternoon fashion show over, my aunts would leave with a white-wine headache and garbage bags filled with my mother's unwanted clothes. Even as a girl, I understood that these afternoons, as fun as they were, walked a fine line for my mother — one that lay somewhere in between being a wonderfully generous sister (neither of my parents could ever have been faulted for any lack of generosity) and a kind of self-aggrandizing gesture that allowed her to lord her fabulousness over her own family.

But then it did also always seem to be appreciated, if only thanks to my aunts' good manners.

ONE MIGHT THINK THAT a family as interested in looking good at all times as the family I grew up in would have stacks of supporting documentation to verify how gorgeous we all were. But this was not the case with my family, who never seemed all that interested in recording our Kodak moments for posterity, nor, truth be told, in the act of taking a photograph in general. Indeed, I can't recall having to stop and smile and say cheese all that often, except perhaps if it was a holiday or we were on vacation somewhere. And usually that was because somebody else might have been around who was a shutterbug.

Still, I suspect that the chief reason Jen, Josh, and I don't have all that many photos of our childhoods is because my mother never bothered to properly organize or store any of them. In fact, the only thing she did with the few vinyl booklets of pictures we got back from the developer's (those being the days before digital point-and-shoot, when you actually had to bring physical canisters of film to a place like Black's before you could even see what was on your camera) was to sift through them and immediately throw out any unflattering ones of herself before burying the loose remainder, in no particular order, in an unspooling rattan trunk to fade and gather mould in the basement. Of course the few really stellar shots my mother allowed us to keep were on display in a collection of silver and Lucite frames artfully arranged on the baby grand piano in the living room. The one that nobody in our family ever learned how to play.

It wasn't until years later, once I became a mother myself, that I discovered that this editorial approach had been her modus operandi all along. A realization I came to when she advised me to stop allowing myself to be photographed in the early morning hours with my brand new baby before I had the chance to shower, dress, fix my hair, and put on at least some lipstick.

"You don't want your kids to see every picture of you later and think you looked like a mess all those years," advised my mother, shaking a long finger of disapproval.

Advice which I quickly dismissed at the time as absurdly self-involved, if not vain and petty. And now, of course, I sometimes regret not having listened to her. When I look over the albums I faithfully made of our children's early years (no ridiculously random tangle of family photos shoved away into a cabinet in my house!), I am largely pictured either in a ratty T-shirt or bathrobe, my unwashed hair a mess. Smiling and happy in almost every captured moment, for sure — but thanks to having ignored both my mother's example and her advice, my own chances of being remembered by my children as a fashion icon after I'm gone are slim at best.

AROUND THE EIGHTH GRADE, when I hit puberty full-on, I shocked my mother by turning out to be someone else. I was already blonde and blue-eyed, unlike my dark and hazel-eyed mother. But instead of growing from the small and skinny girl in the middle seat of the front row of every class photograph into my mother's tall, slim, and elegant kind of womanhood, I stopped at five foot four and a half and turned curvy and voluptuous, with big round breasts that were immediately embarrassing.

No matter how I dressed — and I tried hard not to dress in any way that emphasized my boobs or my waist so I wouldn't look like Dolly Parton — I got catcalls at my primarily boys' school and whistles on the street. The whole event felt like I had been body-snatched and given someone else's physical form. Someone sort of tacky and low-class, like a milkmaid on a chocolate box or a slatternly barmaid in a bad British comedy.

That this assessment was one my mother shared was made pointedly clear by her horrified reaction when she saw me spilling out of my tailored blouse. Or her alarm every time I reached for another piece of cheese or came home from school and made myself a snack of cinnamon toast. One weekend my high school friends came up to the cottage, and even though Iva and Monica were perfectly thin, we were all instructively served salad plates with undressed tuna, celery, and carrot sticks, monastically accompanied by dry tranches of melba toast, like it was lunchtime at the fat farm. But it was clear to me that whatever I ate, or didn't, I was never, ever going to look the way my mother did.

Which didn't stop her from taking the opportunity, on

occasion, to portray me, unkindly, as a sort of clomping goof. Once when I was in my awkward early teens, my mother and I were at our neighbourhood Shoppers Drug Mart, and we bumped into an older girl I knew from school. After a brief exchange in which I thought I had managed fairly well not to seem too uncool, the minute the girl turned away my mother started into her unflattering imitation

"Um, hey," my mother said, her head hanging down between her bent-over shoulders, feet shuffling underneath like a dog slinking away after it's just been punished.

"So, yeah—um, bye." This last bit delivered in the same beta pose and the voice of a developmentally slow learner.

"Stop it," I whisper. "She can hear you!"

"Looks good, don't you think, Karen? Really cool," says my mother, now shuffling through the aisles, still comically slumped over with the terrible loser voice getting louder so that other people are now staring.

"Stop it, Mom!" I'm now on the point of tears and begging. But she is just starting to enjoy herself.

"Yeah, I'm Karen and I'm so cool that I have to walk around like this all the time," says my mother, now giggling at her imitation as she continues following me around the store. Until she stops in her tracks and looks right at me. "If you stood up straight at least you might look a little bit more appealing."

Perhaps I wasn't quite ready to throw my shoulders back because my shoulders weren't square, like her perfect clothes hangers; they were round and growing rounder with the weight of new breasts. Sure, I was pretty enough that boys my age liked me, but pulling off my mother's level of glamour was going to pose a challenge. My clothes didn't flow just so over my frame, but gathered and gaped and rumpled. My feet weren't long and sculpturally bony, but average-sized and merely pretty; my fingers weren't long and dramatically knuckled, just capable and ordinary. Whenever she would coax me to slip them on just for fun, my mother's grandly oversized diamonds and jewels came off as more absurd than elegant—a state of affairs which may have irked my mother even more than it ever did me. Not to say that I ever fully recovered from failing the fabulousness test at the starting line with my self-image entirely intact.

In any case, as my mother freely offered, my looks were more of an "acquired taste" than those of a conventionally attractive beauty ("such as herself" wasn't added, although it hung there in the air).

"You know you aren't everyone's cup of tea, sweetheart. But you do have looks that will be appreciated by the right kind of person," offered my mother, unbidden. "Your father and I have always laughed and laughed about the funny little way you always pump along with your arms, just the way you did when you were a little girl."

I imagine I was supposed to be comforted by this notion that my appeal was something rare and precious or limited to the discerning observer. But then, I never had the other hard-as-diamond qualities my mother had in spades: the strange depth and funhouse mirror-quality of her change-able passions. Her wild love, dazzling in its complexity, that could also cut you where you lived at any time. Perhaps I was always too straight-ahead, too blonde and guileless a sparring partner to be entirely up to her scratch? But then, there was a part of her that preferred even her child to be her straight man.

IT'S MY HIGH SCHOOL semi-formal. This isn't really all that big a deal, not at my former all-boy's high school full of undiagnosed Rain Men who are already bent over on one side from carrying a briefcase full of books in their teens. Plus, it's the '70s, so we are supposed to be all-natural, Irish Spring girls with folk-singer hair and untinted Blistex on our lips who aren't into what we call "appearances." (Today's selfie-mad Kardashian wannabes with their contoured makeup and Hervé Léger Band-Aid dresses would simply have been laughed out of school). Nonetheless, I have agreed to go with Peter, a guy in my class with unfortunate skin whom I've barely spoken three words to in my life, and as the special night in the school gym draws closer, I realize that I really don't have anything to wear. All my girlfriends have gone out and bought special dresses for the occasion, so a cute top and flared jeans are out. But my mom and dad are away, out of town on a trip somewhere like Rome or Santa Fe, so an emergency fashion purchase is not an option.

Although I haven't really asked my mother if I can borrow something of hers to wear, I rifle through her fabulous closet. Most of it is simply absurd on a fifteen-year-old. Too wild, too grand, too big, too fancy, too much of a "statement." Finally I settle on one rather low-key Sonia Rykiel wrap dress in a plain black jersey with a bit of a ruffled cap sleeve that I have never even seen on my mother. Since it's a bit large on me and, even when fully wrapped and tied, a bit too revealing of my newly busty state—plus perhaps a bit summery for early March—I decide I will simply resolve the problem by wearing a white wool ribbed turtleneck underneath. I'll finish the outfit with a pair of dark knee socks with my black patent lace-up Kork-Ease platforms, pull the front bits of my long hair back into a Guinevere-style ponytail, slap on a dab of pink blush and a spritz of L'Air du Temps, and I'll be good to go.

The night itself comes and goes without much drama or excitement. There is the usual gossip in the girl's bathroom about who really likes whom and who had been out smoking dope in the sheds behind the school. Peter, happily, is not expecting much from my accompaniment other than a dance partner, which, believe me, was challenging enough in an era where you had to switch from the slow dance parts and then break apart for the really fast ones in the same endless recording of Led Zeppelin's "Stairway to Heaven" or Don McLean's "American Pie"—either of which were certain to be the last dance of the night. Back at home afterwards, I return my mother's dress, safe and sound, to her closet, careful to place it in exactly the same spot where I first found it. There is no way she will ever find out that I wore it without asking.

Weeks later, long after my parents' return, I have forgotten all about it until my mother confronts me, more smirking than angry. "Did you go into my closet while we were away and borrow that Sonia Rykiel dress?" To this day, I have absolutely no idea how she figured it out. Did our au pair rat on me? (It was the British one, Nicola, I think, at the time). Who knows? As we all knew perfectly well, my mother was a witch.

What is worse is that she seems to know all about my outfit. And she doesn't think much of it. "And you actually wore it with a white turtleneck underneath?"

She laughs incredulously and uproariously, as if this is the most hilarious misstep that has ever occurred in fashion history. Long before the dawn of reality TV or shaming on the Internet, my mother decided that humiliation, apparently, was to be my punishment.

For years, I had to endure the telling of the story as an example of how hopeless I was. At a ladies' lunch or even a cocktail party, whenever someone might compliment me on my outfit, she never tired of sharing how I hadn't always had the greatest fashion sense.

"Once, when we were out of town, Karen 'borrowed' this black jersey Sonia Rykiel dress from my closet to wear to her school dance," she would begin, with a broad smirk. And the last line was always, "And she wore it—can you believe— with a white wool turtleneck underneath!" before bursting into loud peals of laughter, ash dripping from the cigarette in one exclaiming hand and a glass of red in the other.

Thinking back on this now as a mother, I wonder why it was that I was left to myself to find something to wear to my semi-formal. True, it was the '70s, and we chickens were comparatively free-range. But it never occurred to me at the time that it was her complete and utter lack of interest in my little life that was really the story. And that maybe it was more revealing of her failure to measure up than mine.

So lessons were learned, though not perhaps those my

mother had intended. Once I became a mother of a daughter, not only did I try to stay interested and involved in her challenges (potentially to a fault, like the rest of my "over-parenting" generation), there was no question that I would never, ever have made fun of my child's attempts to look grown-up and pretty, pathetic and fumbling toward adulthood as they might have been. Because there is nothing more wounding when you are in that most vulnerable of states than to look into the dazzling eyes of your mother and see, reflected back at you, your goofiness, and her distaste.

GLAMOUR, UNFORTUNATELY, doesn't age particularly well. Its appeal comes with a best-before date. Unlike its emissary and representation on earth, the diamond, which endures every hardship and knock life throws at it without losing its sparkle, the ego essential to pull glamour off successfully becomes dried-up and bitter as, over time, the perceived slights and injuries twist the soul.

I saw it happen to my mother, who was more able to be generous with me when I was an unthreatening child, rapt with attention at her dazzling performance, than when I became a potentially critical adult. True, my mother loved the years when I was living the student life, and would drop by our parties to hang out with my friends, who, new to her charms, would indulge and even enjoy her grandeur; fresh blood, as far as she was concerned, for her ongoing impersonation of an aging Holly Golightly, or more appropriately perhaps, Rosalind Russell in *Auntie Mame*. I cannot count the number of times she held court at my parties while

I was busy rinsing glasses at the kitchen sink. And then my friends would invariably run over to tell me how lucky I was to have such a cool mother.

After our first child, Sophie, was born, I remember being completely stunned by my mother's uncanny gift for dropping by to "help with the baby" at the very moment in the afternoon when I had just successfully put her down for a nap. Instead of being able to take advantage of the one tiny slice of respite I had in a near-twenty-four-hour shift of child care to perhaps lie down for a small nap myself or, say, read the front page of the newspaper or take a shower, there I would be, nearly falling down from lack of sleep and covered head-to-toe in baby spit, serving my mother lunch every other afternoon (at a set table with wine and the proper linens, naturally), while having to somehow generate sufficient enthusiasm through my mommy fog for her stories. And then the moment we would hear a cry from Sophie's crib, she would be off, looking down at her gold Rolex—"I can't believe how late it is already! I must get going!"—leaving me with a crying baby, a pile of unwashed dishes in the sink, and another long night ahead.

For a couple of years after Sophie was born, there was a misbegotten period when my mother invited me (graciously, it's true) to work with her in her decorating business so that I wouldn't have to go back to working full time (the law, with its rules and fine print, was never for me. Truthfully, I had always wanted to be a writer, despite my parents' insistence on a professional degree. Before going on maternity leave, I had been working all hours in publicity and promotion for a film company called Cineplex Odeon—a fun job involving late nights and a lot of travel that wasn't going to work well for a young mother). We had a few laughs, many long lunches, and of course I did manage to absorb a fair bit of design knowledge just by being her sidekick/straight man.

Unfortunately, our collaboration came at the moment when her star began to wane, and mine began to rise.

Many mornings she just wouldn't show up because she "had a bad night and hadn't slept well," which usually meant she had been up till all hours fighting with my dad and drinking, and needed to spend the next twenty-four hours in her darkened bedroom. This despite the fact that she had a day of client meetings on the calendar that I would have to either fumble through on my own, pretending my mother had just that moment been called away on some sort of decorative emergency, or try to re-schedule. Indeed, things for her really weren't going well: upon reflection, it was probably at the height of her menopausal madness that she had blustered her way into being appointed the head of the Canadian Opera Company's gala committee, only to be forced to resign in tears because "all the other women on the committee" were conspiring against her. Indeed, the teary calls at that time would have tested the resolve of Mother Teresa. And as much as I adored her, I found myself with less and less enthusiasm for surrendering myself to her ego.

Truthfully, her powers, while still formidable, seemed to be dimming. First it was menopause that kicked her for a loop; under its hormonal shift, my mother seemed to suffer particularly horrible bouts of sleeplessness and snapping irritation. And then, thanks to a lifetime of sucking on Craven "A"s, her joints had begun to crumble just as the hospital wait-lists for knee and hip reconstruction reached all-time record levels, leaving her in near-constant agony. Of course, it's not every woman in midlife who insists on grandstanding throughout dinner, interrupting every story told at the table with a knowing and bitter aside, and then spending the resulting late nights awake with a bottle of Famous Grouse at her side writing out her furious and insanely detailed frustrations and accusations in longhand on a pad of foolscap to passive-aggressively share with everyone by leaving it around for all to see.

The closest she ever got to just being truthful about how awful she felt without the accompanying theatrics was one weekend when the kids were little and we were all up at the cottage together. She was dragging herself around the kitchen, emptying the dishwasher and putting stuff away in the fridge, and I could hear her actually groaning with the effort.

"Why don't you sit down, Mom, and let me do that?" I said, turning into the kitchen where she was leaning on the counter, slamming the white cupboard doors closed with her bare foot.

"What? I'm okay," she panted, now bending down with some effort to pull out some large cans of tomatoes from a cupboard underneath.

"You know, in yoga they say you're supposed to remember to breathe while you are doing things," I offered unhelpfully, having recently taken up a weekly hatha class. "It seems to me like you're holding your breath."

My slate-faced mother, still in her robe, her hair raised up in the back after a nap, turned and looked square at me:

"Don't do what I did and wear yourself out," she said, before turning back to the task at hand.

Perhaps it was the constant effort of making everything beautiful — which she herself had insisted upon — that was so very draining? Even at our outdoor picnic table on the deck at the cottage, the table was always set for meals. Dinner — no matter whether it was just us and we were having my mother's famous ribs or it was Julia Child's *paupiettes de veau* for a special occasion — was always brought to the table on beautiful antique platters and served family-style with interesting horn-handled or Danish Modern serving spoons, and the table was always set with pretty napkins and little decorative ethnic-patterned bowls for condiments.

When she was little, my sister would be grumpy about being asked to set the table, which would annoy my mother.

"When you do something, please do it graciously!" she would scold.

For my mother, putting on your best and bravest face in public wasn't only a matter of style but basic etiquette. About others we might pass on the street with their faces unconsciously set in sadness and misery, she would regularly advise, not particularly *sotto voce*, "Everyone would look a lot more attractive if they just went about with pleasant expressions."

Indeed it was my mother who was the self-appointed CEO of Making Everything Beautiful around us, as if the very razzle-dazzle of it all would somehow shield us from all the ugliness in the world. Things could still get ugly very quickly, however, especially when my mother would get everything to the table and my father would take his sweet time joining us, an unfortunately consistent habit of his which, understandably in my mother's mind, demonstrated his complete and utter disregard for anyone else and thus drove her completely insane.

"Perce!" she would yell from the table. "Dinner is going to be cold, after all this!"

No answer.

"Where on earth is your father?"

And one of us would be sent to find him only to have to report back that he had just stepped into the shower.

"I have a beautiful dinner here ready and waiting on the table and your father decides that this is the perfect moment to take a shower! Jesus Fucking Christ!"

Tossing aside her (ironed, linen) napkin and pulling away her Breuer chair from the harvest table, she would then leave us three awkwardly sitting at the table, taking her wine and her book to her room and slamming the door behind her. It would then be our job to pretend that we weren't the slightest upset by the scene, just as our father would, once he finally joined us. As if Mum not being there with us at the other head of the table was just normal, or, more precisely, as if her absence should be ignored because she was just nuts.

IT IS HARD, it would seem, to be an icon. To really be able to pull it off, nothing bad can ever happen to you, otherwise you will reveal your less-than-diamond status. Regardless of my mother's perverse insistence that nothing was ever less than perfect with her — or any of us, so long as we simply refused to acknowledge it — she wasn't really okay, and that presented a problem. Surely along with her diamond sparkle came the impossibility of its diminishment?

This problematic worldview, combined with her resulting penchant for self-pity and self-medication, proved a dangerous and volatile cocktail that left her subject to mood swings that varied from sobbing and needy to harsh and vengeful.

It might not have helped that she could no longer turn everyone's heads just by walking into a room while my father still looked like a blonde Zeus. Or that given that neither of them ever actually planned on becoming old enough to retire, let alone saving anything to retire on, my parents started worrying quite seriously about money. And then there was the emerging annoyance of having to share the spotlight of fabulousness when she still wanted to bask in its warming glow for just a little while longer.

Just as my mother's own business had begun slowing down alongside her ability to manage it, I had begun finding my own voice as a writer. First, writing about design and style in the aforementioned shopping column called "Super Shopper" in *Toronto Life* that landed me on the magazine's cover, twice, along with some writing awards. This column led to another in *House & Home* magazine and then a weekly column in the *Globe and Mail*—and by my third decade (which my mother always referred to, rolling her "r's" as a woman's "prrrime"—she adored everything, naturally, to do with the imperious Maggie Smith in *The Prime of Miss Jean Brodie*), I was happily married with two beautiful kids, I had written a popular book on Toronto, was busy appearing on television and radio to talk about style and trends, and was in the midst of creating a TV series for the Life Network called *The Goods*. When I began getting such recognition for my "Noticed" column in the *Globe and Mail* that I started getting noticed while walking down the street, my mom's reaction to my success could best be described as mixed.

While always a faithful reader who would sweetly call with admiring comments the morning my column came out, I suspect she also rather enjoyed sharing with others (particularly those friends whose own adult children might not have been doing so well, say, going through a divorce or just having lost a job) the tales of my latest triumphs, because ultimately they would reflect on her and what a great job she did as a mother.

And then, in the same breath she'd have used to gush about how brilliant I was, she, in true Susan Young fashion, would deliver a stinging slap out of nowhere just to remind me which one of us was the real diva.

"I'm sorry but I think that's just a dreadful print," my mother once offered, upon my excited reveal of a curvy old armchair that I had just had re-upholstered in a vintage, green-and-white watermelon-patterned fabric by a Swedish mid-century architect that I had gone to some lengths and expense to score.

"I guess I just don't 'get it.' But then, your taste has always been much more 'trendy,' I suppose, than mine."

Or, "That's a lovely picture of you, dear, in this month's *House & Home*. But maybe you should reconsider that haircut. And I'm not sure Lily is doing the same thing lately with your highlights? Maybe you should ask whether she is doing something different, because I think it's looking a little more yellow than usual."

Or, even better: "Daddy and I are so pleased for you, sweetheart. And just so amazed by everything you have been able to accomplish. What a star you are. You are really so much better at self-promotion than I ever was!"

Really, the gall of it would just leave one gob-smacked. But what was truly dazzling was that she could get away with saying whatever she happened to feel at any given moment not only to us, but pretty much anyone she came into contact with: waiters, doormen, receptionists. And they would all just be so amazed, or amused, by her nerve that she was still widely admired.

"You're Susan's daughter, aren't you?" I would hear— and still hear quite often, whenever I might bump into any of her old acquaintances in the design trade, or find myself at an arts event or charity fundraiser mingling with society ladies of a certain vintage. What I used to hear was "Susan is so talented" (or "so brilliant," or "such fun"). What I hear now is, "She was a great lady, you know, your mom."

What is always left unsaid, although I cannot help but feel it hanging in the air, is that whatever I may accomplish in my life, nobody will ever describe me in that way. It is somewhat ironic, perhaps, that it was precisely because she truly didn't give a flying fuck about what anyone else thought that my mother was always way cooler than I will ever be. But such blitheness as she had as an operating principle turns out to be something that cannot properly be passed down a generation; being the daughter of such a sparkling personality means that, from childhood, your own spark is tamped by the anxieties and worry your mother simply refuses to take on.

Like a great big solitaire set against other, lesser stones, my mother never seemed all that eager to cede her central role as fascinator-in-chief, or to make room for others to shine. While I would like to be able to report that over time things improved as she mellowed with age, passing the torch was never to be her forte. As we, her children, grew into our own, less malleable, adult selves, it became more difficult for all concerned that, to her mind, everything about us — from the way that we looked to our achievements — was actually meant to reflect upon her. Whether she just couldn't see herself fading into being a bit player in the background, or had effectively worked against that outcome by ensuring we would never fully realize our own brilliance is something I am still trying to understand.

Seven

BARBRA STREISAND'S "GUILTY"

MY MOTHER, WHO, in life, had never failed to announce her presence, had been dead a full year with no marker on her grave. After the nightmare of having to pack up my parents' apartment while trying to find some kind of place—any kind of place—that might take our dad, who was now clearly past coping, my sister and I were barely speaking, our brother had gone back to his busy life in New York City, and basically we had all retreated into our separate lairs to lick our wounds. It seemed weird to me that losing our mother had driven us apart rather than bring us together, but my friend Martha nailed it when she observed that a death in the family doesn't necessarily mean that everyone suddenly behaves the way they do on a Hallmark made-for-TV special.

Since it was starting to feel absurd, if not somehow disrespectful that there was just a muddy patch in the ground where our mother was buried, the first thing that occurred to us was to do something super simple — a plain grey tombstone with just our mother's name etched into it along with the dates she had been born and then died. Mom had always preferred things to be restrained and elegant, right? Grey stone, check. Simple, dignified message, check and check.

But then, when I saw the cheap-looking greys of the stone from the mortuary — which seemed more like composites from China than the beautiful old Vermont stone she would have approved of — and the laser stonecutter's ugly new digital fonts, I just knew she would have hated all of it for being so subpar. It seemed all wrong, like we were just trying to get the whole memorial thing over with, which felt like a bad attitude when dealing with eternity.

In the months after my mother died, I had taken up the habit of going for a walk in the cemetery where she was buried. I didn't sit at her grave and try to talk to her or anything. I would just check in, leave a pretty stone for her on the spot like a good Jewish girl, and enjoy the quiet.

One bright and clear day in early spring when I was on one of these walks through the grounds, I found myself admiring the fanciful stonework of the graceful old monuments and their expressions of loss — the weeping sylphs in their stone draperies, the pleading, childlike angels, the Grecian urns and vaults. The sun was bright against the bare-limbed trees and white snow, and the shadows of the monuments were long, which made them all the more lovely and melancholy.

It occurred to me that these little memorials were all just follies, really, as foolishly romantic as anything people ever built to last forever, or as the very thought that the life of one soul in the immense tide of human history ever mattered. And no matter how much that person was missed, even the ones remembering them would soon, too, be forgotten. Actually, if you took away their sad purpose, these futile markers could easily be taken for whimsical garden ornaments, which they were, really, except in places chosen to remember those we have lost. And then the idea came to me: Mum had always been all about surrounding herself with beauty. Why should her final resting place be any different? If she had wanted to leave anything behind, it wouldn't have been some grim historical plaque, but something delightful, in and of itself. An object whose sole purpose was to be visually pleasing.

Veering off the cleared paths, my boots filling with melting snow, I tromped the cemetery grounds until I happened upon an art deco urn on a crypt with nice, formal lines. The urn was something that, had my mother come across at some antique dealer's, I could just imagine she would have had to snap up right then and there, toss in the trunk of her car and victoriously install on the front steps of one of our homes to Make a Design Statement.

I knew having it copied for her grave wouldn't make for the most typical tombstone. It would actually be more like a garden planter. But the fact that it would remain empty but for the occasional fallen leaf seemed somehow right. On my way back to the car in the lowering sun, I was surprised by the sudden blaze of a bright red cardinal, a bird my mother had always loved, alighting on the bare branch of a tree like a flower against the white snow.

Whether or not I could believe this was some kind of sign, its trill of song above my head sounded to me like approval.

IT'S AROUND MIDNIGHT AND I'm just coming home to our Fuck-You Forest Hill House after being out with a bunch of my friends. My friends are all boys, because there are more of them than there are girls at my secondary school. They are also all a couple of years older than me, so they have introduced me to evenings such as the one I have just had, smoking a joint behind the repertory theatre on Bloor Street, which was playing something Italian and arty (all the better to be stoned in order to take it in on a deeper, more visceral level, was our set's operating logic), followed by a greasy moussaka at our friend Bob's enviously *bohème* Annex student apartment, washed down with several glasses of cheap white vermouth on the rocks (an aperitif I have ceased to enjoy thanks to my early over-enthusiasm for it).

Opening the side door, I find the house pitch black inside, but there is no need to try to be quiet. My mother is sitting in the dark living room, smoking and drinking. And Barbra Streisand and Barry Gibb are loudly reaching a poignant crescendo as their passionate voices meld together with my mother's own: *"And we got nothin', and we got nothin'—to be guil-ty of / Our love, could climb any mountain, near or far, we are—and we'll ne-ver let it e-e-end..."*

It is 1980, and so Barry Gibb and Barbra Streisand, whose high-volume hairdos and matching white silk shirts are locked in a cheesy embrace on the cover of Barbra's new album *Guilty*, are currently on constant rotation on my mother's playlist—a playlist which, per tradition, is limited to just one wildly overwrought and extremely emotive recording, played over and over again for maximum overkill. Preferably in a dark room late at night so my mother can get weepy and carried away with the grand sentiment of it all. As far as my mother was concerned, the more emotionally loaded the song, the better to wallow in its excess of feeling—glass of red, Craven "A"s, and a lump of self-pity at the ready.

My mother's musical favourites were the divas who sang as if their very lives depended on it, swollen, purple hearts pinned bleeding on their sleeves: Barbra, Natalie Cole, Roberta Flack (her version of "Killing Me Softly" saw major play), Anita Baker's ardently overblown vocal performance on *Rapture*, and a super-sad album of world-weary Leonard Cohen covers sung by Jennifer Warnes. Each, in turn, enjoyed their big moment. As a propaganda artist of her own emotional terrorist regime, my mother was brilliant: it was always clear that regardless of whichever recording artist was enjoying significant rotation at the time, the tragic words they were singing were to be understood as my mother's own. A highly effective audio form of the classic guilt trip one would have to try to tune out not to hear.

BARBRA STREISAND WAS BORN in 1942, six years after my mother, in Williamsburg, Brooklyn. A headstrong, grounded Taurus, Barbra is not, like my mother, a witchy, sensitive Pisces. And unlike my mother, Barbra was not a born beauty; according to Barbra herself, her own mother discouraged Barbra's grand ambitions because she thought her daughter was too unattractive to be successful as a performer. Big-nosed and buxom, with a broad Brooklyn accent, Barbra was born a Jewess. My elegant-limbed mother was only a convert, having dutifully studied the basics of Jewish life under a rabbi before taking a ritual bath of conversion known as a *mikvah* in order to be considered an acceptable bride for my father—a guilt dip, I suppose, that empowered her forever after to administer the full Jewish mother's guilt trip.

Also unlike Barbra, who had one overindulged and perfect son during her eight-year marriage to Elliott Gould, my mother had three overindulged and perfect children in a marriage that lasted her lifetime. Like Barbra, my mother was a big fan of the bold and sensual femininity of New York designer Donna Karan. Unlike Barbra, who wore her hair curly in the '70s, my mother never once succumbed to a perm.

Although Barbra famously suffers from a crippling stage fright, she has little cause for insecurity, given that, well into her seventies, she is arguably still the top-selling female artist of all time, along with one of the performing arts world's few EGOTs (winners of an Emmy, Grammy, Oscar, and Tony). My mother, although recognized in local design circles, never got the glory she felt she deserved.

Barbra, who started her career singing in small clubs, has said that to overcome her fear of performing, she imitated the broad style of the drag queens she used to work with, which is interesting because she is now a staple of the drag review—if not a living gay icon. What Barbra and my mother most shared, however, and what gave them both an iconic quality, is that they were so fiercely themselves. My mother, who displayed a penchant for Barbra's high-camp glamour, might never have truly got her chance to vogue in the spotlight, but she did have Barbra to sing the words.

IF DANCE STYLES ARE somehow reflective of that dancer's personality, my parents each had remarkable, and remarkably distinctive, ones. Regardless of whatever song or musical genre happened to be playing, my dad would move to the music in exactly the same way: his fists curled up into his armpits like a blonde Rocky Balboa, his big shoulders and upper body moving in tight little circles as if he were out jogging on the dance floor. His long feet, underneath, doing the occasional little skip-hop, he would always play for a laugh to those assembled, as if to say, This isn't a very serious business, dancing, is it?

If my father was all about his upper body, my mother's dance routine emanated from somewhere in the hip. As if performing some updated, rock version of the Lindy Hop that she must have learned in high school, she would first place one toe out to the side and then, pivoting from the hip to the ball of that foot, twist that leg in time with the music, loudly humming her version of the melody, her eyes typically closed in emotive appreciation of the moment.

As always, they made for a memorable pair.

IT'S A SATURDAY AFTERNOON in the winter of 1971. I am ten years old. Per usual, I am stretched out on my absolute favourite perch, a long, kilim-covered pillow in front of the living-room fireplace in our Millbank Avenue house; I am reading *The Lion, The Witch and The Wardrobe* for the third time and listening, over and over, to my absolute favourite album, Carole King's *Tapestry*.

As Carole starts into the opening chords of "Natural Woman," my parents, who have been upstairs "taking a nap" most of the afternoon, sail into view in the front hall. Mum is in one of my dad's blue-and-white striped shirts with no pants and Dad is in a towel with no shirt and their hair is messy.

"You make me *fee-eel*," my Mum sings loudly along with Carole, smiling wide, as my Dad spins her around our front hall-turned-dance floor. "You make me *fee-eel* like a na-tu-ral *wo*-man."

My Dad dips her dramatically, which makes my Mum laugh. I applaud the two of them from my pillow perch, and they take a grand bow as if they have just performed in front of a large audience on *The Ed Sullivan Show* before they head into the kitchen.

Cut to 1979, a summer morning. I am home from my first year away at college. My sister and brother and I are lounging around the circular glass table on the deck outside the kitchen. I am reading the paper and drinking black coffee from a blue-rimmed Dansk mug. My sister is sipping on hot water and lemon instead, an annoying health fad that has recently taken off amongst my family, who insist, to the confusion of all waitstaff, on it being brought to them in restaurants, which drives me crazy. My brother has his feet with their long toes curled on the back of my chair. Having poured milk into his bowl, he is patting down the cereal segments with his fingers before eating it, which also drives me crazy.

My Dad, shirtless in a pair of Adidas running shorts, is already greased and on a lounge chair on the grass behind us in the sun, his square jaw jutting into his tri-fold reflector, a stack of magazines and a bottle of Perrier at his elbow. The flare from the sunlight coming off the reflector and hitting his gold Rolex is blinding.

"Does anyone feel like eggs?" yells my mother from the kitchen, where the radio is playing behind the open screen doors. Fully absorbed in soaking up as many UV rays as possible, my father doesn't answer.

"I would have some eggs," I say to no one in particular.

"Not for me," says my sister.

"Fried," says my brother, slurping up the milk in his bowl with a spoon.

Behind the screen doors, the opening chords of Bob Marley's "Could You Be Loved" are suddenly cranked up on the radio and my Mum, hair still wet from the shower, freshly dressed in a crisp white linen shirt and pleated shorts, boogies out onto the deck in time to the music, loudly singing her personal take on the lyrics.

"Good to be lo-o-ve! Oh, yeah! Let me lo-ove!"

This, too, drives me crazy, but still I get up and get down with the rest of them, all of us now doing our best imitation of reggae dancing around the outdoor table before breakfast.

Now it's the winter of 1989, the Berlin Wall has fallen and I've just had a baby. We have named her Sophie. Sophie is six weeks old and perfect, and I'm fat, pale, and weepy with exhaustion because I can't seem to sleep whenever she does, constantly imagining that I hear her crying or that she is just about to wake up. And Thomas, who has just been hired back at his law firm, is working all the time. It's December, so my mother convinces me to fly down south early on my own with the baby to stay with my parents at a house they have rented for all of us in Jamaica for Christmas. As soon as we arrive in the warmth and humidity, baby Sophie, who has been a bit colicky, seems to unfurl and relax. I wish the same could be said for her mother. Without Thomas there for reassurance, I feel nervous about bathing her and whether she is getting enough milk, and my little sleep problem is now epic. The house we are staying in is on the water but also somewhat close to a noisy road, and all night long I am wide-awake listening for my six-week-old baby's breathing.

One afternoon when I am just about to drop, my mother, who is already tan and in her Caribbean groove, persuades me to take an afternoon nap. She and my Dad will look after Sophie, who is asleep in her fold-up stroller in the open-air living room. And for an hour I will retreat to my yellow-and-white bedroom turned cool and dark with the blinds drawn and the a/c on full blast.

When I finally wake up, dazed, hours later, and emerge from my room, the blazing sun has slipped beneath the blue on the horizon, and the air is cooling, perfumed with the night-blooming jasmine by the open doors facing out onto the sea. Van Morrison's "Have I Told You Lately" is playing on the CD player, and my parents are dancing around the living room with my Sophie, who is smiling.

Over the years there were so many opportunities to watch them dance, in all manner of ways: jokingly, to my dad singing his truly terrible version of "Man of La Mancha"; grandly, in the banquet halls of hotels for a wedding or bar mitzvah; and sweetly, in their matching white bathrobes at the cottage on the sand.

It wasn't that either of them were particularly gifted dancers; it was just that in their book, there was no time that wasn't the right time to cut a rug. Why the hell not enjoy yourself? Who gives a damn what anyone might think or whether anyone is looking? If there was one constant through our succession of different homes it was that there was always music playing—from the pop hits on the radio in the bathroom in the morning, to the car stereo set on CBC's *Saturday Afternoon at the Opera*, to the albums (and then 8-tracks and cassettes and CDs, their cracked cases piled in the side panels of car doors and stacked in wicker baskets on the shelves of French armoires) that played like soundtracks for different eras, and whose lyrics became as familiar as a nursery rhyme or prayer.

And there were the live concerts: outside, in summer, at the open-air stadium at the CNE where we would go and see James Taylor and Michael Jackson, my father dependably interrupting the performance of my all-time favourite songs trying to flag down the woman at the end of our row selling bags of popcorn and peanuts.

The summer when we were all together in Italy, we took in a magical, open-air performance of *Aida*, out under the Mediterranean stars in an ancient amphitheatre in Verona where they paraded real live elephants in exotic dress onstage for the famous triumphal march. And one memorable night when I must have been around nine or ten, when my mother took us three little kids to see Gladys Knight & the Pips at what was then called the O'Keefe Centre, and I remember being amazed (Toronto being so very white-bread back then) by the beautifully dressed black people filling the theatre and everybody up on their feet dancing in the aisles.

New Year's Eve, an annual occasion which my parents were against celebrating in the typical fashion for its forced, cruise-ship hilarity, was always an all-ages family dance party at our house. This was typically held either down south on the beach or in the open-concept living room of our cottage up in Collingwood—usually after a horse-drawn sleigh ride through the snowy farmers' fields and gingerbread villages atop the Niagara Escarpment, which my dad would organize with a local farmer whenever we spent the holidays skiing. Stripped down afterwards to our thermal underwear, we would dance after dinner on the sand-coloured broadloom in front of the stone fireplace to pop hits of the era like Madonna's "Holiday," Boy George singing "Karma Chameleon," and UB40's "Red Red Wine," sometimes just the five of us, sometimes with our friends, and then our kids. Or, before we filled the bedrooms of the cottage with kids of our own, my parents' friends, who would come up north for the holidays and stay with us—friends like Harvey and Sylvia, and Gary and Jeanne, who, together with their kids, would feast with us around the big pine harvest table and then dance by the roaring fire. To replenish the firewood, we would open the sliding doors and form a human chain from the stack under the deck to the fireplace, scraping off the ice and snow from the logs before tossing another one on the fire, the night air bracingly cold and starry outside the sliding glass doors to the big white lake with its frozen waves, iced upon themselves layer by layer like a naturally occurring *mille-feuille* in the dark.

Always up for a party, my parents would still be hurt and peevish well into their seventh decade should we ever fail to include them in one of our own. Three months before my mother died, I remember my parents amongst the last to leave a holiday party at our house, too feeble by then to join in the dancing but having cleverly ensconced themselves near the ham I had put out by the kitchen so that my mother could harass and interrogate any takers.

Given that we videotaped many of these occasions back in the day on our brand new Sony Handycam, I might even have been able to relive the glory days and actually see them dance again, just like the soul song says—except that now the small square cassette tapes are so outdated we can no longer play them.

IT'S MARCH BREAK, 1976, and we are all, with the exception of our father, down in Longboat Key, Florida, in a rented three-bedroom condo at the Colony Club—a tennis resort with low-rise, taupe stucco modular casitas covered in bougainvillea overlooking the Gulf of Mexico, where, every March, we Snowbirds flock for a bit of sun to tide us over. My mum loves this beach for its wide, pink seashell-strewn stretch of sand and the diving pelicans with their comically huge beaks and skinny legs that she always says remind her of my father. My tennis-mad siblings love the all-day tennis clinics, which are directed by the famous coach behind the careers of Jimmy Connors and Chris Evert. And we all love the Colony restaurant, where waiters in white linens toss Caesar salads tableside, and the beach bar, where they play Jimmy Buffett and serve hamburgers in baskets with kettle chips, and you can get a table on the beach in the sun.

As experienced vacationers, particularly here on this beach at this resort where we come every year, our days quickly melt into a schedule of *au courant* enjoyments: morning walks, stretch classes, and spa treatments, followed by rounds of tennis, sunbathing, and games of beach backgammon, before showering and getting ready to go out for dinner, bronzed and moisturized, in our Lacoste shirts and white pants.

If it ever dares to rain or any of us becomes too sunburnt, we get into our giant American rental car to drive into nearby Sarasota to go shopping for more Lacostes and Ralph Lauren polos, our hair flying around our aviator sunglasses as we cross the bridge over to St. Armands Circle in the open convertible. With the car radio set to a local hits station, the soundtrack to our backdrop of palm trees and white condo towers against the sparkling blue ocean is what I always think of as Florida music: the ultra-smooth, easy-listening, mind-bleaching R&B of Luther Vandross and Christopher Cross.

This year, however, something is off as far as Mum is concerned. Her birthday is on March 19, which, like mine, three days later, always falls in the middle of spring break, so we are typically away on vacation to celebrate them together, with dinners at a fancy restaurant which start with champagne on our balcony and end with a cake and candles brought out by one of the waiters as a "surprise" at the end of the meal. Except that this year, my father — presumably travelling on business — isn't here with us, and so nothing, *nada, niente*, we three kids can come up with from the roster of Fun Things We Do in Florida is giving my mother the least bit of enjoyment. A state of affairs she makes abundantly clear by sighing over breakfast, refusing lunch, and taking to her air-conditioned room for the afternoon.

Worried that my mother is clearly not feeling sufficiently special on her special day, I, at fourteen, the eldest in the party of disappointing underage companions my mother is stuck with all alone in paradise, frantically flip through the glossy *Fine Dining in Sarasota* magazine on the rattan-and-glass coffee table in our condo, looking for somewhere fancy enough to make amends. Somehow we haven't yet been to the Upper Deck, which appears to have five stars and seems to be a local favourite, so I call and make us a reservation for dinner.

"Hello, I'm looking for a table for a party of four tonight; the name is Young," I say, as instructed from the time I was in the first grade, when my parents first started making me call restaurants — because knowing how to talk on the phone and book a table at a restaurant was "an important life skill," like knowing how to properly shake hands (not limply, but firmly, without squeezing but with confidence and conviction), and possibly also because they thought it was sort of funny, having a child call a restaurant for them.

Amazingly, the Upper Deck does indeed have a table, so

I book it for eight o'clock, which is when we usually prefer to dine, because it gives us ample time to get dressed and ready. And then I tell them that we have a birthday in our party, the birthday girl's name is Susan, and could we please also have a cake, so hopefully everything will be okay and my mother will be happy, even though my dad isn't here for the occasion.

And then I tell my sister and brother, who are flopped on the couch in the living room after a full day of tennis clinic and fully absorbed in an episode of *M*A*S*H*, that soon we are going to have to get ready to take Mum out for dinner. And I go and knock on the closed door to my mother's room.

"H-hhello?" Mum calls out in a muffled and phlegmy voice from under the covers. The wall-to-wall taupe draperies in her room, which is as cold and dark as a fridge with the bulb out, are drawn closed. There are lipstick-marked mugs and half-empty glasses and pill bottles scattered on the bedside table. The rumpled bed is covered with magazines and my mother's inside-out clothes are piled on the beige lacquer chair.

"Hi, Mum, so I booked us a table at the Upper Deck for dinner!"

"What's the Upper Deck?" she asks, with little interest.

"You know, that place in St. Armands that looks really nice, the one you always say we should try whenever we drive by? I booked us a table at eight o'clock for your birthday dinner!"

"I don't remember it," my mother says, tossing aside the covers and dragging herself upright as if emerging from some great, weighty depth. "Do we like it?" she asks, blinking.

"We have never been, but it looks really nice."

"Okay, I guess I had better get ready then," she says, with absolutely zero enthusiasm.

"C'mon, Mum, it will be fun! I'll tell Jen and Josh to get ready. Why don't you wear that new outfit..."

And so it goes, with fourteen-year-old me dragging the listless troop first into the car, and then into the restaurant, where my mother is mostly silent and staring into space throughout the three long courses, and my brother and sister and I try to fill the space by being funny and chatty about the other people at the Colony, my brother reciting full passages from his record of *The Goon Show*, which he knows by heart, to amuse my mother, but she is having none of it.

Finally the cake, which is chocolate with mocha icing and is lit with many candles and has "Happy Birthday Susan" written on it, just like I requested, arrives with a flourish at the table.

"Make a wish, Mum!" we three exhort, after our vigorous performance of "Happy Birthday." Blowing out the candles, she looks around the table at us, and instead of smiling her bright smile and thanking her three beautiful, wonderful children for making her birthday fun, big fat tears roll down her face and then she is actually, openly sobbing, right there in the fancy restaurant.

It doesn't matter to her that we are just kids and it's not our fault. She wants us to know that nothing we can ever do will make it okay.

YEARS PASS. IT'S MARCH BREAK, 2003, and since Thomas and I are both too busy with work to go on vacation and Sophie is on a school exchange in Paris, we decide to fly our ten-year-old son Philip, who would otherwise have nothing much to do on his own in icy, dull Toronto, down to Sarasota to stay with my parents.

For the past couple of years, this has been a successful plan. My parents, who now spend the winters in Florida so that my increasingly lame mother can avoid the ice and the cold, always welcome the company. Plus, it's fun for my kids to be down south and have some time on their own with my parents, who spoil them with outings to touristy Florida things like SeaWorld and the Disney theme parks that Thomas and I are less enthusiastic about (i.e., would sooner die before doing). Usually the two of them fly down together, but this time it will just be Philip.

Three days in, however, we get a call in the middle of the night. It's Philip, sobbing. "Na-an...and...Za-ade are fighting!" he cries, hiccupping his words. My preternaturally mature ten-year-old son, who never succumbs to drama, is so upset he cannot stop crying long enough to get the words out. "They are yelling these horrible things at each other! I couldn't stand it. It's so horrible I had to run out of the apartment!"

"Oh my God, sweetheart, I'm so, so sorry. Where are you?"

"I'm on the beach somewhere, it's da-ark..." says my little boy, his teeth chattering between sniffles.

My heart is in my mouth with fear—and with blind, white fury. Seven whole days without drama was too much to ask? My parents couldn't have just kept it together for

194

the one week when their grandson was alone with them in their care?

"Hold on, honey, it's going to be okay. You just stay where you are and I'll call Josh to come and get you. He's coming right away, okay?"

Thank God my brother Josh and his kids happen to be staying somewhere nearby. Later, after Josh manages to air-lift Philip out of the crisis zone and home to us the next afternoon, when I speak to my brother on the phone about what went down, he says, "It reminded me of myself when I was little, seeing him all alone and crying like that because of Mom and Dad."

Even now, I don't know if I will ever be able to forgive them for this. Particularly since my mother never once offered a single word of apology. As per tradition, the two of them just went deep undercover for a couple of months until it was too late for me to bring it up again in conversation. ("I don't know why you would have to bring that up," my mother would say crossly, if I ever dared point out any transgression. "Here we are having such a nice time, and you just have to go and put a damper on the whole evening.") The only thing different from how it always played out was that this time, it was about my child's hurt, not just my own.

My parents might never have felt the least bit guilty about their behaviour, but I was wracked with it. In believing that they would not necessarily act the same way with their grandchildren as they had with us, I had failed to protect my own children. A slip I still feel guilty about because more than anybody, I know how scary it was to be trapped between the two of them at their worst. And how hurtful it is to have the people who are supposed to be taking care of you care only about themselves.

ONCE MY OWN KIDS hit their teens, it became clear—after the repeated shocks of my parents arriving on our doorstep squirrelly, bizarre, and extremely late for family occasions—that the primary source of tension in our home wasn't coming from any of the four of us but from my increasingly impossible parents.

Somewhere, after years of suffering their wild tantrums, of coming across the mad ravings of my mother's angry letters, of putting up with her erratic behaviour and disturbing phone calls, it all just became too much.

Somewhere amidst my mother screaming into the answering machine: "Just who do you think you are?" after some imagined slight. My father, by this point easily wound up, her menacing puppet, chiming in on the other receiver: "You little piece of shit!"

Or being called away from dinners—"Your mother is walking funny." Or, "She can't get up. I think she has had a stroke"—and running over only to find the two of them impossibly engaged in some psycho-drama worthy of a Southern playwright, then fully, shamelessly, in total denial the next morning. Or my mother calling at all hours, alternately in accusatory rage or pathetically self-pitying about my father's increasing confusion: "You children will have to find somewhere for him to go. I can't take it anymore!"

And then, inexplicably, yet entirely unapologetically, from my mother after she threw our father out and onto my doorstep: "It's always the children who have to deal with these things."

My mother had played it all so cleverly all those years, laying in all the trips, all the treats, all the best schools so that she never had to feel a drop of guilt over anything, no matter what kind of drama she felt like staging or pot of mischief she felt like stirring.

"We gave you everything!" my mother would yell into the phone, whenever I might summon the nerve to question a dubious plan. Or "How dare you!" whenever I might try to resist whatever she was trying to unload onto me, making me feel like the worst, most ungrateful child ever.

Best was her accusation — after I'd endured the wild rollercoaster of her mid-life hijinks during the years I worked in her office — that I was to blame for the winding-down of her interior design business. "I had a perfectly good business of my own and then you had to come and ruin everything," my mother once offered in her own, entirely guilt-free assessment of the Susan Young Design years.

I am still so sorry, my beautiful, maddening darling. It is true, you did, you did: Give Us Everything. I still feel awful that I couldn't save you. Even worse that I didn't try hard enough. But I had to stop trying to make you happy because that was never, ever going to happen.

A realization, which, despite its essential truth, still never manages to free me completely.

BARBRA, ROBERTA FLACK, MADAME BUTTERFLY — all the divas sang for her. To this day, I can hardly hear the opening notes of the first song on the second side of Dusty Spring-field's *Dusty in Memphis* without my eyes immediately filling with hot tears.

"Can't I cry a little bit? There's nobody to notice it. / Can't I cry if I want to? No one cares..."

Of all of her greatest hits, "Just One Smile" was my mother's chosen theme song. As the late-night soundtrack of my early childhood, it always seemed like Dusty was really singing in a recorded version of my mother's true voice, saying what she really wanted us to understand: that all the sadness in it was actually my mother's own.

So many years later, if I'm ever in the mood to just let go and cry my heart out, all I have to do is lay the needle down on that record's crackly vinyl groove, and I'm right there, with my mom, crying softly and singing along with Dusty there in the dark.

Eight

THE VENETIAN MIRROR

NOW THAT WE HAVE finally got my father into long-term care on a locked floor for seniors with dementia at a residential hospital (an enormous challenge which involved grim tours of nursing homes and facilities, the intense lobbying of hand-tied social workers at governmental agencies, and a short stay — his, not mine — in the psych ward at Mount Sinai Hospital), there is this enormous sense of relief that he (and we) are finally safe now, and that somehow we have survived the worst of his increasing mania and paranoia. But the burden has not entirely lifted. Even though my father is no longer very responsive and isn't able to say very much, I still have to go and visit him on a regular basis. It is terrible to see him in this state and this way, a man who used to shower fifteen times a day now with dirty hair and food on his shirt. The guy who used to nag us about being inside on such a beautiful day doesn't want to leave the stale air of his stinky locked floor. And still he paces like a caged animal.

The whole picture is all wrong: he still looks like an aged Richard Branson or Ralph Lauren, with his long blonde hair and in his button-down Oxfords and jeans, but there are diapers underneath the denim and he has to be fed with a spoon.

My sister is very good about it all. She visits him and feeds him green seedless grapes one at a time like he is an overgrown child, asking questions he will never answer. Mostly oblivious, in good moments he seems almost soothed by her presence. But it is also obvious that he feels relieved when the strain of our visits comes to an end, so he no longer has to try to pretend to be a normal functioning person. What is difficult for me is that I don't seem to elicit the same kind of benign response. I don't know if there is something about me — something in the way I carry myself, or something in my mid-life physicality that ticks him off — but occasionally some lizard aspect of his brain seems to click in and he starts to look at me with intense hatred and anger. I know, because he is my father, why he is looking at me in that way. I know that sometimes, in a brief flash of cognition, he thinks that it is my fault, that as the eldest, as the one in charge — that I am the one who must have put him there in that hellhole. That I have taken away his freedom and taken control. I know this partly because when he was still able to speak, these are the kinds of accusations he would hurl at me, along with all kinds of other craziness involving people with guns coming to get him, which managed to get him locked up in the first place.

But the other thing I know is that sometimes when he

looks at me, he sees my mother. I can tell by what I see in his eyes, which is most definitely not paternal love, or even love for my dead mother, but the kind of burning hatred only she could elicit from him on occasion, and most definitely more often by the time she, at her vengeful, operatic peak, had reached the age that I am now. My father was once a gentle person who could painlessly remove a splinter from a small child's finger with the calm and delicacy of a gifted pediatric surgeon. An exemplary grandfather of small children who truly adored my son, Philip, who would cuddle up under his arm to watch tennis on TV on the modular leather sofa at the cottage. And who first taught both my kids how to ride a bike and then how to drive a car. To some degree, my mother probably pushed him into madness with her endless provocations, her wild refusal to be tamed. And yet he was always prone to the kind of fury that scared all of us, but only she really suffered.

This is now my burden, even more than the horrible, depressing task of going up there to visit him: that in his rare moments of recognition, what he sees in me is her, but only in all the ways that she was maddening and impossible and infuriating. Reflected back at me in his glare is contempt for my feminine wilfulness, my refusal to *just listen* to him. But all that's left of his psyche is something dark and furious. The only benefit, I suppose, is that it helps me to understand why my mother so desperately wanted out of this life and was so very ready to die.

IF THERE WERE ONE THING, one material object that might somehow be able to express—or indeed, reflect—my mother's taste and style it would have to be a mirror. While almost any type of mirror might do—and indeed every house she ever decorated, including every house she and my father ever lived in themselves, was liberally appointed with them—the absolute top of the line, the pick of the litter, the Waldorf salad, if you will, in her collection of mirrors was what she referred to, with some reverence, as "the Venetian mirror."

Of course it was not the only memorable mirror in the house. There was an art deco mirror in a heavy, Picasso-like wrought-iron frame adorned with rather thorny looking iron roses that always hung, somewhat menacingly, either in a hall or occasionally above a sink in a powder room, in whatever residence my parents happened to be living at the time. There was also a huge octagonal piece that looked like an enormous ashtray—but with a mirror at its centre, surrounded by a heavy border of tan-coloured bricks like a paved walkway in a California shopping development; my mother must have found during the '80s, as there was no other logical explanation for it.

I remember it looming over a French marble console in the open living/dining room in my parents' two-bedroom condo, although I note, from a May 1987 issue of *City & Country Home* which featured my parents' Rosedale Palladian house on the cover, that this same insane-looking art piece/mirror had once stood watch there above a fireplace in the front entrance, smack dab as you walked in the door.

There was also a huge rectangular mirror, with a carved frame my mother had "painted out" in grey to match the walls, and another large oval one, possibly Victorian in origin, with a wooden foliate frame, which my mother lacquered a glossy white and always hung in a guest bathroom, typically against a wall painted an opaline green for its cool, watery, "refreshing" quality. Intuitive to the core, my mother always operated from these sense-memory impressions about decorating—which is why it is so interesting to reflect on what it was that fascinated her so about reflection.

These grand mirrors, as I've described, kept company with all the other mirrored and metallic objects glistening in the light from the glass tabletops everywhere in her interiors. Never one to miss out on the opportunity to maximize this light-show effect, my mother would also place even more sparkling *objets* in front of these mirrors in order for their respective, reflective backsides to be reflected, in turn, on and on into infinity.

Against her monochromatic palette of pearl-grey, a bowl of white roses or French tulips always sat on our rather formal Georgian dining table, the cut flowers placed in a cut crystal bowl on an ornate and slightly crooked Victorian silver-footed pedestal, the base of which, naturally, was lined with mirror. This curiosity always sparkled as if deliberately underlit beneath the twinkling glass wedding cake of my mother's nineteenth-century Russian chandelier. And each and every opportunity my mother had to toss in even more mirror to the mix—say, by installing wall-to-wall mirror in a bathroom, lining a niche in the dining room, or even, in their last home, covering the exposed supporting columns of their open-concept condo in so much floor-to-ceiling mirror that it became almost impossible to avoid running into your own reflection — Mum took it, and, true to form, ran with it into extremist territory.

Of course, there were other decorative touches and *objets* that were very "her" and as much part of her grand and loopy signature style as her penchant for light play and reflection. Alongside mirror, my mother also loved ostrich eggs, for example, for their creamy-shelled orb forms, which, like shark's teeth and horns, she raised on Lucite pedestals so that they seemed to float above tabletops. She absolutely lived for the glam and glitter of chrome and brass in open étagères and table bases; likewise for animals cast in bronze and fired in porcelain and indeed for all manner of taxidermy, from antlers to zebra rugs, fur carpets, and pillows (an old lynx coat she had refashioned into a carpet for our sunroom continually shed like a massive dog). Also the world-beat exotica of Buddha heads, Chinese lacquered boxes, and celadon urns; African wood carvings, Bessarabian carpets (we had a gorgeous tomato-red one at the cottage under our dining-room harvest table which somehow disappeared); Mennonite quilts, Ikat throws, and Kilim pillows. When it came to art, her tastes veered toward anything organic, geometric, ethnic, or abstract and contemporary; in the case of upholstery, she preferred largely monochromatic solid colours in highly tactile weaves of satin and velvet (texture was all-important, prints an unnecessary visual distraction). Window coverings weren't her thing: for her, Roman blinds and California shutters trumped the fuss of drapery (and sheers she absolutely loathed). As far as she was concerned, there was always room for travertine marble and potted palms, along with stacks of art books and tribal baskets filled with magazines;

antique silver trays and candlesticks; and almost anything art deco or Georgian. It all sounds very contemporary: her list of "likes," her mix, but that's how she was, a sort of witchy visionary of a designer, who whipped it all together by feel and instinct. But whatever the source or inspiration for this intuition, it was at its essence almost childishly fascinated with sparkle and reflection. Apart from her penchant for going over the top with glitz and glam, was it possible, like Dorian Gray in reverse, that her mix was some type of spell or enchantment and she was using all that mirror as a sort of shield to protect us all from harm?

Of these various shields, it was the aforementioned Venetian mirror—interestingly, in a shield-like shape—that was the ür-mirror in her funhouse. If you have never seen an antique Venetian mirror (although you most probably have come across contemporary facsimiles of them, now readily available from China), suffice it to say it is a sort of mirror-upon-mirror, first created by the Murano glass artisans in sixteenth-century Italy for the palazzi of noble families. Notable for their etched and bevelled borders, and often found in oval or cartouche-like forms, these mirrors are like drops of chandelier glass or pendant earrings, writ large, for the wall. The real ones are priceless—early examples of the mercury-backed glass made the trade secrets of the Murano artisans who had developed it so prized that they were imperially summoned by Louis XIV to work their magic on the Hall of Mirrors at Versailles. While my mother's is indeed antique, it was still of course only a reproduction of one of those truly precious ones. Nevertheless, so securely did it occupy the A1 location above the fireplace in the living room of my parents' Rosedale Palladian, I can scarcely remember our years in that house without its silvery, faceted surface immediately coming to mind.

Where there was mirror, there was also smoke-coloured satin. And my mother's mercurial presence, dazzling in the shimmering endlessness of its reflection.

IT IS SATURDAY AFTERNOON on a clear, bright day in May that somehow, uncannily, the organizers of the Rosedale Community Association manage to nail each and every year weather-wise for their fundraising effort in the park behind our house. The event, which is rather unimaginatively, if quaintly, called Mayfair, features a kids' carnival of rides and games and a sale—garden plants, old books, and home-baked Upper Canadian offerings like butter tarts and Nanaimo bars, all laid out on fold-out tables that were set up the night before on the field around the tennis courts and the outdoor skating rink. For the adults (and the near-adults carrying fake ID), there is always an outdoor beer garden in which to while away the afternoon tossing back brewskis with old private-school chums in the sun just like you were up on the dock in Muskoka, while the kids run around outside going wild on cotton candy and too many popsicles. So established is this event that every "nice" Toronto family with ties to ye olde Establishment quarter, even those who no longer live nearby, make sure not to miss it—with the exception of my parents, who have zero interest in this sort of thing, even if it's literally in their own backyard.

After trolling the tables of used housewares in the skating-rink area for vintage treasure accidentally donated to the rummage sale by the clueless denizens, my then-boy-friend Thomas and I, who have bonded over our mutual love of mid-century modern, join our friend Fred in the beer garden. Fred isn't his real name, it's actually his middle name, but of course there were too many Roberts in his camp cabin so he is well known to everyone with social links to the Toronto Golf Club or Camp Kandalore as Fred. Luckily he has three first names, having been christened Robert Frederick James at his Anglican church in Lawrence Park, so any one of them, really, might do.

Fred is blonde and prep handsome and great fun when loaded, and not "out" yet, even to himself, so he stays pretty much loaded (and, still, at least at this stage, quite fun) most of the time. He also went to Jarvis Collegiate for a couple of years before being shipped off to boarding school in New England, so he knows most everyone in this jocular and orthodontically perfect crowd.

We join him at a table full of white people quickly turning red under the suddenly scorching spring sun. The table is sticky, the beer is warm, and everyone in their striped shirts and Teva sandals is already yelling over everyone else and laughing loudly because they have had a few. At our end of the table, the three girls with sleek, blonde ponytails poking through the backs of their baseball caps start looking bored. Today they would have had their cell phones out, but back then, in the early '80s, it was time for a diversion.

"Karen's house is that big white one over there," Fred brags on our behalf, pointing to the white Georgian-style house backing onto the park which does look grand, even from this public angle.

"Oh, really!" The ponytail girls, who have up until this moment been vigorously ignoring both Thomas and me, immediately start perking up.

Cat-in-the-Hat Fred is at my side, whispering in my ear. "Charlotte and Bev and Claire *really* want to come and see the inside of your house. Do you think we could just pop by and you could give them a quick tour?"

The minute we are inside my mother's pearl-grey and coyote-lined lair, I realize this is all a terrible mistake. I can see Charlotte and Claire and Bev's eyes rolling as we enter our front hall, with the enormous eight-foot Buddha head perched on a brass pedestal in front of the Warhol print of a blue-faced Mao. But I am forced, out of politeness, to continue.

"Yeah, so this is the sunroom," I say, pointing in the direction of our classically proportioned glass conservatory which my mother has lined in grey suede and velvet and bedecked like Catherine the Great's winter sleigh with Chinese lacquer cabinets sitting on furs. I just know these girls were raised in houses where the dull, dependable dens are painted primrose yellow and appointed with tartan wing chairs. They will have drapes, and these drapes will be too short and made from dowdy faded chintz, but that will be perfectly acceptable since they were installed in 1962. "Um, and here's the living room," I say, gesturing wanly toward our glistening living room with its silver satin modular sofas, Billy Baldwin slipper chairs, and glass tabletops sparkling with various objects of fascination all framed by the house's Palladian windows.

Above the mantel, which my mother has "painted out" in monochromatic pearl grey, is the vast, endlessly reflective emptiness of my mother's beloved Venetian mirror.

Behind me, as I continue my limp impression of Vanna White, I hear Charlotte whispering snidely to Claire: "Where are all the books??"

I want to stop and tell them to leave. I want to show them that there are tons of books, mountains of them, which my mother devours and then throws out, upstairs. I want to tell them that my mother is a great woman of style and they just don't get it. Instead I just pretend I didn't hear and miserably press on.

THANKS TO THE NUMEROUS myths and fairy tales threading throughout the history of Western civilization, it is almost too easy to diagnose my mother's obsession with mirrored surfaces. In her version, she was an interior decorator whose creative challenge was to cast light around a room. Of course she was also a beautiful woman who liked what she saw looking back at her from a mirror, and was perhaps bolstered by the pleasure she took in her own reflection. But then she always preferred to live in myths and stories — casting herself alternately as the triumphant heroine or the poor little victim — rather than in the ugly daylight of what others might call reality.

To the ancient Greeks, mirrors were so powerful they could be used as weapons. The mathematician Archimedes was said to have invented giant mirrors to repel the Roman fleet during an attack on Syracuse in 212 B.C., aiming the sun's rays on Roman warships until they caught fire and burned to a crisp. In his battle with the hideous, snake-haired Medusa, whose very look could turn a man to stone, the hero Perseus used a mirrored shield to divert her image, thus enabling himself to slice off her ugly head without being transformed into a Corinthian column.

But then, in the instructive logic of legend, being bewitchingly beautiful is dangerous enough. Consider poor dumb Narcissus, who was so smitten with his own reflection in a pool of water that he literally pined away with love, for himself. And the flawlessly exquisite yet poisonously vain queen in Snow White, perpetually consulting her own mirror only to discover that there might be someone else, someone younger and more pure of heart, out there in the fairy world who was yet more beautiful than she.

Even today, mystics seeking to commune with spirits or envision the future stare into reflective objects—mirrors, knives, crystal balls—in order to fall into a trance and tune into the invisible spirit world. And of course, as we all know, if we are unfortunate enough to break a mirror, it will result in seven years of bad luck—starting out with the tiny shards of glass that you have already stepped on immediately after breaking one, and usually barefoot.

I'M MEETING MY MOTHER for lunch at one of her regulars, a French-themed bistro called Le Paradis that she frequents because it's in the design and décor district, next-door neighbours with fabric showrooms like Brunschwig & Fils and Robert Allen so everybody there knows her, and the menu lists classic things she actually enjoys like steak frites, quiche Lorraine, and red wine.

It's been a while since I've seen her because she has been recuperating from a procedure I wasn't supposed to know about in the first place, which means she has been in hiding mode. We never discussed it in advance, probably because she knew I would be disapproving. In short, it is the first time I will see her after her facelift. And on my way over, I feel anxious about what she is going to look like. Will she still be all bruised and puffy? Or will she already have that weird, overly smooth and pulled-back look that women have after they have messed around with their faces? Perhaps there are women out there that I'm not even aware of who have so successfully undergone facelifts that the results are undetectable, but most everybody I've encountered who's undergone cosmetic surgery doesn't look younger or "refreshed," just weird, like someone from another planet on *Star Trek: The Next Generation.*

Walking into the restaurant, I see her immediately at her regular spot on the banquette. It is not quite as bad as I had imagined. She is not particularly bruised or puffy. She does not look like the Bride of Wildenstein. It is still recognizably her sitting there. But it is also definitely her with a facelift.

I join her at the table. We chat about the usual things, what the kids have been up to, when she and Dad are booking their winter vacation in Longboat Key, what I'm writing about this week for the paper. We look over the menu, hear about the daily specials, and agree that the *soup du jour*, a cauliflower puree, sounds good. We order our lunch (*salade niçoise* for her, an omelette for me), some mineral water and wine, and still she has not mentioned a word about the glaringly obvious fact that she has just undergone surgery to alter her appearance. The fact that I am supposed to play along and pretend, the way she is pretending, that the face looking back at me is the very same face she had when I last saw her, is starting to make it hard for me to swallow. I was never a part of this decision, but I am supposed to act as if it never happened.

As they take our plates away and we order coffee, my mother leans back, raises her head as if peering at herself in a mirror, turning her face this way and that in my direction, and says, "It looks pretty good, don't you think?" At this moment, something rises within me and all I can do is get out of there, immediately. Scraping back my chair, I make a run for it.

"I have to go to the bathroom," I offer, by way of weak explanation.

Sitting on the toilet in the quiet of the ladies room, my head in my hands, I am trying to understand why I cannot even muster the ability to say the natural, normal thing to her in response: "Oh, yes, they really did a good job, you look just great." What an impossible idiot I am. Maybe I can't bring myself to lie. But can't I just come up with some neutral answer?

After a couple of minutes of hiding there in the bathroom, it comes to me that what I really am is angry. Angry that my mother has gone and done this to herself without even talking to me about it. Angry that I am supposed to play along as if nothing is untoward about the fact that she looks completely different and, like always—as with everything that goes down within my parents' orbit—as if nothing has ever happened. But mostly I am angry that she has robbed me, her daughter, of her real face. I will never be able to look on the unaltered visage of my mother again. It will not be her real face that grows old in front of me. It will be a fake face, a post-surgical face that I will have to look at in place of where my mother's actual face should be. A face that was the first thing I ever saw in the world and that I loved.

Reflecting back on our completely ridiculous lunch, of course I understand that she was entirely within her rights to do what she wanted with her own self. She did it for herself, and not for me, and she, a beautiful woman who was no doubt witnessing the fading of that legendary beauty in the mirror, and the coincident weakening of her powers, with some fear and regret (nature being the unfair mistress that she is, my father of course still looked like a million bucks). But still I felt like I'd been robbed.

GROWING UP, I DIDN'T often hear that I looked like my mother. My sister was the beauty, I was supposedly the clever one, and our little brother was simply perfect. But my fair, blue-eyed colouring was the opposite of my mother's dark, hazel-eyed witchiness, and the squareness of my jawline was much less like her oval-shaped face than the caricatures she would draw of my father's. When I was little and people would tell me that I looked like my six-foot-four father, whose shoes in the front hall were like boats on my feet when I shuffled around in them, I found it silly that I could be a little girl who looked like a great big man.

The physical differences between my mother and I became even more glaring when I hit my teens and morphed into a curvy Jewess instead of a younger version of my mother. But then a strange thing happened. As my mother entered mid-life, she lost her arresting angularity and got softer and rounder (she also began to suffer from a number of physically limiting ailments, including crumbling hips and knees, and wasn't able to be that active, which probably contributed). After years of covering up the grey in her hair until her natural colour was almost snow white underneath, she could no longer get the ladies in the colour room at Michael Kluthe to tint it dark enough without it looking (in her words) "like a wig," so she started sporting more of a medium-fair, variegated honey hue (later, in a more exaggerated Cruella De Vil phase, this was dyed darker and was accompanied by two white stripes of un-tinted, all-white hair framing her face, in the manner of Susan Sontag, or a skunk).

The result of this transformation of my mother's was that as she entered middle age (and I, simultaneously, lost some of my girlishness and became more womanly), we started to resemble each other more closely. And people started telling me how much I looked like her for the first time in my life.

I HAVE OFTEN WONDERED if in my choice of girlfriends I have somehow subconsciously sought out small reflections, like those tiny, sewn-on Indian mirrors on hippie blouses and bedspreads, that remind me of my mother. Steph is just as sexy, femme, and generous as my mother. Sue often reminds me of my mother with her penchant for non-sequiturs and her fine-boned, dark good looks. Leanne shares my mother's grandeur and intuitive brilliance; Ann, Liz, Ellen, and Martha her humanity, insight, and lightning-quick wit.

I have a friend named Kate who makes me feel like I must be a good enough person simply because she has continued to be friends with me since we were four. The story is that our mothers—both extraordinarily good-looking brunettes with oversized personalities to match—met and naturally connected in the park when we two girls were small. Clearly, they liked what they saw in each other's reflections: Carol, too, was tall and dark and clever, and, just like my mother, as much admired for her sass and irreverence as her good looks. Both of these remarkable women were, remarkably, married to almost ridiculously handsome, tall, blonde men, both of whom were starting out as young lawyers, and both women had little blonde daughters in the same kindergarten. Eventually our two families came to resemble each other even more closely, as our mothers, in turn, each gave birth to two more children—a boy and a girl—at which point, we mirrored each other almost completely.

Kate and I don't particularly look alike—she is taller and sportier (and, as my mother might readily have offered here, more conventionally good-looking) than I am—but we are still often mistaken for sisters, which is funny because we might as well have been. Kate and I practically grew up side by side, spending our weekends in the city largely at the Royal Ontario Museum (fascinated by the dioramas of anthropologists in the field wrapping up dinosaur bones), sleeping over at each other's houses and spending weeks in the summer at each other's cottages at different ends of the Great Lakes.

Kate now claims that she actually spent a lot of this time in the company of my mother, as I would often wander off in some cloud of my own to read in my room during her visits. I recall her as a child being terribly allergic to everything, except that she had a more vigorous taste for scary things like haunted houses, roller coasters, and horror movies than I did. In any case, all that time at my mother's pointy elbow proved formative; Kate is now an interior decorator, and best of all, we have somehow managed over the years to stay great friends.

COMING OF AGE AS I did in the '80s, truly a dreadful cultural moment as far as I am concerned — from that era's music (I mean, Air Supply? Wham!?) to its neon and acid-wash and the primary-coloured, Tinker-Toy clumsiness of its architecture and Memphis Group design — it's almost impossible for me to understand its current stylistic revival. I get that this makes me sound terribly old. As an aging hipster myself, I fully understand that this generation's nostalgic re-appropriation is laced with irony; but it was all so obviously hideous for anyone who lived through it that it's hard to imagine any of it would ever come back into fashion. But then, if one's own era serves as a sort of reflection, it would seem that, in the way that we start needing reading glasses as we get older, it gets harder and harder over time to clearly see what's in the mirror.

My mother, for instance, who came of age at the height of the Rat Pack/Scandinavian Modern era, just loathed Mid-Century Modern. Wall-to-wall sheers under drapes;

boomerang coffee tables; those sober teak dining sets with their Lutheran democratic good taste—all those plain and clean-lined things I loved—just gave her the willies. In fact, anything made out of teak—from a Danish cheeseboard to one of those eminently practical sideboards with the sliding front cabinets that today's hipsters have made into cocktail bars for their condos—she just couldn't stand. Which was great as far as I was concerned, because I was able to appropriate her entire early portfolio of Danish Modern. A mere child when such modernism was the prevailing fashion, I happen to adore everything to do with it. Whereas for my mother, the battle against the earnest teak-and-twill modernism of her own time was one she fought with glass and mirror until her death as a sort of decorative point of honour.

Silver satin, however, straight from the set of a Hollywood Regency–styled New York townhouse in some '40s madcap comedy from her childhood—well, now you're talking.

And then there is the case of my mother-in-law, who grew up in the era of the Art Nouveau—or *Jugendstil*, as it was called in her Prussian neck of the woods—a whimsical, naturalistic, highly ornamental style of carved flowers and fairies which she forever ever after wholly despised. And then what decorative style is she most drawn to but the comparatively restrained, Biedermeier style of the mid-nineteenth century—a style that was the height of fashion in the period just before she was born.

If style operates as a sort of cultural mirror, perhaps we simply cannot truly enjoy the prevailing one of our own time—much in the way that we are never pleased with our own reflections?

My mother-in-law tells a funny story about being on a moving escalator in a department store and seeing someone she vaguely recognized and must somehow know, and then waving at them and seeing them wave back—until she realized that the entire time she had been looking into a mirror. And the face politely smiling back at her was her own.

NOW THAT I AM approximately the same age as she was when I had Sophie, the growing similarities between my mother and my aging self sometimes worry me. It's not a simple open-and-shut case of looking into the mirror and seeing my mother, which seems to be a consequence of aging that's almost generically—and genetically—unavoidable.

What worries me more are the little signs and signals that must have formed part of the giant cocktail of increasing panic that brought someone as indomitable as Susan May Lambert Young down before her time. It was clear that the maddening irrelevance and invisibility that seem part of a woman's lot after fifty here in North America never really sat all that well with my mother, who, like some wrinkled and out-of-control toddler, grew increasingly loud and shrill and demanding of our undivided attention—an unattractive, hormonally-fired combination with which I am unfortunately starting to relate. Fantasists to the core, my parents refrained from ever sharing the bad news with any of us that it is hard to be a grown-up—perhaps because they simply refused to acknowledge it themselves, getting older without getting any the wiser. Certainly my mother never really grew up. She just got old and sick, while behaving more and more like a willful child.

And then again, as a creative genius with too much energy to spare, she also found herself under-employed in her later years, particularly after we three children were gone, and even more so once she was no longer able to run around town all day to job sites and showrooms. Like me, she never really had any hobbies outside work and raising a family, which must make for a hell of a long day once you are lame and in pain and trapped in your seventies in a two-bedroom condo with a crazy person. Of course, despite her many protestations to the contrary, she never really took much care of herself, or ever really did that much in the way of exercise — another maternal tradition which I seem to be carrying on into the next generation, having had a fear of all athletic activity since being scarred for life by the horrors of phys. ed. in grade school. (Although it was truly hilarious how vigorously she would protest: having attended precisely three yoga classes at a midtown studio, my mother was once asked to contribute a quote for that studio's advertising brochure. Her quote: "Yoga has changed my life!" was a never-ending source of amusement to us three forever after — a joke that, like any other made at her expense, she never found the least bit funny.)

Now, every single similarity that reminds me of her, every little twitch and twinge I feel in my joints on bending or waking, is terrifying. In the way that my toothbrush now resembles hers, with the ring of red lipstick around its middle, I too am starting to thicken in the places that she did; the wrinkles that have suddenly appeared in the skin above my knees now look exactly like hers at fifty. Like her, I am constantly rummaging through the rooms of my house, or my handbag, in search of a pair of reading glasses. Sometimes a knee, or a hip, or even my fingers ache—are these the first signs of the terrible rheumatoid arthritis that ended up crippling her? Destiny is awfully hard to bear, let alone avoid.

Not like I'm trying particularly hard to live my life better than she did. I too like to drink—and eat and shop and travel and spend money like water without having to consider the consequences. Just like her, I have been extravagant in my sun worship, and irregular if not pathetic in my attempts at regular exercise. Not exactly joiners—just like both of our parents—our social circles too seem to be the only thing contracting more than expanding. Sometimes I think what really killed my mother was a combination of loneliness, decrepitude, and pointlessness, a state of being that she could literally no longer endure. True, I never smoked, and my husband, with whom I have a very different relationship than the one my mother had with my father, has—so far, at least—not shown any signs of becoming any crazier than he already was when we met. But still, as the prospect of the end draws closer, it's becoming clearer on reflection that what the future holds is that you get sick and old and then one of you dies. That my mother would have definitely preferred to have been the first one off the pier (not having quite lived up to the rock-and-roll standard of having died young and stayed pretty) is entirely obvious.

After my mother died, and I was struck from the blue with a ridiculous case of *mal de debarquement*, a mysterious form of post-sailing vertigo that seems to be suffered predominantly by women in their fifties (as if we weren't a sorely tested group enough), I made an appointment to see my family doctor. Our GP is a lovely and very smart woman, who once, years ago, treated my mother for some of her myriad symptoms. Feeling raw in my literally unbalanced state, I shared some of these worries that it was probably unavoidable that I was going to end up exactly like my mother did.

She looked me right in the eye and said: "Your mother was a very different woman than you are." It's an observation that I still sometimes turn to to right myself whenever I'm feeling too dark and Jewish because, whether or not this ultimately is a good thing, or whether it means I have somehow failed to live up to living as large as my mother did, its truth is undeniable.

THE DAY AFTER MY mother died, a long-time friend of hers — a younger and successful real estate agent, to whom she had presumably given tons of business given how many times my parents had bought and sold their various homes and investment properties — very kindly dropped off dinner for us. All of us, shattered, wandering around our house trying to deal with everything that had just gone down, still had to eat. After I sent her a note of thanks for her thoughtfulness, she wrote me back a note which, even after all the craziness we had just lived through, still managed to catch us all by surprise: "I wonder if I might ask for the lovely Venetian mirror that always hung in your parents' living room. While everything she had in her home was beautiful, it is the single object that will always remind me of her."

Maybe it was petty, but we decided that, insofar as any

keepsakes were concerned, my mother's whacked-out '80s mirror with the giant beige frame—along with the commission on the condo sale—would just have to do.

Nine

THE BLACK VINYL
ADDRESS BOOK

AFTER MUM CALLED THE police on our seventy-eight-year-old dad, he wasn't allowed to go back home to their apartment. Which would have been a hard reality for *any* seventy-eight-year-old who'd been married to the same woman for more than half a century to grasp, let alone one with dementia who had to be told, over and over again, why he couldn't go home.

The problem — and really, there were so many problems in the whole situation it's hard to identify the most significant one — was our house, where he was now installed, was only just blocks away from my parents' apartment. And since my father was still at this point insistent on getting himself around and we couldn't exactly lock him in his room or keep watch on him 24/7, he kept wandering over to their condo, fully expecting each time to just walk in the door.

And the poor guys at the front desk had to keep explaining to him that no, he didn't live there anymore and he wasn't allowed upstairs, which was so awful and like a bad comedy sketch at the same time.

Truth was, my Dad wasn't the only one missing my mother. As she had made abundantly clear to all of us by dumping the problem on my doorstep, it wasn't exactly easy living with our father. But then she had simply taken to her bed, just as she had always done when things got difficult. Gone horizontal and hidden away from all of us — ashamed or just exhausted, it was hard to say.

Mornings would be okay with my dad, who would always start the day in a positive frame of mind, certain that today would be the day he could sort things out with my mother and move back in with her, if she would only agree to meet with him. Of course this was all some kind of misunderstanding. He knew he could straighten out the situation if she would just answer the Goddamn phone!

Understandably, his spirits would lessen as the day drew to a close and "the problem" (i.e. that my mother was finally done with him) still hadn't, in his words, "been resolved." Despite my best efforts to keep him calm and comfortable, in the evenings he was restless. As the days of this standoff turned into weeks, my Dad's already tenuous grip on reality started to slip further.

One night after dinner when I was getting ready for bed, I heard my dad, who was down the hall in the guest room, opening doors and calling out "Sue! Susan!!" with increasing agitation. Thomas was away on business and I was the only one at home. For a moment, I was actually afraid of being alone in the house with my own father. A man who'd been so gentle with me when I was little, patiently zipping up my jacket on the ski hill, fixing my hat so my ears were warm, and lacing up my skates at the arena so that my ankles weren't all wobbly but the laces weren't too tight. But at six foot four and 195 pounds, he was still a big guy who could easily go from calm to red-hot fury in an instant even before he was officially diagnosed as a crazy person.

I threw on a robe and summoned the courage to open the door. My seventy-eight-year-old dad was in his white Jockey underwear and a T-shirt. His hair was messy like he had just woken up from bed, and he looked confused to see me.

"I was just looking for your mother," he said, in a small, sad voice before turning to go back into the guest room.

MY MOTHER MADE IT her life's work to surround us with things of beauty, and yet of all of her many special and beautiful things, it is perhaps her ugly black vinyl address book that reminds me of her the most.

An address book is now such a dated item, like those telephone tables people had in their front halls back in the '50s when a house might have had one phone, and talking to people on a party line or even far away (long distance!) was a big deal. But consistently through her entire lifetime, my mother always had an address book on the go. Hers usually had a black vinyl cover, one that, with regular use, would become cracked and sticky to the touch. It was more like a binder, really—a cheap-looking variety from some ordinary office supply store like Staples or Grand & Toy. And it was always sizeable, like a large-print crossword book for old people, because my mother was always almost blind, even when she was younger, although she never really saw much point in trying to remedy the situation (perhaps because all of her reading glasses were perpetually lost, impossibly smeared, or half-broken anyhow).

This charmless oddity in our house of beautiful things usually sat by the phone in the kitchen or the den — wherever my mother happened to have established her Command Central in the house they were living in at the time — a utilitarian treasure of (mostly) practical information and useful contacts my mother had gathered over the years. Deceptively simple and unadorned, it was like an external brain.

That my mother would choose such an ugly thing to serve as her personal databank is interesting enough. But now the black vinyl address book also serves as a reminder of the many working parts of my mother's daily existence. Its abundance of entries, for doctors and physiotherapists, hairdressers and massage therapists, butchers and bakeries — some amusingly intersected, as with the notation for "gynecologist" overlapping that of the Harbord Bakery — as well as the listings for the many trades and services she employed over the years, the cast of characters she relied on to constantly beautify and perfect her person, the homes of her clients, and my parents' own succession of exquisite homes — provided something like a record of her world.

Which is why, after her death and funeral, when we got down to the hard job of disassembling my parents' things and packing up everything in their condo — either to go home with one of us, accompany my dad into his suite in the nursing home, be sold by the contents people, or, finally, to be dragged in bulging garbage bags to the Goodwill—on one of my last trips before closing the door behind me for good I felt compelled to tuck this ugly black vinyl address book in my purse: because it seemed like too much of my mother to simply toss in the trash.

AWKWARDLY OPENING THE FRONT door to my parents' Rosedale Palladian one afternoon, my arms laden with boxes of Passover macaroons and honey cake I have picked up at the Harbord Bakery for the upcoming holiday, I can hear my mother laughing from the kitchen.

Someone must have said something she found amusing on the other end, because when I walk into the room, she is alone, but on the phone. Smiling brightly and beckoning for me to come over, my mother is in a coffee-coloured cowl-necked sweater and a pair of charcoal grey wool trousers. In front of her is a half-empty coffee cup ringed with her lipstick, and, as usual, her black vinyl address book is in front of her, splayed open on the counter like an anatomical organ awaiting vivisection. In one hand she holds a scalpel-like clear plastic Bic ballpoint pen, which she is waving for emphasis, even though the effect is lost on her subject on the other end of the line.

"But, Hallie, you have to admit that I was dead-on!" she yells triumphantly just as I lean in to give her a kiss hello. Her hair and nails are freshly done, and she smells like she just got in from Michael Kluthe. She must have been on the phone for a while already because on the open pages of her

227

address book/anatomical organ she has drawn little overlapping black frames around all of the listed names.

The kitchen air is humid and strongly infused with the garlicky brisket that's behind her in the oven and there's a mess of carrot ends and potato peelings around the sink, which Joyce, or whoever "the help" currently is, will deal with once she arrives. Searching the kitchen counters for a clear spot on which to put down my stack of bakery boxes, I can see that my mother, too, has already been to the Harbord Bakery for the macaroons and honey cake, even though she had asked me to pick them up for her — the duplication of efforts now approaching an annual tradition. Just like last year, we will have enough Passover baked goods on hand to supply the entire Jewish population of the diaspora, should they be inclined to join us for dinner.

THE ADDRESS BOOK THAT I have sitting on the desk here beside me was her last working one. This edition has a zipper that zips all the way around, portfolio style, and true to form, it's cracked and worn at the seams where there's some colourless, fuzzy liner stuff peeking out from under the black vinyl in the corners. On the front, which is, as per tradition, sticky with unknown dried substances, are two yellow Post-its layered over top of each other with scribblings in different inks and pencil. The top one reads: JEN'S NEW CELL # and SOPH'S CELL in rapidly scrawled block letters. The one underneath it has three different numbers for my brother Joshua in New York City, written in my father's extremely neat and precise handwriting, and another number for the wine store underneath Josh's building, which often signs for the parcels we send down by UPS if nobody is home to sign for delivery.

On the inner front cover, randomly stuck into a slotted sleeve meant for business cards, is my mother's membership card to the Royal Ontario Museum, the business card for a social worker in the orthopedics wing of Mount Sinai Hospital, and an official receipt from the same hospital for $15 cash.

There is also a loose and torn page floating atop the ringed notebook that has lost its index holes. On one side is a quote my mother has written out that she has attributed to the late Senator Daniel Patrick Moynihan, who, "On hearing of the death of John F. Kennedy said, 'I don't think there is any point in being Irish (my mother here inserts the word 'Jewish' in brackets) if you don't know that the world is going to break your heart eventually.'"

These words, which my mother obviously found notable, appear to have been written over a faded recipe, perhaps for jam, as it seemed to involve quarts (my mother's writing was never easily deciphered). And on the other side of the piece of paper my *goyische* mother has, to my surprise, written out a list of the twelve tribes of Israel, beneath which is a phone number for someone named perhaps Zendra (or Zenobia?) beside the word "CLOTHING."

It is hard for me to interpret these random scribblings.

Was she preparing to divest the contents of her closet to a woman named Zendra? And why was she brushing up on her general knowledge of Judaism if not in preparation for the end?

Looking through the yellowed and torn pages and their entries — some written in my mother's odd, boxy approximation of capital letters; others quickly scrawled in the wild loops of her illegible script, uppercase letters flamboyantly winged as calligraphy, lowercase ones near-indecipherable nubbins — all randomly entered in faded pencil and ballpoint inks in varying hues of red, black, and blue, I am reminded of the world she built alongside my father, two young people who came from nowhere in particular and managed to pull off a glamorous life. Also how small that world had become near its end.

Inside, too, are numbers and addresses of places she frequented and friends she talked about, like her fellow interior designer pal Bernice, who was always exquisitely attired and made up whenever she managed to make it outside of the brass-and-glass confines of her Manulife Centre apartment (which wasn't often, as she was lame and ancient, plus it took her hours to get dressed). Bernice sported white stripes in her black hair, red lipstick, and a cane, and spoke in the advanced drawl of a West End actress.

There is a number for the nutty and tough-talking Marion, who smoked and drank vodka with my mother in the afternoons and whose late sister Blanche, whom my mother also adored, was scathingly funny about everything from her choice of damask for her wedding dress ("Idiotic! I was as wrinkled as the tablecloth when I stood up after the dinner") to her off-colour jokes about her late husband, actually named Mel, which was perfect.

There is a number for the blonde, blue-blood Harriet, whom everybody who is anybody around town has known as "Sis" ever since her brothers gave her the moniker at six. Sparkly-eyed and still a knockout well into her eighties, despite having been a lively party girl, she is one of those white women who might show up for a formal occasion in a sari, and when entertaining at home, rings a little bell to summon "the help" to the table at dinner.

There are a couple of different entries for Sandy, whom my mother always admired for her intellect and who we used to see on the beach in Jamaica until we stopped going after my father had a business disagreement with her good friends Marion and Tony. Marion is Jewish, originally from Scotland, of all places. Her husband Tony, who is also Jewish, grew up in Jamaica in a fancy family of rum distillers. Here too are the elegant society friends my mother became pals with during her Christie's course in London and whom she would meet for tea, and the few smart and still-married couples my parents went out to dinner with, until it became impossible for my dad to even fake his way through any kind of social occasion. And aspirational contacts like people who wrote columns in the newspaper or used to be on television, whom my parents knew when they were younger—one, a famous writer who lived in their building who has written about his years in Paris with Hemingway, another the rich widow of a late senator—because who knew when you might need to give them a call?

Alongside faded, frayed friendships and the signs of persistent hopes are numbers and addresses of places my mother used to frequent that no longer exist. Antique dealers, like the Prince of Serendip, a red-flocked warehouse crammed with Victoriana and run by two old queens, where my mother used to pop in for brass étagères and bits and bobs of marble statuary. Or Pack-Rat, a now-shuttered Rosedale storefront popular in the '80s for its black leather upholstery and primary-coloured, Memphis-inspired accessories. Elegant Stanley Wagman & Son Antiques, where my mother liked to shop for gifts for important occasions, is still around, however, still filled with hand-picked French deco treasures shipped in by container from *les puces* in Paris, even though Stanley himself isn't. The shop is now run by the late Stanley's ampersand, Warren.

And there are other blasts from the past, listings for long-standing, now defunct "nice" restaurants like Pastis, where the menu ran to classics of the French repertoire, the walls were sponged a reassuring Provençal yellow, and the owner, Georges, an émigré who nonetheless knew his way around Toronto society, would enthusiastically greet each patron by name in a heavy French accent, all of which of course my mother loved. There is also a number for the late John Manuel, the gentlemanly Yorkville boulevardier and designer whose work my mother much admired, who died fairly young, years before my mother, of complications from HIV/AIDS. And the German-born, tough and tiny Lily, the revered hair colourist who, after surviving a childhood of desperation in wartime Europe, emigrated to Canada to spend her days on her feet in the highest heels, pulling the delicate hairs of the city's Jewish elite through a pierced rubber cap with a crochet hook to create the perfect "natural" blonde streaks — before dying, presumably from a lifetime of proximity to the chemicals in hair dye, of cancer. And then there's Farida, the scolding Marseillaise who ran a salon called the Institut de Beauté where my mother would go for expensive weekly cellulite treatments. Each visit would begin with disapproving clicks from Farida as she weighed you in and measured the circumference of your thighs before hooking you up to some strange French contraption involving electro-magnetic pulses intended to smooth and reduce. Unsurprisingly, given that Farida was probably my mother's age, the Institut de Beauté is no longer in the slimming business.

Long lost friends, too, feature in the entries. Some from the Millbank Avenue days, like the birdlike Mary-Ann, whose face I later saw on signs around town as a real estate broker, and the Dutch-born, extremely tan Willy and Andy Eggen, an older, more established couple who used to invite us over to their pool on the weekends before we had one of our own and they moved out west to the lotus lands of BC.

Others were from my mother's hometown of St. Catharines, like the beautiful couturier Mary, whose design sense my mother always revered and whom we used to see sometimes for après-ski up at our cottage after she and her almost cartoon-comically handsome husband, Reg (who my mother unkindly offered was "all looks") retired to their Collingwood chalet full-time.

There is an entry for the wonderfully acerbic Nancy, who shared my mother's quick wit and sense of fun before being sideswiped by a stroke. And then Buffy, my mother's best friend growing up, a hippie and artist who always resisted her own mother's famous elegance. My mother always described falling in love with her on their first day at school, after this strange and scruffy little girl snuck up beside her in the playground and snarled, "Bugger, bugger, bugger!" in her ear.

According to my mother, my father never much enjoyed Buffy's prickly, assertive presence, although I know that she and my mother kept in touch even after Buffy moved away to live in an old farmhouse in Prince Edward county. Oddly, Buffy never showed up for my mother's funeral, but weeks afterward I received a cryptic note from her asking me to call, as she wanted to tell me "a few things about Susan" — an invitation to conversation as potentially intriguing as it was terrifying. What could her friend know about her that I, her eldest, did not?

Some weeks later, I did summon the courage to call her, but after exchanging the usual condolences and pleasantries, I could sense that she had lost her nerve. I'm not sure I had ever fully registered with her as a person of interest on the few occasions we had met over the years; I was just the daughter. Perhaps she decided that whatever dark secret it was that she had planned to share with me had best stay buried along with my mother, which, I have to admit, came as a relief.

There is no listing, of course, for Edith and Bunny — poor Edith having passed away and Bunny locked up just like my dad in some maximum-security zone of a senior's home. Or, for that matter, my mother's formerly dear pals Ann or Cynthia or Susie — all those relationships that got gummed up and worn out over the years like the cover of this black vinyl book on my desk.

A number for the beautiful Jane is here, even though we haven't seen her in ages. I haven't spoken to her since my mom died, even though Jane is the reason I went to Sarah Lawrence College. Tall and angular in the manner of a New England version of Virginia Woolf, Jane grew up in a grand apartment on Fifth Avenue in Manhattan that was rigged to the internal radio of the New York Fire Department—her father Judd was a fire nut who would run out in the middle of the night at the sounding of the alarm to take pictures of the famous fires that hung in the halls of the family's apartment.

We all became great pals on the beach in Barbados: my dad would play tennis with Jerry, my mom would tan and talk books on the beach with Jane and her wisecracking, leathery, and perma-tan mother, who we all called Mrs. Miller—even Jane. A Sarah Lawrence grad with a Harvard doctorate in early childhood education who adopted two kids until she finally had one of her own, Jane was like the smartest, coolest den mother imaginable to our pack of wild beach children running from villa to sandbar. She now runs a quirky old-school summer camp-slash-resort in Maine called Quisisana where the staff are all Juilliard students who stage musical productions each night after serving dinner. She bought it after her husband Jerry died, days after his fiftieth birthday, just like his father before him, despite his refusal of deli meats and his daily tennis regime.

Up until he could no longer recall it, my father would always marvel at his idiocy for failing to take Jerry's early advice and invest in a little company started by Jerry's college friend—somebody named Warren Buffett—which, of course, turned out to be Berkshire Hathaway.

Reading my mother's grubby little address book five years

after her death is a walk back in time, with the added poignancy of knowing how it all turns out in the end. But best of all, every resource and reference is organized according to my mother's strange, personal logic—always a particularly grey and impenetrable area—so perfectly preserved and set down here in her own unmistakable hand.

Tom, from Adanac Glass, is in there, as is Jane from Perfection Carpet and Sylvia from Stone Tile, each of them appearing in more than one alphabetical niche, as if under different guises (like Tom, who is under both "A" for Adanac and "G" for glass). So idiosyncratic was my mother's use of her chosen organizational resource that under the letter "P" is the PARA Paints code for what she described, in her customary scrawl, as "Paint Colour, living room."

It's funny how just seeing their randomly entered names reminds me of my mom, whose solution to any problem or difficulty would be to invoke one of the legends of her address book and their special powers, as in, "Just call Jane from Perfection Carpet, tell her you're my daughter and explain the situation..."

My father, too, had his special resourceful friends: the travel agent Tony (first name Ontario, known to his friends as Tony) Sarracini, who would be constantly recommended as the person to call immediately—first thing on Monday morning—about trying to get anything from seats together on the packed March break flight to Florida to a reservation at the hard-to-get-into Italian restaurant of the moment ("Just call Tony," my father would say. "He'll take care of it.") Oh and poor Jim Katsos, the electrician, whose unique powers my father so believed in that if he'd had his way we would have been calling him constantly. The poor man must now be so relieved that my parents are no longer able to exhort us to contact him, let alone place a call to him themselves.

Listings for trades like Ginger's Bath, Paris Kitchens, and California Closets served an obvious purpose; others such as "David, Hair," "Ruth (sculptress)," and "Bill, or Phil McDonald," less so. And then there are the entries which read more like mini-reviews, like: "Kaliyana—summer clothes and interesting stuff." Or offer detailed, if hard to decipher, driving directions to destinations that remain unnamed.

Under "L" there is Laiko from The Workroom, which is now long gone but was where my mother made sure to have all her custom headboards and Roman blinds made. Though it always cost a fortune, my mother would insist, with her somewhat racist perspective, that it was worth it, as the somewhat dour and rigorous Laiko and her team of Japanese seamstresses were almost obsessively meticulous. And under "A," presumably for artwork display and presentation, good old Neil Sharkey, who would come for an afternoon to each of our new houses after they were carpeted and painted to help my mother professionally hang all her art.

But where is Frank Ignani? Presumably gone to painter's heaven by now, but for decades it seemed he almost lived with us—like that painter in *Murphy Brown*, except Frank was his complete physical opposite. Frank was slim, pointy-featured, and elegant, and he and his meticulously attired crew were also kept constantly employed, maintaining every inch of my mother's painted-out moulding in perfect nick with creamy applications of lustrous semi-gloss (always in oil, never latex—"Iss no good, iss no last, thees plastic stuff," Frank would affirm, in between smokes in the garden, while on a break). Each morning Frank and his crew would appear fully dressed for their task in chef-styled white jackets and trousers and little small-brimmed hats, their brims emblazoned with the logo for PARA Paints, like cyclists racing in the Tour de France. I remember their tools, too, always kept in perfect order in a small and tidy semi-permanent installation in the basement, their expensive brushes perfectly clean at the day's end. Beautiful tools no weekend amateur would ever think to invest in or maintain to Frank's exacting standards.

Frank lived on the lake in Mimico with his family and we were once invited there for a huge Italian dinner with many courses that lasted for hours. The house, which was simple, but on an unbelievable lot that sloped right down to the water, must be gone now, no doubt replaced by some bloated plastic palazzo. (And no matter how grand the plan of that modern McMansion, the paint job inside could never measure up to one of Frank's.)

How horrified my mother would be, I often think, to see the crude ugliness of the world she left behind.

The pages under "H" in my mother's address book contain several otherwise unidentified listings—which to me can't but read like cries for "Help," although they probably refer more to that of the domestic variety rather than anything existential. Entries for nails and facials, too, figure prominently as pure categories, with numbers but no names to go on. Under "C," one can find "construction guy," also unnamed, but with the helpful addition, in brackets, of "(fence)." Under "G," of course, is the number for "Lamp Guy." I burst out laughing when I saw that in the Ns, my mother had written down a telephone number for someone listed only as "Neighbour."

And then it's just sad when I see her pencilled-in notation, under "D," in small capital letters, presumably written when she could no longer even make it out the front door to the LCBO, for Dial-a-Bottle.

Ten

SAMSARA BY GUERLAIN

I OFTEN DREAM OF my mother and in my dreams she is still alive. Sometimes the story is that she didn't really die but had simply had enough of all of us and ran off to live incognito and on her own in a small apartment. When I discover this I am both relieved that she is actually alive and deeply hurt that she would lie to us and let us go through all the pain of losing her. Or it's a dream that takes place in some alternate universe where she never got sick and old and is still pronouncing on things in her impossible way and dispensing the same unsolicited advice as she did in her prime, and I am annoyed by it in exactly the same way I was when she was alive.

My daughter Sophie says that she too often dreams of my mother. And that sometimes, when she wakes up after dreaming of her, she swears that her bedroom actually smells of my mother's perfume.

The other night I dreamt that I was with my friend Martha and her two daughters, Nuala and Lucy, who in my dream are still teenagers even though they are now young women. All of us are sitting around the coffee table in my living room and I am trying my best to engage the girls in the conversation by doing a sort of simultaneous, UN-style translation of what my mother, who is sitting with us at the far end of the table and characteristically banging on about something or other, is actually trying to say.

Gesturing over to my mother, saying something like, "Well, girls, you know how Susan…" and, leaning in toward them to fill in the background, I try to explain whatever nonsense my mother was just going on about, which in the dream is unclear, when I see that the girls are totally silent and looking at me wide-eyed as if I am completely insane.

Martha, who in real life has an innate understanding of human dynamics and always seems to know what is going on even when I am cluelesss, leans over and very, very gently says to me, "Kar—the girls don't see your mother here with us now because your mother is dead."

It is unclear to me even when I wake up whether Martha could see her too, or whether my dream-mother was invisible to all but me. The only thing that is certain is, like the lingering scent of her perfume, she is gone but refuses to be forgotten.

IT'S BEEN A LONG DAY. Ever since I ran out the door first thing this morning for the hairdresser's, wardrobe choices in one hand and a coffee and my notes for the day in the other, it's been non-stop action. We are in the midst of shooting *The Goods*, this TV show my pal Martha and I came up with for the Life Network, and we had the brilliant idea to shoot it out on location, so not only am I on camera all day talking to people and trying to be interesting, I have to fix my makeup and change my outfit for different episodes in between locations in my car. It's our second season and they want fifty-two episodes (in something like sixty-five shoot days), so my schedule is beyond packed. Some nights, after a full day on camera, I have to run out after dinner to one of the editing suites (we have two going full tilt, 24/7, to meet our delivery obligations to the network) to look at footage or to the recording studio to do voice-overs. As if that weren't quite enough on my plate, one morning a week I have to file my newspaper column before running to the office to meet with the production staff to go over that week's stories for the show. Plus one week a month, we are on the road, shooting all day in another city, which is fun, but exhausting, doing all that packing and unpacking and worrying about the kids' schedules for the time I'll be out of town. And at the end of each day when I am in town, just like tonight, I have to run home, be a mother and a wife, make dinner, and get my two school-age kids bathed and into bed.

Whenever we speak on the phone and I mention even in passing how gruelling I'm finding my schedule and how exhausted I am, my mother is still unimpressed. "Well, you do have Beth," points out my mother, who, since her thirties, has relied on a significant support staff to do everything from slice the vegetables for dinner to iron my dad's jeans, despite never taking on a project anywhere near the scale of this one. I know that she is too envious of the opportunities I've had to be able to be truly sympathetic, but it is still a drag to hear her bang on about my good fortune and how much easier everything is for me because Thomas is so helpful, etc., etc. Particularly those nights when she calls late and I can hear in her slurry, stupid voice that she's fully loaded. Sometimes I grit my teeth and try to just put up with the barely veiled insults and the long, drawn-out pauses that come before she starts crying. Other nights, I just don't pick up the phone — thanks to a wonderful new development we pay extra for known as call display.

Tonight I rush in the door to find the kids in a dull, glazed heap in front of the living-room television. Sophie and Philip, who have likely had a long day at public school, look tired. They barely acknowledge my presence, but as soon as I join them on the sofa, I know that my mother has been here because I can smell her on their clothes and in their hair. Beth, the unbelievably even-tempered and patient living saint who has been our nanny since Sophie was six months old, walks in before heading home.

"Mrs. Young was here," says Beth. "She told me I could go home but she seemed like she maybe had been drinking, so I stayed until you came."

No wonder the kids are so tired. I thank her and tell her goodnight, silently thankful that my mother has given up and left before I got in. Beth has put out a little snack for the kids (cut-up apples and carrots) to keep them going till I got home for dinner, but the poor things have had to deal with my mother. I go and open the windows wide to let in some fresh air before heading to the kitchen. The smell of her in the house is so strong it's almost nauseating.

SMELLY, DRAMATIC, AND LOUD, along with being a knock-out in the looks department, my mother didn't tread lightly. Whatever fancy car she was driving was always banged up and battered as if she had a sideline in the demolition derby. On closer inspection, her designer clothes were always spotted with bits of food, her hair flecked with debris; her dinner plate looked like a Jackson Pollock after she had done with it.

And yes, she did also make a big olfactory impression. Back when she openly smoked, she smelled of cigarettes. Later in life, a near-constant fug of vodka emanated from her pores (anyone who thinks vodka is odourless has never spent much time in the company of someone who drinks a lot of it). Throughout, top notes of Listerine, which she swigged from a lipstick-marked bottle she kept in her purse, added to her unique personal aura. Perhaps as a result she began dousing herself extremely liberally with fragrance. The way some people might use body lotion or moisturizer, my mother used perfume. Her chosen scent thus formed no small part of her lingering impression—so much so that after even a short visit with their grandmother, my children's fresh young heads would, somewhat disturbingly, reek, deep into their scalps, of her special *odeur*.

When I think about it, my mother's favourite joke her entire life involved perfume. It was a silly, knock-knock kind of joke, but it drove her into fits of laughter every time she thought of it.

"Why do I get a headache whenever I use toilet water?" my mother would ask innocently, only the mischievous yellow gleam in her eyes giving her away.

Even though I knew perfectly well where this was headed, I would play along and ask why she thought it was that toilet water in particular gave her a headache.

"Because the toilet seat keeps falling on my head!" she would shriek with the glee of a five-year-old who had never before heard anything so hysterical.

While she was more likely in practice to employ heavy doses of *eau de parfum* than the toilet-water version of a fragrance, of course every single thing in her closet, let alone the satin and fur-lined surfaces of her succession of interiors, smelled as if she had sprayed it with her scent like an animal marking territory. Whenever you sat down on one of the chairs or sofas, an enveloping cloud would rise up from the upholstery like a Susan May–scented air freshener. And long after she had left any room she ever entered (including the rooms of my own home following one of her state visits), the *sillage* of her scent would linger on, wafting up from the carpet and lurking in corners.

Scent, like music, has an ephemeral quality that is nonetheless expressive. That the scents we are drawn to somehow correspond to our stage in life and have the ability to convey our moods are things that I learned, like most everything I know, from breathing in the air around my mother.

When I was a little girl and my mother was aspiring to the classic chic of a Parisienne, I recall her chosen scent as the ladylike, somewhat powdery Madame Rochas.

As with an Hermès scarf or a Ferragamo pump, it was a

somewhat safe, conservative choice, veering on the edge of matronly but exuding old-world good taste and sophistication, particularly on a younger woman; it was like choosing to wear a simple black sheath dress to a cocktail party. And of course it was, just like everything desirable back in the early '60s, from Catherine Deneuve to the recipes in *Mastering the Art of French Cooking*, almost essentially, iconically French.

Like the legendary Chanel No. 5—the world's bestselling scent ever since Marilyn Monroe scandalously quipped that it was the only thing she ever wore to bed—Madame Rochas is what is known in the highly technical world of fragrance as an "aldehydic floral," a scent that manages to be crisp, yet warm, with base notes of sandalwood and amber, and a heart of rose de Mai, jasmine, and lily of the valley—all "lifted" with synthetic aldehydes and top notes of bergamot and lemon. To me, Madame Rochas still smells assured and deeply feminine, if a little dusty with time, like the far corners of a lingerie dresser drawer that is rarely opened. If it were a colour, it would be an old-fashioned, European rose gold.

The next scent I recall my mother wearing was the splashy, pungent Joy by Jean Patou, marketed as "the world's most expensive perfume" back in 1929 at the start of the Great Depression—a somewhat counter-intuitive approach that proved remarkably successful. Despite its famously steep price, which was justified by the wild extravagance of its makers' distillation of the precious essences of some ten thousand jasmine flowers and twenty-eight dozen roses to create just a single 30–ml flask of the *parfum*, Joy is still, after Chanel No. 5, the world's second best-selling scent of all time.

Reputedly the favourite scent of Jackie O, which is how I suspect my mother first fell under its sway, and packaged in a smashing, Baccarat-like bottle with a golden thread wound around its neck, Joy enjoyed a cocaine-like bump of popularity again in the early '70s. Such a status object was the bottle alone that I remember my mother's half-empty one on display against a glass mirror in our front hall powder room back in the day. The very essence of excess, the self-described "light avalanche of flowers" of its honey-like liquor was an instant signifier of extravagance and opulence, capturing that era's embrace of over-the-top luxury. All you needed was a small drop of this bottled joie-de-vivre, and you smelled like you had spent a wild night in a bed of roses. (Or, more accurately, according to its packaging, a bed of roses topped with ylang-ylang, jasmine, and tuberose with base notes of sensual musk, sandalwood, and civet.) It's been a while since I sniffed an open bottle of Joy, but I imagine that if I did, I would get an instant headache.

Joy might have been the perfect scent for a diva-in-training, one merely approaching full flower. But it required Yves Saint-Laurent's notoriously stinky Opium to take my mother's growing powers of sensory occupation to a whole new level.

When Saint Laurent launched Opium in 1977, newspaper accounts report that the legendary fashion designer threw a party in New York's East Harbor on a ship called the *Peking*, which he filled with exotic treasures from the Orient including a thousand-pound bronze Buddha surrounded by mounds of white Cattleya orchids; society scribe and Studio 54 regular Truman Capote reportedly stood, oracle-like, at the helm.

This no-holds-barred approach was echoed in the thick, spicy wallop of the scent, which crammed, amongst other essences, jasmine, carnation, myrrh, patchouli, clove, cinnamon, vanilla, sandalwood, incense, and musk into a distinctive red plastic case fashioned after the lacquered boxes called *inro* that were traditionally worn under the kimonos of noblewomen to hold perfumes, herbs, and medicine.

My mother, already a huge fan of both YSL and pretty much any and all representations of Oriental exoticism, wouldn't have needed much prodding to have tried the scent, which immediately caused a sensation with its controversial name and highly sensual ad campaign featuring naked women, including, in the Tom Ford days for the house, a gorgeously milky Sophie Dahl in the throes of what looked like drug- and sex-inspired ecstasy. No stranger to controversy over ad campaigns, having himself posed naked (but for his trademark spectacles) for his first men's scent, Pour Homme, back in 1971, Saint Laurent was (somewhat fairly, in retrospect) accused of glamourizing drug use via the new scent's name, which of course only helped to turn Opium into a pop phenomenon. And the spicy cinnabar-red of its logo was right on the money. If the woman who wore Madame Rochas or Chanel No. 5 was buttoned-up and classic, this was a big, bad scent for a woman who took no prisoners and harboured many, mostly naughty secrets. No Catherine Deneuve in a tailored suit or even Jackie O in her oval sunglasses and white capris here, but a full-blown Madame Butterfly onstage at the Met—or one of the power bitches with their giant-shouldered taffeta gowns from TV's *Dynasty*.

It was a scent by Guerlain, however, that, during the last decade of my mother's life, she so liberally applied that she was almost dipped in it. Combined as it was with alcohol and mouthwash, this was the enveloping toxic cloud that marked my children's heads and remained trapped in my mother's clothes and in her furniture after she was gone. According to the folks at Guerlain, in 1989 Jean-Paul Guerlain himself created Samsara for the love of his life from opulent florals such as iris, narcissus, violet, and rose with juicy top notes of ylang-ylang, lemon, and peach. It freaks me out just to read, on the brand's corporate site, of Guerlain's almost Jungian intention:

> Samsara signifies "eternal rebirth" in Sanskrit and is part of the "wheel of life," a religious reference of Tibetan Buddhism. It evokes the perpetual voyage from one existence to the next, an invitation to serenity and harmony... The bottle is a flamboyant red, a sacred colour, which evokes through the fullness of its shape a statue of a Khmer dancer. The stopper echoes the shape of the eye of the Buddha, a symbol of meditation, which leads the way to supreme awakening.

Sometimes near the end it felt like my mom knew she was on her way out of this life. If only I could believe that a meditative state of "supreme awakening" had marked her final journey.

FRAGRANCE HAS AN OLD STORY, perhaps one as old as narrative. Along with sacrificing men and beasts, early, terrified pagans burned fragrant offerings like herbs and roots as a plea to their gods for protection. Incense, which has been found to exist in relics as far back as 2000 B.C., not only served to perfume the mystical path to the spirit world, its scented smoke was considered purifying. In ancient Assyria, incense was burned for cleansing after sex, like a smoke bidet. In other parts of the classical world, meanwhile, the perfumed smoke was for setting the scene before getting it on, much like lighting a Diptyque candle and putting on some R&B today. Both Sappho and Ovid wrote on the erotic properties of incense, and it is said that Egyptian women used to fumigate their vaginas—while conveniently also perfuming their clothes and hair—by smoking them with myrrh (apparently some Yemeni women today still stand, skirts open wide, over incense burners, although I cannot confirm that I have ever observed this fascinating-sounding ritual first-hand).

Like the ancient Greeks, the Egyptians burned perfumed resins as offerings to their gods (giving us the name "perfume" from the Latin *per fumum*, meaning "from smoke," via the Roman observers of these rites). They also wrapped their dead Pharaohs in cloth infused with aromatic oils to assure their papyrus boats would float on into the afterworld for eternity.

Actually the ancient Egyptians were particularly nuts about fragrance: Egyptian noblewomen were said to have sported cones of perfumed wax embedded in their coiled hairstyles. Each of these crazy head-candles contained a wick that, when lit, released a slow trickle of scented wax that enveloped them in fragrance (too bad about the melted wax over all those asymmetrical flax tunics). Cleopatra herself reputedly travelled with so much scent on the sails of her barges, one could smell her approach across the water.

My mother, then, who was typically more connected to pagan ritual than any more contemporary form of observance, was merely making like her distant diva ancestor. But there was also something of her strange otherworldliness in this heavy perfume habit. One that she could keep conveniently obscured under all that captivating, scented mist.

IF MY MOTHER HAD been born in Salem, Massachusetts, during the time of the witch hunts, I have absolutely zero doubt that she would have ended up burned at the stake. Never the most tactful in her sharing of various readings of situations or predictions of what would come to pass (typically delivered for added emphasis with the theatrical accompaniment of a sly, knowing brow and a witch-like, pointing finger), she would never have been able to keep her special gifts of observation to herself, let alone under the necessary wraps.

And really, it was uncanny the things she would say. One summer, while I was in graduate school, my mother and I took the opportunity to travel together for a few days in Paris before meeting up with the rest of the family for a holiday at an Italian villa (memorable, ever-afterward, for my father's truly terrible Italian — of a skirt my sister was trying on, he suggested to the boutique owner that it was perhaps "*piccolo grande*," meaning, in his highly simplified version of the Italian language, "a little too big." Also, how the Italian farmers laughed after him, "*Scampi, scampi*" whenever my dad went for a run around the fields of grapevines near our villa — at that time absolutely no one ran anywhere in Italy unless perhaps they were being chased by the *carabinieri*). Back in Paris, my mother and I shared a tiny and dark but dead-chic room at L'Hotel on the Left bank, famous as the last stop of the brilliant Oscar Wilde. This was before the hotel had been renovated and spruced up as it has been today, and I recall there was a live, if shopworn, feathered green parrot in the bar, where my mother held court in the evenings with the resident bohemian, mostly gay male, clientele.

After a few wonderful days of hanging out in grand cafés, shopping in boutiques, and wandering through museums, I mentioned casually, over a glass of Chablis, largely for the sake of conversation, that I had met a boy that year at school who was spending his summer fighting fires in the wilds of British Columbia. I said nothing more about him, other than that he was tall and funny and seemed nice. At that point, I wasn't particularly sure myself how I felt about him. We had only just become friends and the only reason I had brought him up in conversation was to describe his unusual summer job. But the very first thing my mother said, looking straight into my eyes (and this was hardly the kind of subject she was particularly obsessed with or fixated on), was that this boy I had so casually just mentioned, the one I hardly knew and whom she had never met or even heard a word about until that very moment, was — "Mark my words, Karen"—the man I was going to marry. A statement that was so out there that it was completely and utterly absurd. How could she possibly arrive at such an extreme conclusion? What on earth could she possibly be basing it on? And then the weirdest thing about it was that she turned out to be right.

And then there was the time, after Thomas and I were indeed married, that my mother told me I was pregnant before I myself had any idea of this sudden physiological turn of events—a snap diagnosis based upon nothing more, according to her, than the way my voice sounded ("fuller") while we were talking *over the phone*. To this day, I still cannot fathom how this feat of communication was possible. But that was what it was like to know my mother. And then an enormous amount of what she said was just outrageous bullshit tossed out entirely for effect, but one never really knew, and of course that was all part of her mystique.

It is entirely possible, however, that as a witch who could occasionally see into the future, she also had the ability to curse or smite you with a glance if she so chose. I remember how, some months into this same pregnancy my mother had first intuited, I was feeling quite pleased with myself because, following the personal instruction of none other than the scandalous Christine Keeler (whom I happened to have been squiring around on a publicity tour for a film called *Scandal* about her involvement in the notorious Profumo affair), I had been rubbing olive oil on my pregnant belly to prevent stretch marks—a strategy which appeared, at least so far, to be working. A happy state of affairs which I innocently reported to my mother, who, it must be said, had ended up terribly scarred from her own pregnancies. All she said, looking at me sideways across my midsection, was, "Well, they do tend to come in a bit *lower* down." And then lo and behold, undressing that very night I felt compelled to look down, way down, underneath my growing belly—to discover that despite my daily Christine Keeler–prescribed ministrations, the first signs of what looked undeniably like stretch marks had decided to make an appearance.

And then our darling first child, Sophie, whose earliest essence my mother had somehow intuited, ended up with Susan May's same mischievous smile, her same improbable hazel eyes that light up like topaz, and her same deep and mysterious understanding, way beyond my operating level (naturally, my mother offered during my pregnancy, not once, but on several occasions, that she felt that the name "Susan" was really a very lovely name for a girl). And then the two, who did not end up sharing the same first name (I'm such a party pooper) nonetheless turned out to be soulmates. By the time Sophie was old enough to be a bona fide companion (which came early in my Sophie's case), she and my mother would meet regularly for tea, where they would show up dressed to the nines and share secrets for hours like two sleek and beautiful felines.

"Nan is so amazing. She just *gets* everything," Sophie would say, her lovely wrist festooned with a pretty new bangle from my mother's collection. "I can talk to her about anything and I don't have to go into any kind of long drawn-out explanation."

The note from my mother, folded and stuffed into Sophie's purse afterwards, would often, like her birthday cards and letters, feature a stylized line drawing, usually of Sophie's lovely face, quickly sketched in black ballpoint pen on simple white writing paper with the words, "Love, love, love you"—always written on her notes to each of us three times, as if the ritual of putting down in print her extravagant devotion might somehow impart extra love and luck.

When I think about it, my mother's entire relationship with any science or philosophy was a more medieval sort of metaphysics—the kind of old wives' wisdom based on early concepts such as the humours. She truly believed, for instance, that dining rooms and sets of china should never, under any circumstance, be blue. ("It's a bad colour for digestion.") According to her, people such as herself, born under the sign of Pisces, "All suffer problems with their feet." While the advent of windy weather could be counted on to cause scenes because "Wind makes people crazy."

Another suspicious factor that might have weighed against her with the Puritanical townfolk of Salem was my mother's almost unshakeable belief in ritual. Being the main acolyte of the one true church of Susan May inside her own head, these little rites she practiced and incantations she uttered were not prescribed by any mainstream, widely accepted faith, but rather were observances entirely of her own making. Of course she would never have described them as such. To her, it was just the way things should be done.

Along with practically bathing herself in her chosen incense and repeating certain phrases for emphasis like "Love, love, love," my mother never left the house without applying several rounds of dark eyeliner and bright lipstick and several layers of big, bold jewellery—and was incredulous that I didn't always do the same.

"You know, whenever I heard your father pulling up in the driveway, I would just run to a mirror and put on a little lipstick," my mother would inform me, instructively. "Every woman looks better with just a little bit of lipstick on."

If she were getting ready to go to a party, before putting on any makeup, she would go to the fridge, take out an ice cube, and rub it over her face, with extra attention to the under-eye area. "It gets rid of any puffiness," she would explain.

If we were down south or anywhere tropical and she came across a hibiscus in flower, she would immediately pull off a single bloom and stick it behind one ear, as if she were Carmen Miranda about to start a musical number. If we were up at the cottage or anywhere near a body of water, she would start her day with a "morning swim" which was more of a dip than any committed form of exercise; somehow, though—perhaps one summer at a cottage with my grandparents on some northern lake somewhere—she had mastered what must be acknowledged as a nice front crawl, and would always emerge from the water smiling wide and gasping with refreshment like someone in a Nestea ad.

After an afternoon nap, which she would always refer to as "crawling back into bed," she could then be counted on to emerge half-dressed in one of my dad's T-shirts into the kitchen to "have a little *schtikl* of something," typically a crust of bread, unceremoniously ripped off a baguette, or a chunk pried loose of whatever might be leftover in the fridge, eaten with her hands and standing up, because that way it didn't really count.

Her preferred cup of coffee was served "black, black," a form of stylistic repetition she might also employ to describe temperature—as in "watch out, that plate is hot, hot"—or depth of colour—so that a sky being described as "blue, blue" might be like the colour reached when the ordinary blue of the sky is mathematically squared.

As a creative person, the strange argot of the design world was her true second language. It was tremendously unfortunate, for instance, if your interior or outfit lacked "flow." Flow, to her, was a good thing and absolutely essential, somewhat like the Chinese concept of "chi," to both the creation of ambience and one's all-around happiness and well-being. If your interior was so unfortunate as to lack this particular quality, it was likely that you hadn't started out with a "good overall concept" and then "carried it through."

Anything well-proportioned, sparkling, or notable that caught her eye might prove to be "a good example of…" (fill in the dots here, from French deco to the "craft tradition following the Brighton Pavilion"). If not, it would be simply written off as "purely ordinary"—a slight in her books if there ever was one, meaning that it would be unlikely to assist in the greater effort of Making a Design Statement.

To that end, there was no such thing as overstatement. A book she enjoyed would be "a great read," possibly "tremendous," or even "significant." A night at the opera would be "magnificent," "superb," or perhaps even "a total disaster." Nothing was ever just "nice," or "fine," or, God forbid, "pretty," my mother being entirely dismissive of mere prettiness in favour of people, material objects, events, and phenomena that could be described as somehow "interesting" or, her all-time favourite descriptive, "important."

Heavy of foot and a smasher open of doors, you wouldn't only sense her approach from the familiarity of her perfume but also the musical accompaniment of her presence. The clash of an armful of bangles, the jingle of a Navajo belt slung low over the hip, the drop of her tapestry handbag on the floor, or the clang of an earring against the phone receiver—the animate sounds of her well-chosen accessories formed part of her greeting and the orchestral prelude to her arrival as much as the language of her dress.

My first language was my mom's own, and it was as all-enveloping as her perfume. When we were little and she was tucking us into bed, she would draw letters on our backs with a great flourish, and we would have to guess what the letters were, which always felt sort of tickly and incredibly relaxing at the same time. And then she would sing us her own Broadway-style variation on the tune of "Goodnight Ladies": "Goo—ooo-d night, Karen (or Jennifer or Joshua), see you in the mo—or-ning," before kissing us loudly with a smack on the ear and whispering, as if it were a secret incantation, "Sleep tight, don't let the bed bugs bite."

I was instructed, early, never to step on cracks. To look down my nose or toss salt if I were ever to say anything that might encourage the gods to think twice about our good fortune.

Sometimes even now when I cross the street, I can still hear the musical nursery rhyme my mother taught me about pedestrian safety when I was little: "Look to the left and look to the right, and you'll never, ever, get run O-ver." It was reassuring, the way my mother always sang it like a protective chant whenever we crossed the street together. And then, when it came time to teach them about cars, I sang it myself to my own children.

While it might have kept us from being completely flattened by a passing vehicle, it was no guarantee that we would never be hurt.

IT IS AMAZING TO me still, even as I write these words, that my mother remained so plugged in to her own inner voice throughout her life that she even knew when she was going to die. I got a call from her one morning while she was in Mount Sinai, supposedly "recovering" from her last surgical procedure—the one before she stopped being able to breathe on her own and ended up on a ventilator in the ICU.

"Karen, you have *got* to get me out of here! These doctors here are trying to kill me!" she was saying, in her usual overemphatic fashion, except this time with some real underlying panic.

Not knowing what else to do, and, basically trying to just get her off the phone so we don't have to talk about her dying anymore, I tried my best to calm her down.

"You're in one of the best hospitals in the country, Mom. I'm sure you are getting the best possible care. And besides, where else am I going to take you? Please stop worrying, I am sure you are going to start feeling better soon."

But of course, and as always, she was right.

Eleven

SILVER SATIN SOFAS

AFTER THE WORST HAS really happened and my mother
dies, and it's determined that in order to pay for my father's
care we will have to put my parents' condo on the market,
it dawns on us that we have to somehow start dealing with
all of the stuff that's still in it.

Before we even sit down to start dividing the spoils (one
family get-together I am not particularly looking forward
to), the idea comes up that maybe we should get some sort
of assessment of what some of the major pieces are worth,
so that we can each make an informed decision about what
we might want to keep and what we should try to sell.

So I call my friend Steve, who happens to run a major
auction house and so is fully *au courant* on the market value
of antiques as well as works of contemporary art, both of
which are well represented in my mother's collection. A
lifelong work which, I am only just beginning to discover,

seems to have largely survived my parents' various moves and attempts to downsize. In fact it has survived so well that, opening drawers and closets, I am shocked to find bits of broken Georgian silver my mother must have held on to since her windfall in the haunted house on Millbank, stacks of linen, and all manner of glass vases and multiplicities of serving pieces literally stuffed rows deep into each nook and cranny of their surprisingly capacious condo storage. And that's not counting the obvious stuff that's right out there on full display, like my mother's huge, nineteenth-century Russian crystal chandelier, hanging above the Georgian mahogany dining table which in turn is surrounded by chocolate-brown suede Breuer chairs on the Aubusson carpet, all of which is set in front of a French nineteenth-century *grise* marble-and-iron console that's naturally flanked by a pair of enormous Chinese celadon planters — sitting watch over all of which is the Yves Klein–blue face of Chairman Mao by Andy Warhol. And that's just what's in the dining room.

Steve kindly agrees to meet me one morning the following week at my parents' place and help me sort it out. Having arrived early, with a fortifying Americano in one hand and a foolscap pad ready for taking notes in the other, I open the sliding glass doors onto the balcony to let some fresh air into the stale apartment. Sitting down on one of the silver satin sofas, I am immediately enveloped in a residual cloud of my mother's Samsara perfume, now even more nauseating, like the overpowering smell of lilies on a coffin.

I don't know if this is just a holdover from the intense strain of watching my mother slip away into final unconsciousness, or exhaustion from the months of worry and hospital visits, but here, in my parents' uncomfortably quiet apartment, empty now except for all their beautiful precious things, I am completely overwhelmed by the task ahead of me. It is all, quite simply, too much.

Not only does this job of disassembling this *gesamtkunstwerk* of my mother's seem impossibly insurmountable, like climbing a slippery satin Everest, but at this precise moment, with the clear light of day shining into the room, suddenly Susan May's special grey just looks shabby and sad. All of her beautiful things, so artfully arranged, now seem worn and tired. There are cracks and flaws in the frames and edges of marble and mirror, and the once gleaming silk and satin surfaces are stained and frayed at the seams, like theatrical costumes backstage after the house lights have been turned on.

When my mother was alive and at her best, everything had seemed so beautiful and sparkling, but slowly, over time, it had all become ugly, and almost false. This shift of perception came on so swiftly, it felt like I had just been awakened from a spell in a ballet based on a fairy tale. And I hadn't really even noticed everything changing around me in the last act until it was over and she was dead.

IF MY MOTHER WERE a superhero — and at the height of her formidable powers, her "prime" as she would have called it, that never felt entirely inconceivable — her secret power would have been the ability to transform any living space into something beautiful, and her cape would have been a silvery grey.

From the day she left Queen Mary Drive to begin creating homes of her own, from our first upper-duplex flat to my parents' last condominium apartment, my mother took on a succession of increasingly fabulous spaces, each with their own challenges (and, at least at the start, with very little money to work with), and managed to turn them into her own exquisite fantasy of the good life, one that was sumptuous with rich tactile surfaces shimmering with light and beautiful, notable *objets*.

Like nearly everything about my mother, her grey was a special mix. The complete, enveloping feeling of entering her rooms was like flying into the middle of a cloud on an airplane, or slipping into the cool of a silvery lake. Every surface was composed to come together as a visual symphony of monochromatic elegance with her at the baton. An orchestration of greys sliding into silver that was designed to shine and sparkle in highlights, yet ultimately to sweep one away with the all-encompassing totality of its vision.

As far as my mother was concerned, taste could be good or bad, but never without importance. Beauty to her was a truth, perhaps the only one really worth living for. And over the decades, Aubusson by armoire, bibelot by bergère — all gathered on trips and spotted with her educated eye in antique markets, art galleries, and ateliers — she built and carefully curated a sort of impenetrable fortress for us, where nothing ugly was permitted to enter and every angle provided a visual delight. Seamless, always, in its use of her signature grey on everything from the walls to the furniture and the broadloom, her vision, realized, was so ultimately her. And while she was alive, we all were

264

engulfed in the magic and mystery of its silvery sway.

Here, from a magazine story I wrote for a September 1999 issue of *House & Home* on their latest residence at the time—a semi-detached Rosedale townhouse in "original condition" on a ravine, which my mother attacked with a full-frontal renovation after reluctantly parting with the grander home on the park where my husband and I were married—is my mother on her own design scheme: "I lived with this grey, which is really a dove-brown colour tinged with purple, for years...But the most important thing about all-grey is the way it flows."

Beside the story's gorgeous opening shot of her grey dining room is a picture of my mother talking on the phone in her all-grey kitchen. Her hair is quite short, shorter than I remember, and the wings framing the sides of her face have not yet been left to reveal the natural silver underneath her professionally-coloured chestnut-brown hair.

Nonetheless, in an accompanying (grey) sidebar are Susan's Tips on Going Grey. "Pick the right grey. Good greys aren't true grey, which is too blue and cold...Grey you can live with is the colour of warm, natural stone."

Thinking no doubt of her most fanciful addition to this perfect grey envelope of refinement, her living-room furniture—a pair of square-shouldered contemporary Lawson sofas and an armless side chair with a decorative scroll back—all absurdly upholstered in glistening silver satin, as if from the movie set of a Hollywood film about a glamorous New York debutante, my mother goes on to add: "One of my favourite looks is classic '30s Hollywood glamour. I love shine and reflection and my grey actually enhances the light."

Like the great starlets of Hollywood studios, who knew just where to stand and offer their good side to the cameras, star quality in decorating, according to my mother, was all about the manipulation of light. In order to soar above the realm of the expected, her signature colour scheme had to transcend grey's earthly hues into the metallic range.

As she prescribes: "Maximize your light. All-grey can look dull without reflection. Add shine with glass, mirrors, satin, and silver."

Like one of my mother's main gurus, Billy Haines, a failed actor who achieved renown for his ultra-glamorous Hollywood Regency–style interiors, my mother even looked at material for its light-conveying qualities. "Think of texture itself as an accent — it will add light. Introduce the sheen of silk and the gloss of lacquer, marble, and stone. Satin with flat linen velvet is divine . . . All my furniture was upholstered in this wonderful silver satin to catch the light and it just works."

Add her characteristic vigorous and sweeping flourishes of one heavily be-ringed hand for emphasis, and you get the picture.

OF COURSE, MY MOTHER always imagined herself a star. And she never wanted to be anything but extraordinary. Perhaps the best illustration of her level of commitment to living beyond the pale was her decision to upholster her living-room sofas in an extremely delicate and costly silk satin from the venerable fabric house of Scalamandré that was the colour of mercury. Highly impractical, absurdly fabulous, it was a bold stroke meant to stave off the commonplace by being so over-the-top, it would be forever memorable.

What my mother had, even more than her uncanny intuition and decorating smarts, was style. Style in the way she dressed and the way she spoke and the way she thought, which is a rarer gift than many.

When my parents' last dog, a huge, handsome, but not overly bright yellow Lab named Dexter (who actually, on reflection, looked an awful lot like a canine version of my dad), grew too fond of spending his nights snoring atop the gleaming silk satin of the living-room sofas, my mother devised a preventive measure that was wonderfully clever while also demonstrating a certain visual consistency and material logic. Every night before turning out the lights and heading up to bed she would instruct "the help" to roll out sheets of tin foil over the sofas' delicate seat cushions. As a protective barrier, it proved surprisingly effective, the loud crinkliness of the foil scary enough to dissuade poor, dumb Dexter from climbing up to sleep like a fairy-tale prince on the delicate satin sofas. From a purely visual standpoint, the improvised metallic slipcovers were also so smashing atop the silver satin in her all-grey interior that it looked as if she had custom-ordered them from Alcan.

AT A CERTAIN POINT I just stopped going out for lunch with my father. It probably seemed abrupt (and perhaps, given where he ended up, on the edge of selfish), but really it was about self-preservation. I just couldn't take the head trip he could be counted on to lay on me about my mother.

"You know, your mother really is a serious alcoholic," my father would say, biting into his ham and cheese (on rye, with mustard). "No, I mean serious. She really needs some help. The other night I came home and she was just wasted. I mean really, really loaded," he adds, loudly slurping his soup. "Clearly she had been drinking all day. And it was just five in the afternoon!"

Pushing away the sympathetic thoughts I just know he is aiming for with this unwelcome information (poor, poor Dad and what he has to put up with!), I ask whether they might, just possibly, have had a teensy disagreement or maybe even a fight the night before.

"Well, I can't see what that might have to do with it!" my father says, smacking his crusts down on the little sandwich plate, clearly indignant with offence. I am just supposed to be listening to him and feeling sorry for his plight, not asking annoying questions.

"Well, maybe Mum was feeling upset because you have been yelling at her?" I ask, quickly adding, "Of course, I know she shouldn't drink so much. But don't you think it might be hard sometimes living with you, too?"

My Dad's unbelievably square jaw somehow gets squarer, his Windex-blue eyes narrow into splinters of ice, and I can see the veins in his neck bulging.

"Where on earth did you get the idea I was yelling?" my dad yells, banging his plate on the counter so that the other patrons at Cake Master start to look at us. "Your mother is the one with the problem! She should be in some kind of institution. I don't know why this conversation has started becoming some kind of crazy feminist accusation session."

And then, after a beat, the inevitable, "This is totally inappropriate!" (One of my father's favourite phrases of condemnation, entirely indicative of his worldview: it is he who sits in judgement, while the rest of us must aspire to meet his standards.) "The point I am making here is about your mother…"

Whatever had gone on between them or whoever bore the chief responsibility for the volatility of their relationship was a constant grey area. The only truth one could ever come to was that nothing between the two of them was ever going to be black and white. More like an impenetrable grey that matched my mother's signature colour scheme. And one that my siblings and I were made to feel was the evocation of some kind of terrible sadness they each were suffering and that we were somehow supposed to try to fix, which of course would always be impossible.

And then, after the latest crisis or blow-up or series of accusations, our strange and self-involved parents would retreat into the perfect beauty of their gunpowder-grey lair to lick their wounds and hide, incommunicado, until the mist had settled and they could emerge again, looking fabulous and in high-spirits as if nothing unpleasant had ever happened inside their silver cloud, either the week before or, ever in their lives, really. And we three would be forced to play along and pretend it was all just as perfect and beautiful and sparkling as it looked, because that was the unspoken deal.

GREY HAS A BAD reputation. The colour of nuns' habits and soulless armies of identical suits in the financial district, it has associations of dullness and conformity. According to surveys in both Europe and America, grey is one of the least popular colours amongst both men and women, although a large segment of the respondents were so indifferent to it, they were undecided (okay, I just made that last part up, but it amused me).

Grey, too, is the colour of ashes, and so a religious symbol of mourning and repentance. It's also the natural colour of undyed wool, so it was first associated with the dress of peasants and the poor, which is how it became the hue of choice for Franciscan monks aiming to wear their humility and modesty on their robed sleeves. Hence the hue's stylistic associations with purity and the resulting spiritual superiority and elegance.

In nineteenth-century Paris, the uniforms of the factories and ateliers were typically grey—*gris*—which gave rise to the female workers being called *"grisettes."* Street prostitutes, too, were known as *grisettes,* even though it's unlikely they adopted the somber tone for their working attire. In Parisian slang of the era, being *gris* also meant being drunk, presumably given that when one becomes even pleasantly inebriated, everything seems hazy.

Our more recent associations with the colour centre around war, industrialization, and the resultant modernism in art and architecture. The Bauhaus, for instance, eagerly embraced it for its Machine Age industrial chic. The colourless hue of concrete and city pavement, grey has an urban, urbane cool. To paraphrase one of my mother's chief gurus, Diana Vreeland, grey is perhaps the richest, thinnest colour on the wheel for its disciplined lack of indulgence. Which is perhaps why the choice speaks of a certain restraint and refinement, with its associations of Zen minimalist architecture and the cool rejection of lesser, brasher colours by stylish refuseniks from Jil Sander to Yohji Yamamoto. Refined and disciplined, true, but at the same time grey defies focus, stubbornly insistent on remaining vague. However one attempts to "read" a grey, it's the direct opposite of black and white.

While my mother was so firmly adamant in her many opinions (particularly on the subject of anyone else's transgressions) that it could definitely be said of her that she saw the world around her in high-contrast black and white, the lens that she preferred to have turned in her direction would have to have been so lavished with Vaseline that any unsightly cracks or wrinkles would have been rendered invisible.

In the end, what interests me most about my mother's predilection for grey in all things is the colour's predominant association with concealment. Think of an *eminence grise* in politics, for instance, the shadowy figure pulling the strings deep in the background behind the empty figurehead in power. Or the multitudes of creatures on earth, from mice and rabbits to whales, whose natural camouflage is to hide out in the open by blending into the landscape as seamlessly as light and shadow.

The very point of grey, even in nature, seems to be that it makes all search for a point pointless. Toss in the smoke and mirrors of my mother's silver-satin design scheme and the haze of it all becomes impenetrable. Somewhat, perhaps, like trying to understand your complicated mother after she has gone — even though that was never a part of her plan.

IT'S CHRISTMAS EVE, and everyone is coming over to our place for dinner because that's what we do to mark or celebrate anything — we cook and eat and give each other presents, even though it's getting harder to muster the enthusiasm to get together because my parents are now so unpredictable and erratic (you never know exactly when they'll show up, and when they do, precisely what state either of them will be in). And of course nobody really needs anything, either, so the presents, even for the kids, who are pretty much grown up by now, have also become challenging.

I can tell by the way my mother lurches in once they finally arrive, and by the strange appearance of her makeup, which looks like she has applied it for the last tragic act of a live stage production, that she isn't in a good place and is perhaps already dangerously fortified with an assortment of pharmaceuticals.

The music is on, the table is set, the fire is lit. I have a gorgeous dinner in the oven. But my mother is already unhappy — most likely because it is my party and at my house when she is the one who should be the Grand Matriarch who hosts everything (despite the fact that she is so lame now there is no way she can manage it). We gather in our own grey living room where I have put out some paté and cheeses and crackers on a wooden board on our own square, glass Corbusier-style coffee table to fortify us until dinner. Thomas brings in glasses and we open a nice bottle of wine and start into the presents.

From my sister, Sophie gets a beautiful pair of bright red leather gloves — something she actually needs but with just the right amount of panache that she seems thrilled with them.

"Oh, I need those!" my mother slurs, reaching across the cheese board and grabbing the brand new leather gloves from Sophie's lap with hands that have just moments before been picking at the paté. "Now these are just gorgeous!" she exclaims, smearing the animal fats on the ends of her fingers into the new leather as she turns them obliviously in her paté-covered hands.

As we try to stop my mother from ruining them entirely, Sophie, who was just delighted with her pretty new present only moments before, bursts into rare tears and runs from the room, and I follow her into the kitchen.

"Why does she have to be like that?" my daughter is crying. "Why does she always have to grab everything and ruin it!"

I rub her back and whisper something consoling. Seeing my own child so upset, I want to slap my mother with the damn gloves, which I know is silly. From the corner of my eye I can see that the veal stew with carrots, which I had ready and waiting hours ago, looks dry and is now sticking to the pan. Clearly, we have a long night ahead of us and the fun has only just begun.

My father has been enlisted to bring in my mother's gifts, which appear to have been wrapped by a group of unruly monkeys and then dropped from a great height (perhaps a moving airplane?) into our living room.

"Karen, darling, this is for you," my mother says with great solemnity, getting teary with her own generosity, handing me what appears to be a large, heavy beach ball covered in tatters of silver paper tied together with a loose knot of navy ribbon. Unwrapping it, I discover she has given me the Victorian silver punch bowl with the silver earrings on its sides that usually sits filled with flowers on her sideboard. An object I have never particularly admired or desired.

"I wanted you to have it, darling," she sniffs, her face contorting with what I can see is a mixture of self-pity and self-congratulation for her extraordinary magnanimity. With tears actually rolling down her face now, like some B-actress in a TV melodrama who has come to terms with a terrible diagnosis, she clutches her hands at her chest, adding, "It's time now that I started giving away some of my most precious things."

I do my best to suppress an unseemly urge to laugh while expressing my extreme gratitude for her truly incredible generosity and then move us all along to dinner.

What on earth am I going to do with this giant silver thing?

THE MORNING I AM meeting Steve at my parents' apartment to go through my mother's things starts out sad and grey and just gets greyer. When Steve arrives, I give him a tour around the grandly appointed apartment, the grey suites of which now feel more like the interior of an overstuffed mausoleum. As we walk through the rooms and I show him the various pieces we are wondering about, Steve snaps away on his iPad, taking pictures of different pieces of art and items of furniture for reference. Sweetly taking in my fumbling attempts to explain what I know of the provenance of each piece, certain themes quickly arise in his responses. First, the bottom has fallen out of the antique market, and second, nobody wants any of these old things.

"Mid-century is still moving, but the market just isn't there for beautiful old French nineteenth-century pieces like these," says Steve, playing with the heavy iron latch on an armoire my mother found at the *puces* outside of Paris and sent home alongside a whack of other, presumably now worthless, French traditional pieces in a shipping container.

"Armoires in particular you can't even give away," Steve adds. "People used to want them as entertainment units for their TV sets, but now everybody just puts their flat screens on the wall."

What about the silver? Looking through the stacks of worn and scratched trays and serving pieces alongside somewhat unidentifiable broken-off bits and bobs of Georgian silver that my mother couldn't seem to part with over the years, Steve offers apologetically: "I'm afraid it's now just going for melt value."

As to such obviously one-of-a-kind pieces as my mother's Russian chandelier and the lovely Aubusson carpet, Steve offers that his auction house has a general sale of furniture and housewares in a warehouse outside the city a couple of times a year, but even the good stuff doesn't go for much.

And the contemporary art? "It's hard to value the Warhol without knowing whether it's part of a series. Sure that's a lovely Swain, but he still isn't getting much. Oh, maybe the Bolduc and the Lorcini might fetch about $1,000 each at auction, so if I were you I would just divide up all the art work between you and your siblings and enjoy it on your own walls."

On his way out the door Steve says kindly, "Your mother obviously was someone who knew her way around beautiful things and amassed a truly lovely personal collection. Its real value, though, isn't in any single piece but in the way that she put it all together."

Buttoning up his coat, he turns around and says, "She must have been an extraordinary woman, your mother," before heading down the hall to the elevator.

IT DOESN'T GO MUCH better with the contents people, who won't accept anything for consignment that is the slightest bit nicked or chipped, which basically rules out practically everything in my parents' house. I find myself getting cross that they would turn down something so beautiful as my mother's lovely and very old Indian brass dowry box because it's slightly banged in on one side, or a pair of French deco faux-bois bedside tables because one is watermarked. Everything in my mother's collection is infinitely more special and lovely than the ordinary, run-of-the-mill dross they have on display in their crummy shop.

So we three are stuck with most of it, unless we want to just give it away, which we end up doing with a ridiculous amount of it, carting over bursting garbage bags in multiple runs to Goodwill so somebody out there will have the thrill of finding some old silver plate or a vintage Armani jacket amongst the bits of old Tupperware and souvenir glasses on the shelves. Trust me, if you ever come across anything amazing at a Goodwill, it's likely because the children who have had to take apart their parents' home have thrown their hands up in despair, having gone temporarily insane.

Still we end up with way too much of it. Having agreed that we will each come up with a shortlist of a few things we really want, we call a family meeting to haggle over our initial choices — an unfortunately grotesque scene loaded with everyone's issues (perhaps unavoidable, given how much we were taught at our mother's knee about the importance of *things*) and then start into sorting the rest, each piece now invoking pity, silently making its case (*Remember me?*), quietly clamouring for safe passage to one of our homes.

Somehow we muddle through. As the clock ticks on the closing of the condo, we engage different movers in a crazed and disorganized fashion, sending some pieces to my house, others to my sentimental sister's smaller midtown semi (which is now as packed as a storage warehouse) — and yet more professional shippers to move some of the fine art and smaller furnishings across the border to my brother's SoHo loft.

Like an archeological dig, the first layers of things removed only reveal further, deeper layers of more things to reminisce over and then decide on: does it stay for one of us to keep or should it go?

Table linens, boxes of candle tapers, and art books might actually come in handy; my mother's seemingly inexhaustible supply of costume jewellery items in their various states of disrepair, perhaps less so. Do we have to keep the family photographs my mother had blown up to poster size that used to hang, embarrassingly, on the dining-room wall at the cottage? Well, we certainly can't give them away to anybody. In the office I find the bags of gifts that we had given them that very Christmas—carefully chosen Italian chocolates, olive oils, and pretty art books I had hoped they might still be able to enjoy—still unpacked, months later, along with the handmade cards from our kids.

Behind one of the sofas I am shocked to find a foolscap pad with a diatribe written out in my mother's unmistakable scrawling hand. It begins, "Who the hell do you think you are???"

I immediately recognize those as the exact words she left me in an angry telephone message over nothing in particular several months ago, which I now discover she had actually written out and rehearsed before leaving it on my phone. What a terrible diva she was! Thanks for the memories, Mum. You were always one with a stiletto at the ready for even the most imagined slight.

If there was one thing I learned growing up in her house, it was that whatever anger or disappointment or vengeful thought ever made it into words, those words, once spoken, never really went away. They just hung there in the air, taking up the space between everyone, like evil thought bubbles in a comic strip that wasn't the least bit funny.

Somehow this only steels my resolve. I will not get sucked into the vortex of taking on all of her sad things, no matter how beautiful and special they might be. A resolution, which, no matter how determined, doesn't manage to free me entirely from the siren call of my mother's stuff.

After almost a week of solid, back-breaking work clearing the apartment, the silver satin sofas sit there accusingly, such a fantastical remnant of my mother that I find myself questioning whether we should part with them at all. Maybe I should consider taking home even just one as a sort of family souvenir? True, they are a bit of a mess, and they reek horribly of her perfume, but they are well made and do have a beautiful shape. Maybe they could be re-upholstered in a more normal, everyday fabric?

Any lingering nostalgia for my mother's silver satin mystery is resolved on our last moving day. The front-door entrance to their condo is fairly small — standard, presumably. But the ridiculous sofas aren't only upholstered in the most absurdly extravagant fabric and stuffed with the finest down, they are custom-made to be extra full and extra long and they simply will not fit through the door. The movers try angling them slightly, tilting them again when they come to the part where they just won't go any further. After a couple of hours of these dedicated efforts it becomes clear that the damn things are going nowhere.

Suddenly I have a memory of a conversation I had with my mother over the phone when they were moving into this very apartment. In my memory, I am making dinner and the kids are crawling around the kitchen floor imitating some sort of animal as my mother is going on about the various travails of her latest moving day.

"Well, we tried everything but the movers couldn't get the silver sofas into the apartment through the door, so I am just going to have to hire a crane," my mother is saying, as the children mew like cats underfoot and a pot boils over.

I take the elevator down to the marble-and-glass entrance of my parents' building to ask the concierge, a pleasant if rather formal middle-aged gay man with apricot-tinted hair who has been watching me come in and out of the building toting boxes and bags of stuff for the last three weeks, whether he has any recollection of my mother hiring a crane to hoist her furniture through the sliding glass doors on the balcony of their apartment.

"Yes, I think I do remember she had to bring those sofas in by crane when they first moved in," he says, confirming my suspicions. Leaning in, he adds, conspiratorially, "But I don't really know how she managed to get away with it. I've never seen anybody else in the building do it since then. I don't even think it's allowed."

My mother might have had the chutzpah to call in the cranes and get the building's approval to lift her precious cargo up five floors into their condo apartment, but I guess it's true: I am not the woman she was.

Since it's beyond ridiculous at this point to even consider hiring a crane to pull two filthy satin sofas that smell like death out from the fifth-floor balcony of their apartment, I take a deep breath and tell the two movers, who have been extremely patient, to go ahead and do whatever they have to do to get them out the door.

The movers are equipped with crowbars and hammers. As if they are about to perform some kind of brutal act that I should not witness, I almost want to look away. It is weird and horrible to watch them start to beat up on the poor, defenseless silver satin sofas, which, after only a few brisk strokes of the crowbar, start to splinter into shards of their formerly glamorous selves, like the bones of dead silver elephants on the matching grey broadloom.

After they are done, and the reverberations of the smashing stop echoing in the now-empty apartment, all that's left are torn shreds of fabric and shattered bits of wood and stuffing, reflected endlessly in the apartment's many mirrored columns. Scented silver scraps of my mother's fabulousness now strewn across the floor, what they resemble most after having the stuffing literally kicked out of them are the fallen remnants of a cloud—as if we could ever really see what's inside a cloud. Or maybe the last ashes of all that was once so glittering and is now gone for good.

My eyes well up as the thought arises that my mother's beloved style statements proved as impossible to sustain as she was. Too grand to exist, truly ridiculous sitting there now all ripped apart, even her silver satin sofas, like everything else, were, in the end, just stuff.

ACKNOWLEDGEMENTS

This book was hard for me to write, although probably hard in a good way. Since writing a memoir demands that you make some sense out of everything that happened, the process came with its own rewards.

First of all, I am grateful for the love and support of my sister, Jennifer, and my brother, Joshua Young, both of whom were always there for me and with me. We had the good fortune to be born into an extraordinary and loving family, and we are still so fortunate to have each other.

I owe a debt of gratitude to Sarah MacLachlan at House of Anansi Press, who first encouraged me to write this book and has been incredibly supportive throughout. Also to my editor, the wonderfully astute and empathic Janie Yoon; Melanie Little for her thoughtful and thorough copyedit; and to my agent Amy Moore Benson, who has been an enthusiastic champion since we met.

I would also like to thank my early readers and dear friends Martha Kehoe, Ann Tenenbaum, Kate Thornley-Hall, Leanne Delap, and Ronnilyn Pustil. Your instincts and insights were invaluable, and thank you so much for putting up with me and cheering me on.

In my research into material culture I am indebted to Dr. Rachel Gotlieb, who recommended the writings of fellow cultural anthropologists Daniel Miller, Judy Attfield, and Arjun Appadurai. As to the history of design and decorative objects, I referred to publications including *The Penguin Dictionary of Decorative Arts* by John Fleming and Hugh Honour (Viking Penguin, 1989); *Pearls* by Fred Ward (Gem Book Publishers, 1998); *Hope: Adventures of a Diamond* by Marian Fowler (Ballantine Publishing Group, 2002); and "A Short History of the Glass Mirror" by Josiah McElheny, *Cabinet* magazine (Summer 2004); as well as online resources such as inspectorinsights.com, perfumersworld.com, and designboom.com.

Above all, I would like to thank my husband, Thomas, for being not only the best person that I know, but my most constant reader. Without his wise counsel, fortifying Manhattans, and expert travel-planning skills, I would have found being an adult impossible. This book is for him and for our two children, Sophie and Philip, who have grown up to be both thoughtful readers as well as truly stellar human beings.

KAREN VON HAHN is a columnist with the *Toronto Star*. For more than twenty-five years she has reported on trends in life and style for publications such as the *Globe and Mail*, *More*, *Fashion*, *House & Home*, *en Route*, and *Toronto Life*. She was also the editor-in-chief of *KingWest* magazine and the host and producer of *The Goods* for the Life television network. Her first book was *Karen von Hahn's Hip Guide: Toronto*.